ADVANCE PRAISE FOR

TRANSFORMING AMERICA

"In this provocative study, Robert A. DeVillar and Binbin Jiang examine the pressures of societal schooling practices, race-based asset accumulation, multicultural education, and metacultural cohesion. I found the book to be the most authoritative work by far on the subject and a landmark. I highly recommend it and applaud its originality."

—Ashok K. Roy, Assistant Vice President for Finance
and Associate Professor of Asian Studies, Kennesaw State University

"DeVillar and Jiang offer a set of well-researched prescriptions for comprehensive and systemic reform in the United States. Their ideas are rooted in an understanding of the complex social and economic challenges confronting American schools. Unlike so many of the policies emanating from Washington and state legislatures, their ideas are sound, practical, and should be heeded if we want to avoid the disaster that awaits us if we fail to bring about the changes that are needed in American schools. Every policy maker who says they want to 'fix' our schools should read this book!"

—Pedro A. Noguera, Peter L. Agnew Professor of Education,
Steinhardt School of Culture, Education and Development, and Executive Director,
Metropolitan Center for Urban Education, New York University

"In this timely and well-conceived book, DeVillar and Jiang persuasively argue that greater United States global competitiveness and economic well-being can only come about if this nation's 'culture of conflict,' particularly around race and ethnicity, becomes a 'metaculture of cohesion.' Through a compelling analysis of current demographics and economics, this country's history of racism, and oppressed groups' unrelenting struggles for equality, the authors courageously and ethically show the way for improving U.S. global standing: eradicate racism once and for all, radically improve the educational opportunities of poor and non-white students, and authentically unify as a people regardless of skin color, social class, or time of arrival to the U.S.!"

—Lilia I. Bartolomé, Professor, Department of Applied Linguistics,
University of Massachusetts, Boston

TRANSFORMING
AMERICA

Educational PSYCHOLOGY

Critical Pedagogical Perspectives

Greg S. Goodman, *General Editor*

Vol. 7

The Educational Psychology series is part of the Peter Lang Education list.
Every volume is peer reviewed and meets
the highest quality standards for content and production.

PETER LANG
New York • Washington, D.C./Baltimore • Bern
Frankfurt • Berlin • Brussels • Vienna • Oxford

Robert A. DeVillar
and Binbin Jiang

TRANSFORMING
AMERICA

Cultural Cohesion,
Educational Achievement,
and Global Competitiveness

Foreword by Jim Cummins

PETER LANG
New York • Washington, D.C./Baltimore • Bern
Frankfurt • Berlin • Brussels • Vienna • Oxford

Library of Congress Cataloging-in-Publication Data

DeVillar, Robert A.
Transforming America: cultural cohesion, educational achievement,
and global competitiveness / Robert A. DeVillar, Binbin Jiang.
p. cm.
Includes bibliographical references and index.
1. Education—Social aspects—United States. 2. Educational equalization—
United States. 3. Education and globalization—United States.
4. Educational leadership—United States. I. Jiang, Binbin. II. Title.
LC191.4.D48   371.200973—dc23   2011023393
ISBN 978-1-4331-0810-5 (hardcover)
ISBN 978-1-4331-0811-2 (paperback)
ISSN 1943-8109

Bibliographic information published by **Die Deutsche Nationalbibliothek**.
Die Deutsche Nationalbibliothek lists this publication in the "Deutsche
Nationalbibliografie"; detailed bibliographic data is available
on the Internet at http://dnb.d-nb.de/.

FSC
Mixed Sources
Product group from well-managed
forests, controlled sources and
recycled wood or fiber

Cert no. SCS-COC-002464
www.fsc.org
©1996 Forest Stewardship Council

We gratefully acknowledge permission to reprint:
"The South" from *The Collected Poems of Langston Hughes* by Langston Hughes,
edited by Arnold Rampersad with David Roessel, Assocate Editor,
copyright © 1994 by the Estate of Langston Hughes.
Used by permission of Alfred A. Knopf, a division of Random House, Inc.

The paper in this book meets the guidelines for permanence and durability
of the Committee on Production Guidelines for Book Longevity
of the Council of Library Resources.

© 2011 Peter Lang Publishing, Inc., New York
29 Broadway, 18th floor, New York, NY 10006
www.peterlang.com

Printed in the United States of America

Dedication

For our children—Nina, Robert, Julian†, and Joy

Table of Contents

Foreword

It's not a fun time to be a teacher in America. Teacher-bashing in the guise of increased accountability is by no means new, but in recent years the venom directed at teachers has been unprecedented. Ineffective teachers, protected by their teacher unions, have been targeted as the major cause both of the mediocre performance of US students on various international comparisons (e.g., OECD, 2010) and the persistent achievement gaps between rich and poor and among cultural/racial groups. Teachers in schools that are perceived to be underachieving have been fired *en masse* despite the fact that these schools are frequently dramatically underfunded compared to more affluent schools, and typically serve students whose families struggle on a daily basis with the effects of poverty. Schools that persistently perform below expectations are increasingly being handed over to private charter school consortia whose teachers are non-unionized and thus easy to fire and replace, as the need arises. The logic is simple and superficially persuasive: *Good teaching is the key element in academic success and consequently poor teaching must be to blame for student underachievement.* Accountability has become the buzzword for school improvement and, in the name of accountability, high-stakes standardized tests are increasingly being mobilized to measure not only the progress of students but also the effectiveness of teachers and the teacher education programs that certified them.

For anyone who aspires to understand the historical origins and current intent of this discourse, Robert A. DeVillar and Binbin Jiang have provided a lucid and at times disturbing account of the roots and current manifestations of inequality in American schools. They argue convincingly that the persistent achievement gaps between rich and poor and across cultural/racial groups are a direct function of the racist social, economic and educational policies that have been characteristic of American society since its inception. The legal landscape has changed during the past 60 years as a result Supreme Court rulings and federal legislation that has prohibited discrimination on the basis of national or racial origin. However, in practice, housing and educational segregation persist, and what Jonathan Kozol (1991) aptly termed "savage inequalities" still characterize the schooling experience of America's poor, most of whom are from cultural/racial minority groups. DeVillar and Jiang, like other progressive scholars in the United States (e.g., Berliner, 2009; Darling-Hammond, 2010), demonstrate that a focus on equity in both the structures of schooling and in pedagogical interactions is essential to transform the process and outcomes of American education.

Unfortunately, equity has fallen out of fashion among American educational policy-makers. Those in power prefer instead to promote evidence-free policies that will, in all probability, exacerbate rather than reduce achievement gaps; the widening of these achievement gaps will, in turn, be taken as further proof that only the private sector can "fix" the broken educational system.

What evidence is there that current policies are evidence-free? A few examples will suffice to illustrate the point. First, under-achievement is not characteristic of all American schools. According to data from the Organisation for Economic Cooperation and Development (OECD, 2010), underachievement is concentrated in schools serving low-income and racially/culturally marginalized students. On the OECD's measure of Reading Literacy, 15-year old American students in schools with less than ten percent of students receiving free or reduced-price lunch obtained an average scale score of 551, comparable to the top performers in other countries; however, students in schools with 75 percent or more of their population eligible for free or reduced-price lunch obtained an average scale score of 446, a difference of 105 scale score points. As pointed out by numerous authors (e.g., Berliner, 2009), low income is associated with a variety of factors that directly affect students' educational prospects such as less access to prenatal care, lower quality nutrition, exposure to lead, less access to books and computers, less experienced teachers, less per-student spending, etc. Further evidence of the impact of socio-economic variables is seen in the fact that interventions to address these factors produce educational benefits. Detailed reviews by Rothstein (2004) and Berliner (2009) highlight extensive evidence that nonschool interventions such as increasing family income, ensuring adequate nutrition, provision of prenatal and general health care were associated with increased cognitive ability and/or academic achievement among low-income students.

These data on the impact of socio-economic variables are consistent with many other large-scale surveys (e.g., Coleman, 1966) but have been largely ignored in current policy debates. Current policies adopt a "no excuses" stance whereby schools (and individual teachers) that fail to raise students' test scores up to grade expectations are regarded as failing and subject to various forms of sanction (such as the firing of school staff and closing of schools). These policies ignore the fact that out-of-school factors associated with socio-economic status (most of which are beyond the control of teachers) account for considerably more variance in achievement than do in-school factors (Rothstein 2004). Thus, it is unrealistic (and evidence-free) to expect instructional interventions or improvements in teacher quality alone to reduce the achievement gap when the bulk of this gap is associated with socio-economic disparities.

The pervasiveness of high-stakes testing has brought about an additional pedagogical challenge for teachers and students in low-income schools. Because the consequences of failing to pass the test are so potentially severe, there is huge pressure on teachers to teach to the test. The curriculum has been narrowed so that, in some states, many elementary school students in low-income areas receive no instruction in science or social studies (which thus far are not tested) so that more time can be spent on reading and math. In some schools, recess has been cancelled in order to maximize instructional time. These pressures are not nearly as intense in schools serving higher-income students because these students are much more likely to pass the test (as illustrated in the OECD data reviewed above). Thus, the pedagogical divide between affluent and impoverished communities has probably never been greater—affluent students get cognitively challenging instruction involving higher-order thinking while impoverished students get drill-and-practice test preparation.

Another example of evidence-free policy making is evident in the use of high-stakes standardized tests with English language learners (ELL). Under the provisions of the 2001 *No Child Left Behind* legislation (NCLB), schools were required to demonstrate "adequate yearly progress" on standardized tests administered to all students between Grades 3 and 8. ELL students were exempted from testing only in their first year of learning English. After that period, their scores were interpreted, along with the scores of other students, as reflective of the quality of instruction in a particular school. This policy ignores the numerous studies carried out in the United States and elsewhere which have shown that at least five years (and frequently longer) are typically required for ELL students to approach grade norms in reading achievement and other academic areas that are dependent on language proficiency (see Cummins, 2000 for a review). Thus, ELL students' "underachievement" on tests administered during the period when they are on the normal catch-up trajectory reveals nothing about the quality of instruction they have received; the data simply reflect the time periods required to catch up academically even under very favourable educational conditions. Yet, policy implemented in the context of NCLB routinely interprets this pattern as a failure of schools and teachers.

In view of the fact that schools serving low-income students and those from culturally and racially marginalized backgrounds have been set up for failure through what can only be described as either cynical or irresponsibly ignorant policies, it is difficult to see why any teacher would be motivated to teach in these schools. However, dedicated teachers *are* teaching in these schools and many are beginning to actively resist their own marginalization and the disadvantaging of their students. This is illustrated in the Grade 1 teacher quoted by Kozol (2007): "I didn't study all these years...to turn Black babies into mindless little robots, denied the normal breadth of learning, all the arts and sciences, all the joy in reading literary classics, all the spontaneity and power to ask interesting questions, that kids are getting in the middle-class White systems."

How can teachers resist the powerful forces that are expanding the pedagogical divide and excluding marginalized group students from powerful learning? What strategies are available to them to highlight the hypocrisy of those who preach the need to improve teacher quality while effectively mandating instructional conditions that reduce teachers to transmitters of test preparation work sheets? In this context, knowledge is power:

- The knowledge that most of the policies that have been mandated under the No Child Left Behind legislation are evidence-free (see Cummins, 2007, for a review) gives educators (e.g., teachers, researchers, parents, and teacher unions) the confidence to demand accountability from policy-makers who have substituted ideology for evidence.

- Knowledge of the pedagogical principles and strategies articulated in this volume under the umbrella of the Expanded Socioacademic Framework (ESF) provide an excellent starting point for bridging the pedagogical divide so that marginalized group students experience the identity affirming and intellectually powerful instruction that is taken for granted by more affluent communities.

However, knowledge of the core research relating to student achievement and the pedagogical strategies that will promote achievement will only become relevant when educators, individually and collectively, recognize that societal power relations are operating to devalue both their professional expertise and their students' intellectual and academic potential. As DeVillar and Jiang point out, this process has a long and ugly history but its current manifestation through discourse and media manipulation is no different in principle from its more overt predecessors. The core insight that derives from understanding the history and current manifestations of the exclusion of socially marginalized students from educational opportunity is that effective teaching *requires* that teachers (and administrators) challenge the operation of coercive power relations. Thus, rather than being complicit in an instructional regime that devalues student and community identity, we affirm student identities by supporting students in carrying out and showcasing intellectually challenging academic work. Rather than participate in the hypocrisy that encourages bilingual students to abandon their languages and cultural knowledge, we enable them to build on this knowledge and use their multilingual skills as cognitive tools to expand their social and cognitive horizons. Teachers who take on this challenge become agents in transforming schooling into education and, as the title of this volume articulates, they also participate in transforming the character and identity of their nation.

Jim Cummins
The University of Toronto, April 2011

References

Berliner, D. C. (2009). *Poverty and potential: Out-of-school factors and school success.* Boulder and Tempe: Education and the Public Interest Center & Education Policy Research Unit. Retrieved 5 March 2010 from http://epicpolicy.org/publication/poverty-and-potential.

Coleman, J. S. (1966). *Equality of educational opportunity.* Washington DC: National Center for Educational Statistics.

Cummins, J. (2000). *Language, power, and pedagogy: Bilingual children in the crossfire.* Clevedon, England: Multilingual Matters.

Cummins, J. (2007). Pedagogies for the poor? Re-aligning reading instruction for low-income students with scientifically based reading research. *Educational Researcher, 36,* pp. 564–572.

Darling-Hammond, L. (2010). *The flat world and education. How America's commitment to equity will determine our future.* New York: Teachers College Press.

Kozol, J. (1991). *Savage inequalities: Children in America's schools.* New York: Harper Perennial.

OECD (2010). *Strong performers and successful reformers in education: Lessons from PISA for the United States.* Paris: OECD. Retrieved January 12, 2010 from http://www.oecd.org/dataoecd/32/50/46623978.pdf

Rothstein, R. (2004). *Class and schools: Using social, economic, and educational reform to close the Black-White achievement gap.* Washington, DC: Economic Policy Institute.

Preface

In addressing the topics that comprise this book, we, in Chapter 1, first address the complex and far-reaching problem our nation faces, domestically and globally, regarding our declining educational performance and geopolitical competitiveness and standing. In Chapter 2, we analyze the root of the continued fragmentation in our country through the examination of the origins of race and exclusion, before turning, in Chapter 3, to the cultural construction and dissemination of racism through entertainment, eugenics and academia. In Chapter 4, we illustrate the selective rise of the White American middle class as a result of government-supported residential segregation and redlining, which not only produced unequal and race-based asset accumulation, but also produced separate and unequal schools, school districts, schooling experiences and academic outcomes among groups.

In Chapters 5 through 7, we focus on the persistent action by minority group members in their common quest for substantive social and educational reforms characterized by equality and equity. We specifically address the great migration by African Americans in Chapter 5; the conditions that promoted multicultural education in Chapter 6; and, in Chapter 7, the continued civil struggle to legitimize and integrate the creative and scholarly contributions of individuals from minority groups and how religion, education and music, influence perceptions and decisions that move us toward further fragmentation or unity. In Chapter 8, we provide evidence that our nation's schooling is generally characterized by exhibiting and reinforcing the continued maintenance and spread of societal schooling practices that are antithetical to favorable schooling experiences and outcomes for students from underserved minority and low-income groups in general. Major schooling factors that researchers identify that contribute to this status quo behavior include resegregation, inconsistent teacher quality, and tracking. We conclude this book with two final chapters. In Chapter 9, we advocate for metacultural cohesion through an expanded research-informed socioacademic achievement (ESA) framework that emphasizes integration, communication, cooperation, critical inquiry and culture; we also integrate the ESA framework within the context of technology-mediated social participation. In Chapter 10, we provide research-informed recommendations—synthesized from various researchers and professionals within or on behalf of educational agencies—to improve the quality of education and that, to varying degrees, support the ESA framework. We also address the recommendations provided by President Obama in a September 2010 interview in *Ebony* magazine, which are different in tone and substance than what he proposed to Congress in February 2009. In closing, we recap the problems and opportunities our nation faces, and propose that we must transform ourselves from a culture of conflict to a culture of purpose to achieve the vision of metacultural cohesion and to ensure that our nation as a whole, as well as its individual members, thrive domestically, and that we enhance our nation's global competitiveness and contributions, geopolitically and otherwise, throughout this century and beyond.

Robert A. DeVillar
Binbin Jiang
December 5, 2010

Acknowledgments

We are delighted and honored to express our gratitude and appreciation to those who provided support and assistance to us at different stages in our writing of this book.

Our profound expression of appreciation to Jim Cummins extends well beyond the substantive Foreword he added to the book, as his friendship and collegiality, and groundbreaking contributions to education and society, throughout the past decades have inspired, buttressed and refined our individual and collective professional perspectives, development, practice and scholarship. We are sincerely grateful to Lilia Bartolomé, Pedro Noguera, John Stanfield, and Ashok Roy for their rigorous reviews and insightful comments regarding the book.

We also express our sincere appreciation to Greg Goodman, as series editor, for his support, understanding and consummate professionalism throughout the demanding process associated with the book's ultimate production. We thank Barbara Morton for her invaluable expertise, collegiality and timeliness in copyediting and formatting the book, and Sophie Appel, Chris Meyers and others at Peter Lang for their helpful assistance and strong support.

In Spring 2009, we each received a Global Learning Grant from the Bagwell College of Education at Kennesaw State University that provided one course release for each author. The grant furnished each of us valuable time in which to gather data that contributed to the completion of the book. In addition, Roseanne Axlen and Jessica Killcreas, undergraduate and graduate students, respectively, at Kennesaw State University, assisted us in collecting helpful research literature and related information. Nadia Clark, also an undergraduate student at Kennesaw State University, assisted us in generating a fine preliminary draft of the index of the book.

For the complex and provocative array of questions, comments and reflections consistently generated by our undergraduate and graduate students, which challenged and inspired us to write a book that would address their intellectual and pedagogical concerns and needs as students and aspiring professionals, we are especially grateful.

We thank all of the above, as well as all those who remain unnamed, and hope that this book will help college students, scholars, policy makers, leaders and the general public in understanding our collective historical roots, our present challenges, and the elements needed for our nation to achieve and live its promise through its cohesive culture and people.

Chapter 1

Education, Economics and Expectations: The State and Sustainability of United States Culture

Concerns?...I'll give you a concern. I mean, you talked about the TARP plan and the stimulus plan and all the plans. And the one word that is missing from this is competitiveness. And to me, that's a really big issue because if we're not competitive, then we've only put a Band-Aid on the problem. We really have to figure out how do we as a nation—everyone has to figure out, every person, every household, every company, every organization...has to figure out how does it [become] competitive....I think education for sure would be front and center.

—Michael Dell, 2009

National Economic Trends

Currently, our national economy remains the largest in the world, yet three disturbing trends over the past 40 years are clear and may even serve as harbingers of a less sanguine future lest we untangle the complex knot that binds us: U.S. household median income, when adjusted for inflation, generally has been stagnant or downward; relative mobility (a change in individual fortunes regardless of national economic growth) is flat or in decline; and, the gap between the rich and the poor is widening. Sawhill (2008) succinctly contrasts the positive trajectory of U.S. family mobility in the past with the negative trajectory and its devastating effects for families over the past four decades:

> Over the long sweep of American history, families have moved up the ladder primarily as a result of the nation's economic growth. In short,

through much of the nation's history, absolute mobility was high. But for the most recent generations, those born after about 1970, economic growth has had less impact on the average family and absolute mobility has declined. Economic growth from the 1970s until now has led to growing gaps between rich and poor. The current literature does not suggest that the rate of relative mobility has changed much since about 1970. If anything, relative mobility may have declined. Inequality of individual earnings, which fell from the 1930s until the mid-1950s in the United States, has been rising ever since. Inequality of family income continued to fall until the late 1960s and has risen sharply since that time. (pp. 27–29)

Today, the top 20 percent of Americans own 84 percent of the nation's wealth, while the lowest 20 percent own 0.1 percent, and, as a nation, we have "the world's second-lowest level of income mobility between generations, after England" (Bennett, 2010, p. 11). Robert Reich (quoted in Rose, 2010b), former Secretary of Labor in the Clinton Administration and now a professor of economics at the University of California, Berkeley, states that "everybody gained" between 1947 and 1975:

> The bottom 20 percent did even better than the top 20 percent. Partly because 30 percent of Americans were unionized, partly because we had a high marginal income tax on high earners, partly because we as a country invested substantially in education and infrastructure. We committed ourselves during those 30 years to broad widespread prosperity of the sort we have not had since. (p. 40)

The current disproportionate figures on wealth distribution actually are more striking when the top 20 percent group is analyzed. Jacob Hacker (quoted in Rose, 2010a, p. 18), political science professor at Yale University, discussing the widening range that the category middle class encompasses as wealth accumulation becomes more restricted in the face of "30 years of rising disparities":

> [M]ost Americans really have experienced very similar developments over the last 30 years, because most of the economic gains have gone to a very small slice at the top. When you take into account income taxes and government benefits and private health insurance and pensions, roughly 40 percent of all household income gains over the last generation, from 1979 to 2007, went to the richest one percent of Americans.

The reality of our broken economic situation—particularly the ephemeralness of abstract, rather than concrete, wealth and how middle class Americans had been compensating for a 30-year period of income stagnation—was made clear by our own national subprime mortgage program debacle, which was, in turn, responsible for triggering a financial crisis of worldwide magnitude that "tipped the entire world economy into a financial blackout" (N. Ferguson, 2010), and, as Shujie (2009) illustrates, eroded public confidence:

> The current financial crisis was triggered by the failure of the US subprime mortgage market. By September 2008, many large financial institutions in the US and the EU revealed massive losses. Four largest US investment banks collapsed and many gigantic commercial banks such as Citigroup, Bank of America, RBS and Lloyds required colossal support from the US and British governments to survive. The collapse in the banking system rapidly affected the real economic sectors, resulting in deflation, sharp reduction in trade, industrial production, share and commodities prices, and employment. *The total collapse of people's confidence became the most vital threat to the world economy and its recovery* [italics added]. (p. 2)

The tragic irony of the subprime mortgage debacle was that more than half of the borrowers qualified for other-than-subprime loans, as Charles Ferguson (Marketplace, 2010), the director of the documentary *Inside Job*, points out:

> There was a bubble, and it was a big bubble and many people bought houses that they couldn't afford and were careless with regard to the loan documentation that they signed. But over half of people who received sub-prime mortgages actually would have qualified for a less expensive prime mortgage. *They were steered into more expensive sub-prime mortgages by mortgage brokers who were paid extra money the more expensive the loan they made was* [italics added]. So it was something that was cultivated, and in many regards, forced upon the American people by the financial services industry.

Our economic circumstance, be it national or family, is not predicted to soon change for the better. Bankruptcies in the United States continued to increase at an alarming pace during 2009, numbering nearly a million (915,552) at the end of the third quarter, up 14% from 2007 (Munns & Metzger, 2009); bankruptcies in 2009 are estimated to reach 1.5 million (Dugas, 2009a), surpassing the 1,089,146 bankruptcies recorded in 2008. Moreover, the vast majority of bankruptcies filed are designated as Chapter 7, which "allows for a discharge of all debt" (Munns & Metzger, 2009), thus reflecting banks' and courts' twofold acknowledgement of borrowers' inability to repay even portions of their debt and right to a "fresh start."

Dugas (2009b) relays news of a research-based work by Elizabeth Warren (Harvard Law School professor, former chair of the Congressional Oversight Panel monitoring the bank bailout and currently responsible as special adviser for creating the Consumer Financial Protection Bureau) and Deborah Thorne that uncovered a fourth disturbing trend: "personal bankruptcy has become a largely middle-class phenomenon led by filers who are college-educated and owners of homes." A related disturbing widespread social phenomenon is that recipients of Food Stamp Program (officially, the Supplemental Nutrition Assistance Program) have risen consistently and significantly since December 2007. In September 2009, more than 37 million people participated in the government program— more than half of whom were children—represented an increase of nearly 35 percent from late 2007 and an 18 percent annual rate of increase; also, approximately 40 percent of the participating households had a member who still earned wages (Baertlein, 2009). Recent figures provided by the U.S. Census Bureau, economic research, and various other sources demonstrate that our overall national economic context is worsening and not predicted to improve in the short term, perhaps even through 2027.

Global Competitiveness

The United States, today, retains its status as the country with the highest Gross Domestic Product (GDP, the value of all goods and services produced within a country in any particular year), producing US$14.142 trillion in goods and services in 2008. But to what degree this status is precarious or even waning, rather than an imponderable, needs to be addressed. Kalwarski (2009/2010, p. 19) points out that this past decade's "increase in U.S. GDP...is the lowest since the depression," totaling less than two percent. Sheer size, after all, as in humans, is not in itself the telling criterion of a nation's health, strength, intelligence or ability. It is, for example, nationally disconcerting that our 1.8 percent growth rate average from 1979 to 2008 falls dramatically short of the nearly 10 percent GDP average growth rate experienced by China over the same period. Morrison (2009) elaborates upon the present and future consequences of China's growth:

> From 1980 to 2008, China's economy grew 14 fold in real terms, and real per capita GDP (a common measurement of living standards) grew over 11 fold. By some measurements, China is now the world's second largest economy and some analysts predict it could become the largest within a few decades. (p. 1)

Reports were mixed in terms of when China's GDP would overtake Japan's, the world's second largest economy, not if. Principal International Inc. chief executive (Asia) Rex Auyeung calculated that China's GDP would overtake that of Japan's in 2010, which has been second only to that of the United States, although some three times smaller at US$4.4 trillion (Loong, 2009). The China Policy Institute of the University of Nottingham (UK) published a research paper suggesting that China's GDP had actually overtaken that of Japan's in 2009 or would do so by 2010 (Si & Fu, 2009). This metric is particularly important as China's GDP per capita, in 2007, was estimated at $5,370, ranking China at 112th among nations and "behind Egypt, El Salvador and Armenia" (Si & Fu, 2009). The multi-faceted question remains as to how and at what pace the wealth that is being generated is being distributed across China and the economic effect of that distribution on the population. The much simpler question of when the Chinese economy would surpass that of Japan's was answered on August 15, 2010, when *The New York Times* reported that China was now the world's second largest economy (Barboza, 2010). Although the current economy of China at $4.9 trillion—measured by its GDP—is substantially smaller than the $14 trillion economy of the United States, China's economy is expected to surpass that of the United States as early as 2027 according to Jim O'Neill, chief economist at Goldman Sachs Group Inc. (Bloomberg News, 2010). It is worth mentioning that, while it took China 32 years to surpass the economy of Japan, it is predicted to only take 17, roughly half, to surpass the GDP of the United States. The second question is more difficult to answer, yet there are current indicators as to wealth accumulation and distribution.

China's soaring economic growth has affected its people along three important dimensions: They are earning more, consuming differently and continuing to save substantive amounts of their earnings. As in the United States, incomes and wealth in China are unevenly distributed; and, as in the United States, the number of millionaires and billionaires rise with each successive year, as does the extent of their wealth. The Boston Consulting Group reported that China had approximately 223,000 U.S. dollar *millionaire* households in 2005; in 2007, the number of millionaires had risen to 310,000, which ranked China as number five globally in the number of millionaires. By 2009, the number of estimated millionaire households reported by the Boston Consulting Group surpassed 450,000, and is expected to reach 788,000 by 2013, leading a senior official at BCG to state: "China is arguably the most explosive wealth market in the world, as rising income and a high savings rate will continue to spur development" (SINA, 2009).

According to the Hurun Rich List, a report that identifies the one thousand richest people in China whose net worth is US$150 million or greater, the number of Chinese billionaires in 2009 was 130, second only to the United States; in 2003, there were no billionaires in China (Hurun Report, 2009). The "can do" entrepreneurial sense is thriving in China, as only one percent of wealth within the 1000 richest people was inherited, in contrast to the United Kingdom's 25 percent and the United States' 35 percent; moreover, the 102 Chinese women (10.2%) who were among the richest one thousand people in China "now make up over half the world's richest self-made women" (Hurun Report, 2009).

In contrast to our own middle class, the Chinese middle class, now second in the world in terms of size, has also been rising at an astounding, breakneck pace. From 2002 to year-end 2008, the Chinese middle class had grown to 185 million people, "equivalent to the entire middle-class increase for India, Russia, the U.S. and all of Europe combined" (Adler, 2008, p. 20). China is projected to surpass the United States middle class in sheer size if not in proportion of population by 2015, at which time its middle class will number 334 million, compared to the projected 314 million in the United States (Adler, 2008). The Chinese government's strategy of building its middle class sector is buttressed by "free enterprise...upward mobility...and near-universal literacy—all key components in the creation of a middle class" (Adler, 2008, p. 22).

The rise in income brings with it a rise in consumption, due to need and desire. In 2005, China's global resource consumer patterns surpassed those of the United States in vital areas, including "four of the five most important commodities: grain, meat, coal and steel;" its consumption of oil, automobiles and corn were second only to the United States, and its mobile phone and fertilizer purchases were more than double that of the United States (Mekay, 2005). In the fourteen-year period beginning in 1995 and ending in 2008, Chinese consumption of meat rose from 11.36 pounds per person to 24.10 pounds per person; the effect this consumption pattern has had on global grain supplies is enormous, as "rising Chinese demand for meat, and the ensuing livestock feed demand, will empty global grain stocks as soon as 2013," according to a recent study, Meat vs. Fuel: Grain use in the U.S. and China, 1995–2008, published by Biofuels Digest (Lane, 2008). Meat consumption in China, which had soared over the 14 years reported upon, nevertheless was still 45 percent below the average meat consumption in the United States (Lane, 2008), a nation with one-fourth the population of China. China now leads the world in energy consumption, a century-long title, however dubious the distinction, held by the United States (China Surpasses U.S., 2010). Zakaria (2008) summarizes our nation's present global competitive position:

> America remains the global superpower today, but it is an enfeebled one. Its economy has troubles, its currency is sliding, and it faces long-term problems with its soaring entitlements and low savings....In 2007, China contributed more to global growth than the United States did—the first time any nation has done so since at least the 1930s. (pp. 217–218)

China's dynamic and disarmingly accelerated development, both internally and globally, casts an increasingly broad and penetrating shadow that economically, culturally and politically implicates the

United States, as a national entity and in our role as a, if not the, foremost global geopolitical presence and model (DeVillar, 2010). Our nation's continued viability as a credible, competitive, contributing and cohesive power within the current light of geopolitical shift depends, in turn, on our ability to relevantly and massively educate our nation's youth to produce sustained successful academic performance outcomes. The degree to which we are doing so is the subject of our next section.

U.S. K–12 Student Academic Performance

Our nation's overall K–12 student academic performance is compromised by one of every three students dropping out from high school during the four-year cycle, and the dramatic performance and completion rate differences among Asian American and White cohorts compared to their Native-, African- and Hispanic-American student counterparts (Pinkus, 2006). Globally, the United States' competitive edge in producing a formally educated workforce, particularly in the fields of science and engineering, is eroding. Other industrialized and developing countries' rates of first university degree holders and doctoral degree holders now compare favorably to those of the U.S., and the percentage of U.S. citizens and permanent residents who major in science or engineering is declining, even as the percentage of foreign students in U.S. universities majoring in these areas have dramatically surged (National Science Board, 2004). Our nation's diminishing ability to build capacity among its native-born or permanent resident K–12 students in this critical area of professional development and expression is visible in high relief when comparing scores from the global assessments: U.S. students' scores in math and science fare poorly against students from Asian and other developed, newly industrialized or developing countries, including Kazakhstan, the Russian Federation, and Latvia (Baker & LeTendre, 2005; Boisseau, 2008; Gonzales, Williams, Jocelyn, Roey, Kastberg, & Brenwald, 2008).

That the persistent disparity in academic performance among students from poor schools and affluent schools in the United States is a salient factor in our lackluster global assessment score competitiveness in math and science is undisputed and well documented

(Gonzales et al., 2008; Nagel, 2008). In 2007, the average math score for all U.S. public school eighth grade students having participated in the Trends in International Mathematics and Science Study (TIMSS) was 508; the average math score for eighth grade students in affluent public schools, where attendance by students eligible for free and reduced-price lunch ranged between 0% to 10%, was 557, whereas that of students attending schools where the range was from 75% to 100% was 465 (Nagel, 2008). Thus, the average math score for eighth grade students at affluent schools is virtually 20% greater than for their counterparts at poor schools, and nearly 10% higher than the overall average U.S. eighth grade math score. Boisseau (2008) reports that 9,723 eighth graders in 239 public schools from the United States participated in TIMSS 2007.

However, test performance by students in poor schools cannot explain the marked differential between our best performing math students and those achieving the top five highest average math scores at the eighth grade. The U.S. overall average eighth grade student math score of 508 differed from their top five country or administrative region counterparts by a range of 11% (Japan: 570) to 15% (Chinese Taipei: 598). The highest U.S. eighth grade average math score of 557, achieved by students from schools having 0% to 10% free or reduced-price lunch, did not place the U.S. even in the lowest average eighth grade math score of the top five, namely, Japan's score of 570 (Mullis, Martin, & Foy, 2008/2009). There were eight countries (or administrative regions) that scored higher in math than the United States, and in five of the eight cases the score differential was not due to chance, that is, each was statistically significant (Mullis et al., 2008/2009).

A more telling statistic relates to the depth and complexity to which students learn how to solve math problems. The International Benchmarks of Mathematics Achievement refer to the four categories of hierarchical skills upon which students are tested in the TIMSS: Low ("Students have some knowledge of whole numbers and decimals, operations, and basic graphs"), Intermediate ("Students can apply basic mathematical knowledge in straightforward situations"), High ("Students can apply their knowledge and understanding to solve problems"), and Advanced ("Students can apply their understanding and knowledge in a variety of relatively complex situations and explain their reasoning") (Mullis et al., 2008/2009, p. 69). Here, U.S. students' scores at the fourth and eighth grades were overwhelmingly concentrated in the lowest benchmark of math achievement: 95% and 92%, respectively, 77 % of U.S. fourth graders and 67% of eighth graders achieved the Intermediate benchmark, while 40% and 10% of U.S. fourth graders and 31% and 6% of U.S. eighth graders achieved scores high enough to place them in the High and Advanced benchmark, respectively (Mullis et al., 2008/2009, pp. 70–71). The percentage of students from the top five countries whose average math achievement scores demonstrate substantive movement toward or placement within the Advanced Benchmark level—representing "fluency on items involving the most complex topics and reasoning skills"—stands in stark contrast to U.S. students' movement toward and placement at this advanced level, both at the fourth and eighth grade levels (Table 1) (Mullis et al., 2008/2009, pp. 70–71).

Table 1

Comparative Achievement in Mathematical International Benchmarks: United States and Top Five Countries (4th and 8th Grades, 2007)

Ranking (4th/8th)		Country	Fourth Grade (% IB Achieved)				Eighth Grade (% IB Achieved)			
			AB (625)	HB (550)	IB (475)	LB (400)	AB (625)	HB (550)	IB (475)	LB (400)
1	3	Singapore	41	74	92	98	40	70	88	97
2	4	Hong Kong	40	81	97	100	31	64	85	94
3	1	Chinese Taipei	24	66	92	99	45	71	86	95
4	5	Japan	23	61	89	98	26	61	87	97
5	-	Kazakhstan	19	52	81	95	-	-	-	-
-	2	Korea, Rep. of*	-	-	-	-	40	71	90	98
9	10	United States**	10	40	77	95	6	31	67	92

Source: TIMSS 2007 International Mathematics Report: Findings from IEA's Trends in International Mathematics and Science Study at the 4th and 8th Grades. Key: IB (International Benchmark); AB (Advanced Benchmark score); HB (High Benchmark score); IB (Intermediate Benchmark score); LB (Low Benchmark score).

* The Republic of Korea did not participate in TIMSS at the fourth grade level in 2007.

**In 2007, U.S. comparative TIMSS International Benchmark ranking in Mathematics Achievement was 9th among fourth graders and 10th among eighth graders.

The science scores by U.S. students in fourth and eighth grades are summed up succinctly in the statement released by the National Science Teachers Association on December 9, 2008 (National Science Teachers Association, 2008):

> The National Science Teachers Association is discouraged by the results of the 2007 Trends in International Mathematics and Science Study (TIMSS). Science scores for both fourth and eighth grade students have remained flat since 1995 and scores for minority students are dismal.

Gender generally did not affect average scores in mathematics across the participating countries at the fourth grade level. This parallel performance course was not sustained, as the difference between boys' and girls' average mathematics score at the eighth grade level was significantly higher for girls across the TIMSS 2007 countries. The average mathematics score for 4th grade boys in the U.S. (532), in contrast, was higher than their 4th grade girl counterparts (526), a statistically meaningful difference. These differences also were visible within the Massachusetts and Minnesota benchmarking participants, although only the difference between the Massachusetts average scores of boys (578) and girls (567) were statistically significant. At the eighth grade level, the average scores of U.S. boys (510) and girls (507) were not statistically significant. With the exception of Singapore, there were no statistically significant differences between the average mathematic scores for 4th or 8th grade boys and girls in the top ranking Asian countries or administrative regions.

Thus, the general trend for the top ranking countries and the United States is that boys and girls perform, on average, equally well on mathematics tests, the exception in 2007 being Singapore. The Program for International Student Assessment (PISA) by the Organisation for Economic Co-operation and Development (OECD) provides another international comparative assessment. PISA compares 15-year-old students in math and science within 30 member countries in the OECD organization. The average PISA score in mathematics was 498; the average PISA score in mathematics for students from the United States was 474, or five percent below the average, which positioned our students in 25th place. Only student scores in mathematics from Portugal, Italy, Greece, Turkey and Mexico were lower, while those of Finland at 548 and South Korea at 547 towered above the average score of the U.S., and more than half of the OECD countries' average mathematic scores surpassed the 500 point mark (16, or 53%) (McKinsey & Company, 2010). In PISA science scores, our profile was equally discouraging: an exact same average score of 474, positioning the U.S. in 24th place, with South Korea (552) and Finland (548) again holding the top two positions—and while our country neighbor to the south in both instances placed at the bottom in mathematics and science (406 and 408, respectively), Canada, our neighbor to the north, scored 5th in mathematics (527) and 3rd in science (527) (McKinsey & Company, 2010).

PISA score results for 2009, which were released in December 2010 (Anderson, 2010), demonstrated that our nation continues to decline in international standing in math (mean score of 487; 496 PISA average), while posting scores that hovered around the average in science (502; 501 PISA average) and reading (500; 493 PISA average). Nevertheless, we continue to lag significantly behind many, if not most, of the thirty-four developed and high-growth developing countries (and "sub-national regions" such as Shanghai, Taiwan, and Hong Kong) that participate in the OECD PISA survey. These scores placed our nation in 17th place in reading, 23rd in science, and 31st in math. Shanghai, China participated for the first time in this international assessment process and topped all three areas with scores of 556 in reading, 575 in science, and 600 in math. Anderson (2010), reported in the *Washington Post* that

> U.S. officials said the results show that the nation is slipping further behind its competitors despite years spent seeking to raise performance in reading and math through the 2002 No Child Left Behind law and a host of other reforms. (para. 4)

Obviously, our nation is not rising academically to the challenge of international competition in mathematics, science or reading, all of which are areas of extreme urgency and relevance to our continued development, innovation and competitiveness, both nationally and globally.

Gordian Knot Dilemma

As a nation, we in the United States are in the throes of a perplexing Gordian knot dilemma that threatens our ability to sustain our national development and global preeminence, particularly in the economic sphere, but also geopolitically. As in the case of Alexander the Great twenty-four centuries ago, there are positive implications if we can deliver the bold stroke required, and severely threatening ones if we continue to attempt unraveling the knot through traditional means. The knot itself is at once a product and expression borne of contradiction: the credo of freedom and equality for all coexisting with rationalized or legalized subordination of groups based on perceived, but always misguided, notions of human inferiority in one form or other.

As Michael Dell points out succinctly in the beginning quote, the threat is as much, if not more, internal than external, and education is key to resolving our dilemma. The pronouncement that our problem is internal and therefore so must be its solution appears increasingly widespread among economic analysts (e.g., Nobel prize-winning economist J. Stiglitz, in Pressley, 2010; Judson, 2009) and journalists (J. Fallows, 2010). The pronouncement has a corollary that stems from analysts' and journalists' early, but not necessarily premature, critique: It is becoming increasingly clear that we, as a nation, are not well prepared to face or resolve our problems (Fallows, 2010). The close to $1 trillion stimulus package was not effective in addressing our national dilemma, much less resolving it. More importantly, the stimulus dollars would not fix, and perhaps may even exacerbate, the philosophical slant heralded in by former President Reagan (1981–1989) that prizes "free market exuberance" coupled with an "unabashed skepticism of government" (Judson, 2009). The accompanying decline of our manufacturing sector and exportation of manufactured goods, the three-decade-long trade imbalance, the staggering levels of government and household debt, the precarious value of the dollar in international markets, and the burden of "imperial overreach" (Jacques, 2009) reinforce the internal nature and crisis of our national dilemma. The notion of imperial overreach, particularly as it relates to wars, is viewed by some international analysts as integral to our culture—that is a *modus operandi* to sustain our *modus vivendi*. The statement by Yu (2008), a Chinese scholar specializing in history, illustrates this perspective:

> [In] order to maintain its hegemonic position in world trade and production the United States always takes augmenting its military strength as the trump card. American military operations abroad have never ceased since the disintegration of the Soviet Union and the drastic change in Eastern Europe: the invasion of Panama in 1989; the Gulf War from 1990 to 1991; the military intervention in Somalia from 1992 to 1993; air raids over the Gulf area from 1998 to 1999; air strikes against Kosovo and Yugoslavia in 1999; the war against Afghanistan in 2001 and the war against Iraq in 2003. (p. 43)

The economic burden of our nation's engagement in Iraq and Afghanistan currently surpasses $1 trillion and, on a monthly basis, exceeds $12 billion (Wolf, 2010). This particular financial burden consistently and substantively contributes to our current national economic crisis and to the flexibility we have in setting amounts of scarce resources to allocate to proposed solutions, say, in education, as well as their degree of comprehensiveness, and the timeliness with which we can initiate them.

Fallows (2010) concurs with Dell that our ability to weather and transcend the current crisis, and effectively address "America's worst economic problem"—which Fallows asserts is the "loss of middle-class jobs"—is through *internal* practices that embrace education and other critical factors, and that reflect a common and comprehensive strategy:

> According to prevailing economic theory, a country's job structure and income distribution are determined more by its own domestic policies—education, investment, taxes—plus shifts in technology than by anything its competitors do....Those policies are ours to change. (p. 48)

Of course, the emerging markets' aggressive, mounting economic inroads that began some three decades ago operate on an ever-greater global scale and continue to barrage our historical markets and resource bases and erode our national confidence. This geopolitical phenomenon cannot be discounted. But the driver that will move us toward sustained development, innovation, and competitive preeminence and the trigger that will release the explosive energy toward our desired national trajectory will be a result of our response to internal matters that will have been acknowledged, addressed and resolved—in spirit as well as in fact.

Our spirit of nationhood—of national identity—relies on belief informed and sustained by faith in the universal principles articulated by our founding fathers in our core documents, most notably the Declaration of Independence and Constitution, and, putatively, by Supreme Court decisions (see GPO Access, 2008). Fact is based on observable measures of consistent, substantive national practice that accurately and proudly reflects our spirit. We have been and are "brilliant in vision and short on execution," to borrow Sir Howard Stringer's phrase in addressing a failed corporate cultural circumstance needing restructuring to regain competitiveness (Rose, 2010a), for we have neither evinced nor developed our spirit in an all-inclusive sense and thus have never attained the heights of practice that our vision promises, and demands, to sustain our national development and global preeminence. Nor have we formed a oneness as a people. In neither spirit nor fact are we, as Americans, as a nation, cohesive. That is our dilemma. And it was for us as a nation as well, when in 1937 the Carnegie Corporation contracted Dr. Gunnar Myrdal, a Swedish social economist at the University of Stockholm, to form and lead a team in the United States to study "comprehensively" what was ultimately titled *An American Dilemma* (Myrdal, 1944), and subtitled *The Negro Problem and Modern Democracy*. The Carnegie Corporation looked to specialists outside of the United States, not due to a lack of specialists within its borders, but because

> the whole question had been for *nearly a hundred years* [italics added] so charged with emotion that it appeared wise to seek as the responsible head of the undertaking someone who could approach his task with a fresh mind, uninfluenced by traditional attitudes or by earlier conclusions [and from a country] of high intellectual and scholarly standards but with no background or traditions of imperialism which might lessen the confidence of the Negroes in the United States as to the complete impartiality of the study and the validity of its findings. (Keppel in Myrdal, 1944, p. vi)

We have managed across generations, despite superb-but-rarified treatments as Myrdal's, to maintain, perhaps even widen, the gap of profound ignorance, stereotypes and distrust toward group differences—which now include class, gender, language, and religion, as well as race and ethnicity. Some of our largest and historically most successful corporations look upon themselves as exceptional and take pride in addressing diversity within their corporate culture more than 70 years after publication of *The American Dilemma*, 50 years after the Supreme Court ruling in *Brown* (1954) mandated desegregation, and 46 years after the Civil Rights Act (1964). A January 2010 National Public Radio (NPR) online article reports that, for every case of a putative exceptional corporation, "there are many other companies that do little more than pay lip service to the issue of diversity," and it is safe to assume that meaningful dialogue regarding diversity remains rare, as Harvard Business School professor of organizational behavior and researcher Robin Ely states in the NPR article:

> People might have a better rhetoric around diversity than they used to. They are trying to indicate a movement away from the past, but I don't particularly see diversity being incorporated in the way work is being structured. It's something that's still taboo to talk about....People are afraid to talk about it. They don't want to offend others.

The tone of F. P. Keppel's Foreword to Myrdal's (1944) *The American Dilemma*, dated December 15, 1942, could be described as cautiously optimistic with respect to race relations in the United States:

> It is a day, furthermore, when the eyes of men of all races the world over are turned upon us to see how the people of the most powerful of the United Nations are dealing *at home* with a major problem of race relations. [original italics] p. viii

It is to be lamented that such a clarion call for change, sounded 68 years ago, continues to fall upon deaf ears within the United States and that eyes, now surely bloodshot 'round the world, have remained focused on our *irresolution* relative to our dilemma of national fragmentation.

Elements Comprising Our Dilemma

Growing Student Diversity

Ironically, the complex elements that compose the knot are well-known. For one, our nation's schools continue their inexorable demographic march toward greater student diversity. Students designated as minority, for example, comprised 41%, or 22,500,000, of the estimated fifty-five million students enrolled in elementary and secondary schools (U.S. Census Bureau, 2006, 2008). Additionally, in 2006, nearly a quarter (23% or 12,650,000) of all students had at least one parent who was foreign-born, and 5%, or 2,275,000, of all students were themselves foreign-born (U.S. Census Bureau, 2008). One in five U.S. students (11 million) spoke a language other than English at home, of which 7.8 million (71%)—more than two of every three students—spoke Spanish (U.S. Census Bureau, 2008).

The continued dramatic growth of designated minority populations—but those of Hispanic and Asian groups in particular—drive our nation's rate of school enrollments. Minority student enrollments in 2003, for example, accounted for 42 percent of public school enrollment, distributed substantively but unevenly throughout the major regions of the United States: 25.6% of all public school preK–12 enrollments in the Midwest; 35.2% in the Northeast; 46.4% in the South; and 54.1% in the West (U.S. Department of Commerce, Bureau of the Census statistics, reported by Peterson, 2005). The percentages in each case were virtually double that of 1972 enrollment figures, other than in the case the South, where the minority enrollment growth expanded by 51 percent: 12.5%, 18.6%, 30.3%, and 27.2%, respectively (Peterson, 2005). Moreover, minority groups will account for 65% of the U.S. population growth in the two-decade period of 2000–2020 (Hodgkinson, 2000/2001).

Continued Polarity in Teacher Demographics

Teacher and administrator diversity, in contradistinction to student diversity, is characterized by an overwhelmingly White presence that remains comparatively fossilized, virtually locked in place. In 2004, eighty-three percent (83%) of the nearly 3.5 million public elementary and secondary teachers in the United States were White (U.S. Census

Bureau, 2004). Since the 1990s, the expectation of heightened competence of knowledge, skills and disposition has extended also to school administrative leaders (Hafner, 2005)—a professional group that is also overwhelmingly White. Ninety-five percent (95%) of public school superintendents in the United States, for example, were reported as White in 2000 (Björk & Keedy, 2001), as were 82 percent of public school principals in the 1999–2000 school year (Gates, Ringel, & Santibañez, 2003). This demographic polarity, in and of itself, would not be cause for alarm were it not for our schools' general transgenerational inability to successfully meet the academic, social and cultural needs of students, particularly those from low-income families and urban contexts. Ben Bernanke (2007), Chairman of the Federal Reserve System, addressing the U.S. Chamber Education and Workforce Summit in Washington, D.C. on September 24, 2007, summarized our national educational dilemma with these words:

> Although the United States has long been a world leader in expanding educational opportunities, we have also long grappled with challenges, such as troubling high-school dropout rates, particularly for minority and immigrant youths, and frustratingly slow and uneven progress in raising test scores and other measures of educational achievement.

In the 2002–2003 school year, for example, approximately 3 of 4 students (74.4%) who began high school in a suburban school district completed high school in the four-year academic cycle; in contrast, only 60 percent of students in urban school districts graduated within the same cycle, or 20 percent fewer graduates than that within suburban districts (Spring, 2008). Students in high economic segregation districts fared even more poorly than in districts categorized as urban, where somewhat more than half (54.9%) of students graduated (Spring, 2008). This long-term failing diminishes the return on the country's schooling investment, particularly the growth and development of capital—whether human, financial, productive or social (Goodwin and Global Development and Environment Institute, 2007)—of individuals, groups and, ultimately, the nation itself as an increasingly productive, internally cohesive, and globally competitive unit. The persistent diminishing returns on our nation's schooling investment, in turn, reinforce physical, cultural, social and economic divisions between mainstream and historically subordinated or marginalized groups (Arneil, 2006).

Segregation and Economics

The second element in our nation's metaphorical knot is its pervasive and exacerbated segregation. By definition, segregation, both social and spatial, separates groups—including by race and ethnic designation—through maintenance of differential clusters of homogeneity, particularly based on economically driven housing patterns (Finkleman, 1992) but also driven by race and ethnicity (Logan, 2007). Thus, the desegregation promise in the United States of *Brown v. Board of Education* (1954) has yet to be realized, as segregated communities not only are still present but growing in distance from one another, as the income inequality that separates the affluent from the poor increases (Mayer, S. E., 2001). Persistent heightened economic segregation, in turn, has been linked to differential educational outcomes between the respective communities (Ainsworth, 2002), where high-income students achieve educational attainment gains within their exclusive, restricted-by-affluence neighborhoods, while low-income students experience decreases in educational attainment (Mayer, 2002). The term *hypersegregation* has been introduced to describe the intense degree of segregation that Hispanic and African American students experience within their schooling contexts, that is, where 90 percent to 100 percent of the student body is non-White. Nearly 40 percent (39.5%) of Hispanic American students as well as African American students (38.3%) attend hypersegregated schools, although in "large central cities in the west more than 60 percent" of Hispanic American students are enrolled in hypersegregated schools (Gándara, 2010, p. 26).

While on a per capita basis, our nation's GDP increased more than twofold over the past three decades, poverty rates for children under six years old (20%) and for adults (10.9%) are higher now than they were in 1969 and 1973, respectively, and the percentage of poor living in conditions of extreme poverty has risen from 28 percent in 1976 to 43 percent in 2005 (Wright & Rogers, 2010). Thus, the dramatic increase in wealth has been accompanied by an increase in poverty rates, and, more disturbingly, an increase in its geographic distribution from a U.S. South concentration to a nationwide presence, and a corresponding shift in poverty rate dominance from rural to central city (Wright & Rogers, 2010). On September 10, 2009, the Census Bureau released its annual report on income, poverty and access to health care—an index of the well-being of average Americans. As Brownstein (September 11, 2009) reports, from the beginning of 2000 through the end of 2008, median household income declined 4.2 percent (from $52,500 to $50,303), poverty increased by 26.1 percent (from 31.6 million to 39.8 million), childhood poverty increased by 21 percent (from 11.6 million to 14.1 million), and the number of Americans without health insurance rose by 20.6 percent (from 38.4 million to 46.3 million).

Despite our nation's vast production of financial capital, we do not compare well with many other developed capitalist countries in terms of poverty rates or distribution of wealth and income. Wright and Rogers (2010) summarize and interpret our comparative status thusly:

> Perhaps the most striking fact about poverty in America is that the United States has by a considerable margin the highest rate of poverty among all the developed capitalist economies....The figures are especially disturbing for children, where the poverty rate in the United States is 3-4 times greater than in many European countries.... [T]o a significant extent this is the result of public policies rather than simply the "natural" functioning of the market. This, then, is one of the crucial defining characteristics of the United States at the beginning of the 21st century: poverty in the midst of plenty, tremendous inequalities in conditions of life and opportunities in the context of an extraordinarily rich society.

As a result, more than a half-century after *Brown*, an increasing segment of our nation's children continues to attend segregated school settings. This pervasive schooling condition undermines not only the operating principle supporting the May 17, 1954 Supreme Court decision that segregated schools are "inherently unequal" and thus "deprive the children of the minority group of equal educational opportunities" (*Brown v. Board of Education*, 1954), but the long-sought promise of comparable educational attainment across all differentiated groups that would result through integrated schooling.

Each generation of post-*Brown* adults, regardless of race, ethnicity or class, continues to bear dramatic, intergenerational witness to our nation's failed promise and obligation to our children and the vast array of negative consequences to our nation and its people that result from our nation's continually dimensioning educational returns.

Our nation's legally mandated societal shift away from segregation has been one in name rather than in result. Given this surface phenomenon, it should not be surprising that differential educational outcomes persist between affluent and poor schools more than a half-century after our judicial—if not cultural—resolve to begin closing educational performance gaps through desegregation. Thus, the phenomenon of segregation, which was once a legally authorized national practice (i.e., *de jure*) that our nation was to dismantle, remains firmly in existence through systematic practice that has been acknowledged to result in or perpetuate segregation but has not been determined to be caused by "*explicit* government policies" (i.e., *de facto*) (Hall, 1992). Segregation of this type continues to exacerbate income inequality and decreases the "life chances" of those stymied by social-spatial immobility, as well as exacerbating interracial tensions and misunderstandings, political marginalization, and overall societal fragmentation (Massey & Denton, 1993). It is a truism that economics and education are two salient, even indispensable, factors that relate, individually and interdependently, to national development, global competitiveness, and self-government. The statement as rhetoric is threaded throughout our national and cultural psyche and is a belief arguably shared by all Americans. It is in our national practice where we consistently fall short, historically and currently. Thus, our national rhetoric, however universally inclusive, can be ultimately judged as national pseudologia—a falsehood perpetrated by those within the superordinate group, a fluid, resilient and adaptive social group who exercise "elite power" as they continually "accommodate themselves to a democratic politics...a defining feature of the American republic" (Fraser & Gerstle, 2005, p. 20).

The most recent adaptive challenge and opportunity of elite rule, according to Fraser and Gerstle (2005), is attributable to a number of salient factors:

Defeat in Vietnam, the U.S. loss of global economic supremacy in the 1970s, the election of Ronald Reagan in 1980, and the difficult transition to a postindustrial computer and information economy. (p. 24)

To the above list, we can assuredly add the multiple, complex and ongoing effects of the present deep recession—which began in December 2007 and was supposedly over as of June 2009 (National Bureau of Economic Research, 2010), although the collective roar that continues due to near-10 percent unemployment rates (substantially higher for many groups once disaggregated by demographic characteristics), the foreclosure imbroglio, our huge and growing national debt, depressed state coffers, and identity fragmentation issues, among other national issues, serve, perhaps justly, to drown out the theoretical voice of good tidings. Amidst, but not because of, the present economic-political context, our national long-term need to achieve measurably substantive equitable inclusion—the legal charge the nation gave to itself on the basis of the watershed *Brown* (1954) Supreme Court decision and the 1964 Civil Rights Act—continues to suffer from insufficient consensus and momentum. The Obama administration, as LaMarche and Bhargava (2010) point out,

has been unwilling and perhaps unable to speak cogently about the persistent racial divide in the country or to propose targeted measures to address structural disadvantage. The need for a strong and effective racial justice movement and agenda is arguably greater now than before Obama became president. (p. 15)

Hence, as has been the case throughout our history, the single greatest barrier to a sustained trajectory of quality educational outcomes and economic development is our continuing lack of meaningful inclusion of all groups into the fabric of our national ethos, culture and society through a leadership agenda—whether at the grassroots level or state or federal—that will initiate and sustain the momentum to fulfill the national promise generated by inclusion. In an increasingly connected and interdependent world, our nation's loss in maintaining a competitive sustainable development across critical forms of capital or in maintaining substantive movement toward an ethos of cohesiveness is definitely another country's or set of countries gain—as comparative economic and educational performance figures cited in this chapter dramatically, and perhaps forebodingly, indicate.

Metacultural Cohesion

Spirit and fact are two interrelated societal characteristics that must co-exist in productive—rather than conflictive—juxtaposition for our nation to achieve *metacultural* cohesion, which is at once the societal dynamism and the unifying force that together embody our prospective collective national being and expression, our present state at any one moment and the sum of our possibilities. We must differentiate metacultural cohesion from assimilation and from multiculturalism. In the case of the United States, the former attempts to change any group's cultural identity to that of the euphemistically designated "mainstream" culture—in fact, the Anglo American cultural model (Gordon, 1964). The latter strives earnestly, awkwardly and, ultimately, unsuccessfully, to produce collective inter-cultural harmony through the study and instructional integration of each group's ever-complex and dynamic individual cultural distinctiveness. The difficulty of the latter endeavor is compounded in great part by the reality of a history of purposeful subordination and the transgenerational marginality and severe group underperformance within and across educational, economic, and political categories.

What do we, as a nation, need to do to reach metacultural cohesion? Our society—here to include all groups, but particularly those within the fluid category termed *mainstream*—must transform itself through the *practice* of universal integration into a state of collective cultural harmony that transcends micro-cultural differences, both perceived and real. Furthermore integration must be *comprehensive, permeating every facet of our society*. In the same manner in which we should not have to question our right to hold and practice fundamental rights—of freedom of expression, of assembly, of bearing arms, of worship, and other vital freedoms—*our adherence to integration must be unquestioned and we must be always prepared to actively defend that right*. In the same manner, as no culture is monolithic or static, that is, each and every culture is constantly dynamic in its myriad manifestations, the attempt to deem members of each cultural group in or coming to the United States as an object of study, as a phenomenon for all students and members of society to understand, is a fruitless endeavor, particularly for classroom teachers, and unattainable as a goal even for the most prepared and diligent of social scientists.

As a nation, we understand, however reluctantly, that the United States is comprised of diverse groups, who, to varying degrees, maintain a shared sense of kinship identity—whether by affinity, by fictive association, or otherwise—and practices. These types of grouping by association may be termed *microcultures*. However, this understanding we have is limiting in that it fragments us, hyphenates us, sharpens the lines that divide us, as we continually seek to identify and value the characteristics that define one's particular group in opposition to any other, regardless of the degree of intensity of perceived cultural distance. Microcultural cohesion at the expense of metacultural cohesion is not the appropriate response to our national dilemma. We must refocus our endeavors toward the larger sense of cohesion we need to attain—that of metacultural cohesion. Metacultural cohesion is also a culturally defined kinship, but in a grand, unilineage sense which O'Neil (2008) characterizes as

> a multi-generational group of relatives who are related by unilineal descent...and...know the precise genealogical link to the founder... Unilineages usually consist of a number of related nuclear families.

Simply stated, as a metaculture, we live our rhetoric, we become the *e pluribus unum*, out of the many, one. The goal of placing metacultural cohesion at the foreground of our national strategies and endeavors, and the emphasis on microcultures at its background, is not to deny the need to understand and continue to take action to eliminate the multifaceted and long-term dynamics of group prejudice and exclusion in our country. It is this balance that we address in the following chapters. Thus, we identify the roots of our persistent distance, distrust and disdain for groups that we at once devalue and subordinate, which inevitably leads to national fragmentation and conflicts with our national rhetoric and spirit. At the same time, we illustrate the changes brought about by persistent struggles by marginalized groups and their advocates for equity—that is, to gain the same rights of access and participation as mainstream members in order that they may derive associated benefits—and thereby participate in and contribute fully within our nation as free individuals. Schooling is undoubtedly the most important and influential formal developmental experience that we offer our nation's children, both as individuals and as community members. It is where we are expected to learn the value of cohesion through the practice of its essential elements: integration, communication and cooperation— in the classroom and on the playground. We therefore examine the extent to which schooling serves all students equally and prepares them for a meaningful future, both as individuals and as future participants in our civic society.

Chapter 2

Race and Exclusion

We hold these truths to be self-evident, that all men are created equal, that they are endowed by their Creator with certain unalienable Rights, that among these are Life, Liberty and the pursuit of Happiness.—That to secure these rights, Governments are instituted among Men, deriving their just powers from the consent of the governed.

—the United States Declaration of Independence, July 4, 1776

This is a country for White men, and by God, as long as I am President, it shall be a government for White men.

—Andrew Johnson, 1866

Origins and Justifications of Exclusion and Discrimination in the United States

Ours is a long-standing dilemma, having its origins, though not its justification, in English-whetted beliefs and practices toward outsiders, such as the native people of Ireland, which Henry II of England invaded in the late 12th century. Irish were designated savages, and, as such, were undeserving of being "*free* men with *rights* that governments must respect...and therefore subject to any sort of cruelty or exploitation at the whims of their conquerors" (Jennings, 2000, p. 9; see also Wilson, 1996). The English monarchy and its representatives committed or allowed atrocities against the Irish, which, by the mid-1600s, included selling vast portions of Ireland, designated as confiscated lands of "rebels" (Engels, 1881/1971), authorized initially by the popularly termed Adventurers Act of 1640, in the reign of Charles I of England, to

enable Corporations and Bodies Politic to participate of the benefit of an Act lately passed entitled *An Act for the speedy and effectual reducing of the*

Rebels in his Majesty's Kingdom of Ireland to their due obedience to his Majesty and the Crown of England. [Italics added]

The Act, passed in 1642, apportioned 2,500,000 acres and "invited the general public to subscribe £200 in return for 1,000 acres of lands, estates and manors confiscated from the rebels;" later that same year, subscribers (i.e., adventurers) could double their allocated acreage by investing an additional twenty-five percent of their current subscription (Manganiello, 2004, p. 10). War, to rulers and nobility, historian J. M. Roberts (1990, p. 475) points out, although expensive to sustain, "seemed a plausible investment" and "in the long run strengthened the state."

By 1650, Irish Catholics, particularly, but also non-Church of England Protestants, continued to suffer under the violent, intolerant hand of Oliver Cromwell's England, to include even being involuntarily displaced from their homeland (O'Donovan, n.d.):

> Government agents were employed to round up beggars, widows and orphans to be transported to the sugar plantations of the West Indies where they became servants and indentured slaves. The Puritan Parliamentarians persecuted not only Catholics but Ulster Presbyterians, members of the Church of Ireland and those of other minority religions. Priests were hanged, exiled or transported to the West Indies and Puritan preachers were brought over from England to replace them.

Karl Marx (1867/1960), addressing seven hundred years of English encroachment in Ireland, summarized the sweeping exclusionary effects of continual, remorseless, intentional religious-based subordination by the English:

> Under William III [1689–1702], a class came to power which only wanted to make money, and Irish industry was suppressed in order to force the Irish to sell their raw materials to England at any price. With the help of the Protestant Penal Laws [1691–1760], the new aristocrats received freedom of action under Queen Anne [1702–1714]. The Irish Parliament was an instrument of oppression. Catholics were not allowed to hold public office, could not be landowners, were not allowed to make wills, could not claim an inheritance; to be a Catholic bishop was high treason. All these were means for robbing the Irish of their land.

Schaffer (n.d.) notes that the Protestant Penal Laws disenfranchised the native majority from all power, both political and economic....By deliberately defining the haves and the have-nots, the politically powerful and the oppressed, on the basis of religion, these statutes had a profound effect, not only on the eighteenth century, but on the subsequent history of Ireland to the present day.

These blatantly belligerent behaviors, fueled by self-serving intolerance toward the rights and lands of groups outside the pale of English identity, as Jennings (2000) and Debo (2003) remind us, anticipate similar beliefs, attitudes and practices by the English toward groups who differed along lines other than religious, including, most importantly, racial. Native American groups and, soon thereafter, African American groups in what is now the United States of America were subjected to intentional institutionalized racism as native lands were coveted by English colonists and enslaved human labor on plantations was deemed necessary (Jennings, 2000):

> The core and dominant part of this empire was England, a tumultuously bellicose land constantly at war either with its surrounding neighbors or within itself. England's colonies in America were founded while the "home" country was in perpetual uproar, burning church primates at the stake, warring with France on land and with the Dutch Status General at sea. With this sort of parentage, the colonists invaded and seized the territories of Amerindian tribes, drove Dutch imperialists away, [and] destroyed Spanish missions to enslave their Catholic converts....Considering their origins, what else could have been expected of those English colonists? (p. 10)

Two prominent early figures in New World-engagement under the auspices of the British Crown, Francis Drake (1540–1596) and Walter Raleigh (c. 1552–1618)—the first, landing somewhere north of San Francisco on June 17, 1579; the second, attempting, unsuccessfully, in 1585 to establish a colony on Roanoke Island, near the North Carolina coast—displayed this same imperialistic arrogance. Drake claimed the lands in the name of the Queen and left a brass plate with the West Coast Native Americans with whom he gathered, which contained the following words (Debo, 2003, p. 39): "Whose King and people freely resign their right and title in the whole land unto Her Majesties keeping." The practice of metaphorical imperialism was known to be toothless by the English, as it applied the settlement-based, counter principle when confronted with Spain's contention that it legally held claim to all North America: "'prescription without possession availeth nothing.'" In 1607 and 1608, Jamestown as a settlement and Quebec as a fort were founded by the English and French, respectively, and, beginning in 1609, the Hudson River was navigated by the Dutch and subsequent settlements established along it, to include Manhattan and Long Island by them (Roberts, 1990, p. 603).

Virginia, established as an English colony, represented the complexity of elements of early migration to the New World lands along the Atlantic seaboard as the colony characterized the explicit and overlapping intentions, both of the Crown and of the individual. Elements included the establishment of agricultural settlements, the development of markets and trade, the extended presence of political power to counter that of other European powers, and the construction of a secure foothold for the spread of Protestantism and religious conversion of Native Americans (Beard and Beard, 1941). All of the above, however, were beholden to "the corporation of capitalists," as this particular mode of commercial entity "planted the first successful colonies and molded their early polity in church and state and economy" (Beard and Beard, 1941, p. 36).

Racial Labeling and Exclusion

The historical manner in which our nation has officially labeled groups and the differential value accorded to each group has had a pronounced, lingering and as-yet-unresolved conflictive role in maintaining spatial and social segregation, well beyond the post-*Brown* (1954), post-Civil Rights (1964) eras, that remains prevalent in today's national climate, both official and popular. This hierarchical labeling of human groups in our nation, of course, was meant to unilaterally favor the group responsible for the labeling—those popularly and officially designated as White, and that also has been known or self-described as Aryan, Anglo, Anglo-Saxon, Caucasian, Euro-American, Teutonic, White Anglo Saxon Protestant (WASP), among others—and served to perpetuate their social, political, economic, cultural and spatial dominion and advantage (Daniels, 1990, pp. 265–284; Franklin, 1965; Gordon, 1964, pp. 84–114; Jennings, 2000). Slavery, for example, in 1760 existed in all the colonies (Kornblith and Murrin, 2005). By 1790, slavery was still legal in every state except Massachusetts, and while 15 percent of American households had slaves, most of the nation's 700,000 slaves—18 percent of the nearly four million people comprising the U.S. population—were concentrated in Georgia, Maryland, North Carolina, South Carolina and Virginia (Rothman, 2005). By 1860, there were four million slaves (5.7 times the 1790 slave population and 13% of the total population) distributed among 365,000 slave holders in a national population of 30 million (7.5 times the 1790 total population), whose presence, as Jefferson Davis, the future president of the Confederate States of America, remarked in 1857, "elevated the White man, and gave our social condition that freedom from humiliating discrimination and dependence among individuals of our own race" (quoted in Rothman, 2005, pp. 80–81). Thus, as Rothman indicates, whiteness not only protected the lower class Whites from the threat of servile conditions comparable to that of Black slaves but also gave them a sense of belonging to a select group whose status was based on race.

Historically, labeling by race has been a pejorative mainstream societal enterprise that precedes our nation's official founding (Franklin, 1965; Jennings, 2000). Race and racism, moreover, formed a critical unifying element between the North and South in our Constitution (1789) at the expense of African American slaves, who "for purposes of apportioning both [Congressional] representation and direct taxes...would count as three-fifths of a person" (Kornblith and Murrin, 2005, p. 42). Moreover, anyone of African descent was denied citizenship as a result of the Supreme Court's 1857 ruling in *Dred Scott v. Standford* (Curtis, 1992, p. 310). While the decision was overturned in 1868 when the Fourteenth Amendment was ratified (Boyer, 2001, p. 289), African Americans' suffrage—their inherent, indisputable right to vote—was another matter. Legislative measures in 1867 (First Military Reconstruction Act), 1868 (Fourteenth Amendment), and 1870 (Fifteenth Amendment) afforded African Americans the legal right to vote, but also left intact the right of states to impose restrictive conditions on suffrage, such as literacy and nativity tests and property holdings. It took the Voting Rights Act of 1965, nearly a hundred years later, to ensure that African Americans, particularly in the South, had the unrestricted right to vote and unconditional access to voting booths.

Race, Slavery and Segregation

Slavery was intact as a common European practice, however controversial or challenged, prior to and during the colonial, revolutionary and Civil War periods of the United States. The forced migration of African-origin people spawned by the slave trade spanned nearly four and a half centuries, from 1442 to 1880, although it was only in the United States that slaves were deemed property, as opposed to being relegated to the lowest rung of the human social order (Tannenbaum, 1946). Thus, slavery—from its introduction by the Dutch to Virginia in 1619 (Jennings, 2000)—was associated with the involuntary, lifelong, inheritable bondage of a particular group of people, who, in the case of our colonial and Revolutionary past, were forced to migrate mainly from West Africa.

Race, of course, has been the overarching criterion of inclusion or exclusion, although culture, ethnicity, gender, religion and language have also served to exclude groups from being embraced by the national credo, and the term has been used to include these different forms (Barkan, 1992; Sowell, 1994). Racial segregation began with the first permanent English colony in what is now the United States (Jamestown, Virginia, 1607) and "that cancer has still been preserved" (Jennings, 2000, p. 25) if not now by law, by custom—again, however controversial or challenged. Transgenerational exclusion has, in turn, thwarted, and even denied, these groups' relevant access, participation, position and influence in the nation's democratic process, public institutions and economic system. Consequently, long-term exclusion has served to significantly curtail their respective political, educational and wealth-producing benefits.

The construct of race has been approached, defined and applied polymorphously throughout our history. Race, moreover, has been the overarching Janus-faced criterion of group inclusion into or exclusion from the full panoply of opportunities in American life. Our national race-based policy was operationally visible in a broad-brushed, officially explicit manner dating from our Naturalization Act of 1790 to the Voting Rights Act of 1965, and in Colonial America beginning in

1630. Haney López (1996) cites the Virginia court decision of *Re Davis, McIlwaine 479* (September 1630) as the "first case in North America to turn on race," which read:

> Hugh Davis to be soundly whipt [sic] before an assembly of negroes [sic] & others for abusing himself to the dishonor of God and shame of Christianity by defiling his body in lying with a negro which fault he is to act Next sabbath [sic] day. (pp. 23–24)

There have been other U.S. nativist restrictions, extending well beyond 1965, that have served to exclude groups from being embraced by our national credo, including culture, ethnicity, gender, religion and language. This officially stated and transgenerationally transmitted and enforced denial of human rights—or their effective thwarting through states' rights practices (Chappell, 2001)—has barred, and by extension, excluded targeted groups' relevant access, participation, influence and position in our nation's political, economic, academic, and socio-cultural institutions and development. Consequently, the respective benefits—particularly in the form of cultural, economic, social and political capital—that would be expected from such wide-ranging and long-term engagement have not materialized to form a substantive part of the excluded groups' general history or profile. Scholars such as Allen (1994) identify our nation's perennial dualistic struggle over its universalistic-inclusionary trajectory and its particularistic-exclusionary trajectory as a *paradox*. However, the reality of our historically embedded socio-cultural phenomenon is more accurately defined as a *contradiction*.

The notion of race served early on to justify practices of exclusion and enslavement, and, more recently, practices of second-class, lower quality and restricted institutional access and participation by groups considered to be outside the mainstream of American culture, and thus not entitled to, or capable of, taking advantage of the nation's benefits. A quote from Edward Long's 1774 three-volume publication, *The History of Jamaica* (quoted in Little, 1952), illustrates the racial inferiority perspective, and thus the rationale for subjugation, trade, enslavement, exploitation, exile and extermination of non-White people, particularly, but not limited to, those of African-origin (see, for example, Frazier, 1957, on the near-extermination of the

Australian indigenous population and the total extermination of the Tasmanian native population, among others):

> We cannot pronounce them unsusceptible of civilization since even apes have been taught to eat, drink, repose and dress like men. But of all the human species hitherto discovered, their natural baseness of mind seems to afford the least hope of their being (except by miraculous interposition of Divine Providence) so refined as to think as well as act like men. I do not think that an Orang Outang husband would be any dishonour to an Hottentot female.[1] (p. 65)

Thus, to the above 18th century author, a female from an African community would be honored to have an arboreal anthropoid ape husband. Long's racist work, which remains in print and available online today, was used in the 1830s by Southerners in the United States to defend the practice of slavery (Horsman, 1981, p. 50).

Renowned philosophers to whom the West has traditionally looked toward to understand and justify its foundations shared and even preceded in print the perspective of Long. David Hume (1711–1776), for example, wrote the essay "Of National Characters" in 1742, and revised it in 1753 to include the following footnote (Library of Economics and Liberty, 2008):

> I am apt to suspect the negroes [sic] and in general all the other species of men (for there are four or five different kinds) to be naturally inferior to the Whites. There never was a civilized nation of any other complexion than white, nor even any individual eminent either in action or speculation. No ingenious manufactures amongst them, no arts, no sciences. On the other hand, the most rude and barbarous of the Whites, such as the ancient Germans, the present Tartars, have still something eminent about them, in their valour, form of government, or some other particular. Such a uniform and constant difference could not happen, in so many countries and ages, if nature had not made an original distinction betwixt these breeds of men. Not to mention our colonies, there are Negroe [sic] slaves dispersed all over Europe, of which none ever discovered any symptoms of ingenuity; tho' low people, without education, will start up amongst us, and distinguish themselves in every profession. In Jamaica indeed they talk of one negroe [sic] as a man of parts and learning; but 'tis likely he is admired for very slender accomplishments, like a parrot, who speaks a few words plainly. (¶ I.XXI.Note)

And, cited within this same document (Library of Economics and Liberty, 2008), Hume asserts that

> you may obtain any thing [sic] of the Negroes by offering them strong drink; and may easily prevail with them to sell, not only their children, but their wives and mistresses, for a cask of brandy. (¶ I.XXI.32)

This particular view of Hume's toward races other than White was, in fact, one of four prevalent views regarding the superiority of the White race and the relative inferiority of all other races (Morton 2002), based on (a) mental and moral superiority; (b) color, that is, whiteness as the reference point for superiority in human nature; (c) evolution, that is, that some races, such as Africans, are a link between ape and humans, or a different species altogether (i.e., polygenesis rather than monogenesis); and (d) lineage, both spiritual and evolutionary, with Whites at the top of the human order.

Publications regarding race, considered scientific, during the 18th century exerted substantive, long-term and extensive influence on the intellectual minds in Europe and its colonies—although flawed in premise and in method. In specific cases, the authors revered, or helped to justify, the Teutonic Anglo-Saxon myth of superiority, both racial and cultural—where freedom, rather than the alleged Roman thirst for power and empire, inherently resided and reigned (Horsman, 1981). Early examples include, among many others, the imminent scientists of their day, Carl Linnaeus and Georges Cuvier, as well as the influential Johann Friedrich Blumenbach, who "considered [the Caucasian race] as the primary or intermediate of these five principal races" (Horsman, p. 46), and English physician John Atkins, who, in the 1730s, wrote: "I am persuaded that the Black and White Race have, *ab origine* [from the beginning], sprung from different-coloured first Parents" (Horsman, p. 47).

Thus, it is to this line of paradoxical universalistic-racialist 18th century thought (strengthened by even more explicit racialist models in the early 19th century) to which the rhetoric—a constant expression of the very beliefs—of the Founders of the United States and their later political progeny adheres (see, for example, Abraham Lincoln's 1858 speech on racial relations). The paradox alluded to earlier is evident in the opposition to slavery held by Thomas Jefferson (although he did not act upon it), on the one hand, and his belief that: "...the Blacks, whether originally a distinct race, or made distinct by time and circumstance, are inferior to the Whites in the endowment both of body and mind" (Franklin, 1965, p. 901). There was contemporary evidence of moral-pragmatist thought that stood, albeit outside our borders in this case, in eloquent opposition to our racist national ideology and practice, but did not reflect mainstream thought or practice in 19th century America or Europe. Lord Acton's admonition in 1862 of the consequences of a racist state remains vibrantly cautionary (quoted in Daniels & Kitano, 1970):

> A State which is incompetent to satisfy different races condemns itself; a State which labors to neutralize, to absorb, or to expel them, destroys its own vitality; a State which does not include them is destitute of the chief basis of self-government. (p. vi)

Yet, this principle was trumped in the United States by its polar opposite, a race-based theory of Aryan superiority formalized by Joseph Arthur de Gobineau (1816–1882) in his *Essay on the Inequality of Human Races* (1853–1855). Gobineau's framework not only perpetuated the myth of Aryan origins and exalted status, but "provided the ideological basis of the superiority of the White race, especially the Nordic branch [which, according to the myth was] endowed with reason and excelling all others [Black, yellow] in physical beauty, which originated in the Hindu Kush region of Asia" (Frazier, 1957, p. 271). In the latter part of the 19th century, the British view of race was explicitly summarized in the words of Seton Kerr, a Foreign Secretary of the British Government, as (Panikkar, 1959)

> the cherished conviction of every Englishman in India, from the highest to the lowest, by the planter's assistant in his lowly bungalow and by the editor in the full light of the Presidency town—from those to the Chief Commissioner in charge of an important province to the Viceroy on his throne—the conviction in every man that he belongs to a race whom God as destined to govern and subdue. (p. 116)

The application of Gobineau's racist view justified conquest, as well as subordination, subservience and segregation, of native and marked immigrant groups—in political, social, professional and religious spheres—and enabled capitalism to spread across Europe (Panikkar, 1959, citing quote of J. A. Hobson):

> The exploitation of other portions of the world, through military plunder, unequal trade and forced labour, has been the one great indispensable condition in the growth of European capitalism. (p. 316)

When transferred to the United States, the view's antipathy toward miscegenation and support of racial determinism struck a harmonious chord with the precepts of the U.S. South's slaveocracy, whose ruling class held power from 1783 to 1865—a feat of longevity that "no other ruling group in American history matches" (Fraser & Gerstle, 2005, p. 17). Gobineau's racial paradigm extended and expressed itself in the separate-but-equal legislation that defined the United States until 1954 and in the subsequent race-based civil rights struggle that followed and clutched the heart and mind of our nation officially through 1965. The mythology of Gobineau's Aryan superiority thrives still in U.S. hate-group rhetoric.

The Civil War and Uncivil Rights

The Civil War (1861–1865) in the United States tested, among other phenomena, the role that slavery would play in the nation. During this tumultuous period, in 1863, Abraham Lincoln, at that time President of the United States, produced two documents that, from the then-tenuous federal government perspective, attempted to interweave the national practice with its rhetoric: the *Emancipation Proclamation* (effective date, January 1, 1863) and the *Gettysburg Address* (November 19, 1863). The importation of slaves had been abolished by the U.S. Congress in 1807, but slavery continued to thrive close to six decades later in southern states. The Proclamation (U.S. National Archives & Records Administration, n.d.) stated explicitly that slaves, at least those within the 10 Confederate states that had seceded from the Union and that were still at war with it—would be "forever free":

> That on the first day of January, in the year of our Lord one thousand eight hundred and sixty-three, all persons held as slaves within any State or designated part of a State, the people whereof shall then be in rebellion against the United States, shall be then, thenceforward, and forever free; and the Executive Government of the United States, including the military and

naval authority thereof, will recognize and maintain the freedom of such persons, and will do no act or acts to repress such persons, or any of them, in any efforts they may make for their actual freedom. (¶ 3)

As the Civil War continued its blood-filled course—ultimately claiming 620,000 lives (Long Island University, n.d.)—President Lincoln, in his Gettysburg Address (Abraham Lincoln Online, n.d.[a]), again stressed the fundamental tripartite relationship of being free and equal, having a voice in government, and being American:

> Four score and seven years ago our fathers brought forth on this continent, a new nation, conceived in liberty, and dedicated to the proposition that all men are created equal. Now we are engaged in a great civil war, testing whether that nation, or any nation so conceived and so dedicated, can long endure... we here highly resolve that...this nation, under God, shall have a new birth of freedom—and that government of the people, by the people, for the people, shall not perish from the earth.

President Lincoln's words of prospective inclusion were expressed less than a decade after the decision by U.S. Supreme Court justices ruled in the *Dred Scott Case* of 1854 (Long Island University, n.d.[b]) that

> Dred Scott could not bring suit in federal court because he was a Negro, not just a slave. No Negro whether slave or free, could ever be considered a citizen of the United States within the meaning of the Constitution.

On December 6, 1865, the 13th Amendment to the United States Constitution, which officially abolished slavery in our nation, was ratified by representatives in Congress from 27 of the then-existing 36 states of the union; four states rejected the Amendment, but later ratified it: New Jersey (1866), Delaware (1901), Kentucky (1976), and Mississippi (1995) (Seth Kaller, Inc., 2009). On July 28, 1868, the 14th Amendment was ratified by 28 of the 37 existing states, granting citizenship to former slaves and all people born or naturalized in the United States, as well as guaranteeing all citizens protection under the law and due process with respect to it (FindLaw, 2010). The 15th Amendment, ratified on February 3, 1870, extended the right to vote to African American men (U.S. Constitution Online, 2010). The voting rights of African Americans, however, were curtailed for the following ninety-five years, particularly in the South, where the majority of

African Americans lived, through racist policies and practices that included the infamous poll taxes and literacy tests, among other restrictive barriers to voting.

Exclusionary behaviors were allowed to prevail under the rubric of *state rights*, but were actively challenged by Blacks and Whites alike during the early 1960s. Perhaps the galvanizing event that triggered the nation and its politicians to finally act was the murder of one African American and two White civil rights workers in Mississippi by members of the Ku Klux Klan in June 1964, although at least 19 known murders since 1955 had occurred, and 19 more would transpire by 1968 (see Southern Poverty Law Center, 2007). Lyndon Baines Johnson, President of the United States, summarized the need for the Voting Rights Act of 1965, which was signed into law on August 6, 1965:

> There is no Negro problem. There is no southern problem. There is no northern problem. There is only an American problem.... Every American citizen must have an equal right to vote....Yet the harsh fact is that in many places in this country, men and women are kept from voting simply because they are Negroes. Every device of which human ingenuity is capable has been used to deny this right. The Negro citizen may go to register only to be told that the day is wrong, or the hour is late, or the official in charge is late, or the official in charge is absent. And if he persists and he manages to present himself to registrar, he may be disqualified because he did not spell out his middle name or because he abbreviated a word on his application. And if he manages to fill out an application he is given a test. The registrar is the sole judge of whether he passes his test. He may be asked to recite the entire constitution, or explain the most complex provisions of state laws. And even a college degree cannot be used to prove that he can read and write. For the fact is that the only way to pass these barriers is to show a white skin.... This bill will strike down restrictions to voting in all elections—federal, State, and local—which have been used to deny Negroes the right to vote.

Excluded groups have continually struggled for their freedom of speech, assembly, and vote, as well as the right to access, participate in, and benefit equitably from American institutions and systems, particularly schooling, property ownership, employment, public services, public office and marriage. Universal suffrage, although not an official requirement for a group's voice to be seriously considered, accords the group prospective power each election year, and therefore a voice that translates into votes. Suffrage, of course, depends on having citizenship status. Native Americans were granted the right to vote in 1924; Asian American immigrants, as a group, were excluded from citizenship or voting in various forms from 1790 until 1943, when Chinese immigrants were allowed to become naturalized citizens—a policy that was extended to all Asian immigrants in 1954 (Daniels, 1992); and women, in 1920 by ratification of the 19th Amendment (Linder, 2009).

Beyond Reconstruction: Segregation and the Undue Process of Law

The era of Reconstruction (1862–1877) did not bring a resolution to the socio-economic plight of the former slaves, now *freedmen*. Black Codes (later referred to as *Jim Crow* laws) were in existence in several states prior to the Civil War (Ohio, 1804; Michigan, 1837) and established in Louisiana, Mississippi, and other southern states beginning in 1865. These codes restricted the now-freed Black individuals' employment prospects, geographic mobility, and related freedoms (Davis, n.d.). The strident opposition to allowing Blacks to access and benefit from the tools used by White culture—employment, schooling, and other forms of development and equality—was heard from President Andrew Johnson's White House, as well as from the streets by way of the newly formed (May 1866) vigilante body, the Ku Klux Klan—organized to prevent free Black males from voting, and Blacks in general from succeeding in their economic endeavors (Simkin, n.d.). Upon vetoing the Civil Rights Bill (the veto was overridden by Congress) in April 1866, President Andrew Johnson's (1865–1869) words expressed clearly his views with respect to the future status of the freed slaves, and U.S. Blacks in general (Simkin, n.d.):

> This is a country for White men, and by God, as long as I am President, it shall be a government for White men.

Andrew Johnson's tenure as president was so disruptive that he was nearly impeached, having survived being convicted by one vote. The text of one writer expresses his legacy precisely and succinctly (Miller

Center of Public Affairs, 2009):

> Andrew Johnson is largely viewed as the worst possible person to have been President at the end of the Civil War.... In the end, Johnson did more to extend the period of national strife than to heal the wounds of war.

Segregation extended beyond the South. In Detroit, Michigan, for example, during the post-Civil War period to the early 20th century, wealth accumulation by a very small segment of the Black population was primarily achieved through real estate investments and speculation, and the opportunities and interest in major business enterprises and positions were low (Katzman, 1975). Furthermore, except for the small Black upper class, the general Black residents' status was caste-like in terms of vertical immobility, class endogamy, and rigid class isolation and insulation (terms used by E. W. Pohlman, 1949, 1951 and cited in Katzman, 1975, pp. 82–83). Public education, prior to the 1840s, was not available to Black children—although their parents and all working Blacks paid the general school tax—so private schools were established in Detroit. While White students were offered 12 years of schooling, Black students were offered only six. Although the U.S. Civil Rights Act of 1875 passed, it was declared unconstitutional in 1883 and, during its life span did not abolish school segregation. Likewise, locally in Detroit, the 1867 and 1869 statutes in Michigan that eliminated school segregation were ignored until 1871. Within this context of constant struggle for access to equal schooling, only the wealthy Black families could, and did, educate their offspring; for the remainder of the caste-like Black residents of Detroit in this era between the 1830s and 1910 (Katzman, 1975)

> ...few Blacks outside of the upper class in Detroit managed to attend high school, and none is known to have attended college.

In the mid-1800s, segregation was a way of life for particular groups. According to Daniels (1991):

> The classic pattern of ethnic succession, by which one group moved out of the slums while another group or groups moved in, did not work for "colored" immigrants. (p. 242)

The national phobia in the first quarter of the 20th century regarding the acceptance of Blacks into White society as equals—including its notions of the racial, intellectual and political effects of miscegenation—was reflected in Dixon's *Leopard's Spots*, published in 1902 (Leiter, 2010):

> One drop of Negro blood makes a Negro. It kinks the hair, flattens the nose, thickens the lip, puts out the light of intellect, and lights the fires of brutal passions. The beginning of Negro equality as a vital fact is the beginning of the end of this nation's life. There is enough Negro blood here to make mulatto the whole Republic.

During the mid-19th century, these attitudes, exclusionary laws, policies and practices, following White American settler patterns, had extended to the western United States. DeVillar (1994, p. 30, citing C. M. Wollenberg, 1978) describes the racist Californian context toward African Americans and other non-White racial groups:

> In California in 1852...legislation also regulated the freedoms of the 2,206 African-Americans (2 percent of the population) who resided there, including the return of fugitive slaves to their southern locations, even though California had abolished slavery in 1849....Moreover, interracial marriages were forbidden, "and people with as little as 'one-sixth African blood' were denied the right to vote, hold public office, and testify in court against White persons" (Wollenberg: 9)...[By] 1855, African Americans were legally barred from attending Californian schools with Whites and, [in 1859], were...allowed...to attend segregated schools with "Mongolians and Indians" on the grounds that "the great mass of our citizens will not associate in terms of equality with these inferior races; nor will they consent that their children do so" (Wollenberg: 13).

From the latter part of the 19th century through the first third of the 20th century, this racist thought and action could still count on the support of the general scientific community in Europe and the United States. Barkan (1992, pp. 2–4) notes that:

> By the turn of the [20th] century, racial theories which constructed a hierarchy of races with the Nordic at the top were considered factual, free of prejudice and generally pertinent to social and political analysis....[T]he inferiority of certain races was no more to be contested than the law of gravity to be regarded as immoral.

The separate-but-equal doctrine segregating "colored races" from Whites, now at the national level, was upheld by the U.S. Supreme Court's decision in *Plessy v. Ferguson* (1896). It remained operative from 1896 to 1954 and was especially deleterious to interracial relations. Support for the separate but equal doctrine was, moreover, widespread across the educational community. Educators generally accepted the practice of separate but equal education, and seventeen states, together with the District of Columbia—our nation's capital—actually established dual systems of public education, while four states reserved the option to do so (see DeVillar & Faltis, 1991, Chapter 2).

Racing and Racializing for Land: Native Americans and Manifest Destiny

Native Americans, the original group of inhabitants in what is now the United States, were singled out for exclusion from the beginning and granted unconditional U.S. citizenship status only in 1924. Nevertheless, universal suffrage was denied them in the states of Arizona, Idaho, Maine, Mississippi, New Mexico, South Dakota, Utah and Washington for decades after the passing of the Indian Citizenship Act, extending even to 1968 (Spickard, 2007, p. 310; Democratic Policy Committee, 2004). Other rights of Native Americans were granted on paper and curtailed in practice, impeding their cultural and economic development. For example, a spate of treaties, beginning with the 1854 treaty of Medicine River, that purportedly guaranteed "the right of taking fish at all usual and accustomed grounds and stations...in common with all citizens of the [Northwest] Territory," actually restricted Native Americans' rights to fish in what is now the state of Washington until a district court ruled otherwise in the Boldt Decision of 1974 (Boswell and McConaghy, 1996), a decision upheld by the Supreme Court in *Washington v. Fishing Vessel Assn.* (1979). *Time* magazine reported in its December 21, 2009 issue (*Time*, Tribal Justice) that the United States Federal Government had settled a lawsuit initiated in 1994 by Native Americans, by agreeing to pay $3.4 billion and acknowledging that "it underpaid beneficiaries and mismanaged revenue from land it holds in trust for more than 300,000 Native Americans under an 1887 law."

Once more, an act of incrementalism is judged as an act of transformation as *Time* reported that President Obama "called the *proposed settlement* (italics added) 'an important step toward a sincere reconciliation' between the U.S. and Native Americans." The caveat tagged on to the end of the news item is that the "pact must be approved by the federal court and authorized by Congress."

    From roughly the late 18th century to the late 19th century, Native Americans in the southeastern United States (the areas of the Carolinas, Georgia, and Florida) comprised the so-called Five Civilized Nations, which consisted of the Cherokee, Chickasaw, Choctaw, Creeks and Seminole. During this period, they had been enmeshed in the rhetoric-practice contradiction, in terms of (a) being excluded as prospective members of American society and moved to reservations far from their native lands by authority of the Indian Removal Act of 1830, (b) being sold as slaves by victorious Native American rival communities through 1750, (c) forming part of the Confederacy and Union during the Civil War, and (d) having African-origin slaves or freemen within their communities up to 1866 (Seybert, n.d.). Their common overall plight, however, was one of forced cultural demise and disintegration through a relentless "legal" encroachment by the ever-expanding United States' Indian policy, which has been "characterized as 'genocide-at-law' promoting both land acquisition and cultural extermination" (Strickland, 1992, p. 577).

    The effects of our Indian Policy—a spiraling, lethal, ethnocentric virus transmitted by U.S. official policy and common practice—was evident to Alexis de Tocqueville in his visit in 1830 to the Eastern seaboard, South and Midwest. De Tocqueville's comments in his prescient and still-salient 1835 work, *Democracy in America*, reveal our nation's duplicity and inspire pathos regarding the plight of Native Americans (De Tocqueville, 1835, quoted in Strickland, 1992, p. 577): "It is impossible to destroy men with more respect for the laws of humanity." He further describes the vicious human, family and generational costs of this externally initiated and perpetrated cultural destruction (quoted in DeVillar and Sugino, 2000):

> It is impossible to conceive the frightful sufferings that attend these forced migrations. They are undertaken by a people already exhausted and

reduced.... Hunger is in the rear, war awaits them, and misery besets them on all sides.... They have no longer a country...their very families are obliterated; their common name is forgotten; their language perishes. (p. 4)

Andrew Jackson, first as a General in the U.S. Army and then as President of the United States, was instrumental in the removal of Indians from the southeast. In his Second Message to Congress in December, 1830, President Jackson stated explicitly, and in straightforward exclusionary-paternalistic language, the case for Indian removal from their lands (Library of Congress, n.d.):

> It gives me pleasure to announce to Congress that the benevolent policy of the Government, steadily pursued for nearly thirty years, in relation to the removal of the Indians beyond the White settlements is approaching to a happy consummation.... It puts an end to all possible danger of collision between the authorities of the General and State Governments on account of the Indians. It will place a dense and civilized population in large tracts of country now occupied by a few savage hunters. By opening the whole territory between Tennessee on the north and Louisiana on the south to the settlement of the Whites it will incalculably strengthen the southwestern frontier and render the adjacent States strong enough to repel future invasions without remote aid. It will relieve the whole State of Mississippi and the western part of Alabama of Indian occupancy, and enable those States to advance rapidly in population, wealth, and power. It will separate the Indians from immediate contact with settlements of Whites; free them from the power of the States; enable them to pursue happiness in their own way and under their own rude institutions; will retard the progress of decay, which is lessening their numbers, and perhaps cause them gradually, under the protection of the Government and through the influence of good counsels, to cast off their savage habits and become an interesting, civilized, and Christian community.... Can it be cruel in this Government when, by events which it can not control, the Indian is made discontented in his ancient home to purchase his lands, to give him a new and extensive territory, to pay the expense of his removal, and support him a year in his new abode? How many thousands of our own people would gladly embrace the opportunity of removing to the West on such conditions! If the offers made to the Indians were extended to them, they would be hailed with gratitude and joy. And is it supposed that the wandering savage has a stronger attachment to his home than the settled, civilized Christian? Is it more afflicting to him to leave the graves of his fathers than it is to our brothers and children? Rightly considered, the policy of the General Government toward the red man is not only liberal, but generous. He is unwilling to submit to the laws of the States and mingle with their

population. To save him from this alternative, or perhaps utter annihilation, the General Government kindly offers him a new home, and proposes to pay the whole expense of his removal and settlement....

There were more than 370 treaties signed with the various Indian tribes—all violated in practice or officially superseded by the U.S. Government, who, by mandate of the Supreme Court in *Lone Wolf v. Hitchcock, 187 U.S. 553* (1903), was "permitted...to appropriate tribal lands and resources under the guise of fulfilling federal trust responsibilities" (Norgren, 1992). As the 1887 Dawes Act demonstrated, lands and resources were for the White populous, as part of its manifest destiny—a point brought home by Lewis Cass, President Andrew Jackson's Secretary of War (PBS, 2003):

> The Indians are entitled to the enjoyment of all the rights which do not interfere with the obvious designs of Providence.

The fate of the Indian communities was the exact opposite, then, of the White rhetoric, as Barraclough (1978) wrote:

> For the indigenous Indians, every American cliché ran in reverse: expansion became contraction, democracy became tyranny, prosperity became poverty, and liberty became confinement.

Cultural extermination rather than cultural survival or assimilation was the goal, as our sinister national policy and practice cast a dark and tragic shadow on—if not making a mockery of—our national founding rhetoric of self-evident equality and of ensuring unalienable rights such as life, liberty and the pursuit of happiness.

Native Americans (interchangeable here with the term "Indians") and Africans and their native-born progeny were not a part of the American Dream, although both groups sacrificed deeply and continually so that Whites could achieve it. And dream it was, guided, in the eyes of many, including Presidents (J. K. Polk, 1845–1849; Andrew Jackson, 1829–1837) and Generals (Andrew Jackson, 1812–1821) and writers alike, by Divine Providence. John L. O'Sullivan, author of "The Great Nation of Futurity," published in the 1839 issue of *The United States Democratic Review* (Volume 6, Issue 23), expressed the same universalistic-as-particularistic beliefs as those of the framers of the Declaration of Independence and the U.S. Constitution—even in the face of slavery and our genocidal— promoting Indian Policy (O'Sullivan, 1839):

> The American people having derived their origin from many other nations, and the Declaration of National Independence being entirely based on the great principle of human equality.... [So] far as regards the entire development of the natural rights of man, in moral, political, and national life, we may confidently assume that our country is destined to be *the* [original italics] great nation of futurity. It is so destined, because the principle upon which a nation is organized fixes its destiny, and that of equality is perfect, is universal.... How many nations had their decline and fall, because the equal rights of the minority were trampled on by the despotism of the majority? It is our unparalleled glory...in defense of humanity, of the oppressed of all nations, of the rights of conscience, the rights of personal enfranchisement....We are the nation of human progress, and...Providence is with us...Yes, we are the nation of progress, of individual freedom, of universal enfranchisement. Equality of rights is the cynosure of our union of States. (pp. 426–430)

In 1845, O'Sullivan explicitly used the term *manifest destiny* in his apologia for U.S. westward expansionism (Thomas, 2001):

> [T]he right of our manifest destiny to over spread and to possess the whole of the continent which Providence has given us for the development of the great experiment of liberty and federative development of self-government entrusted to us. It is right such as that of the tree to the space of air and the earth suitable for the full expansion of its principle and destiny of growth.

The Long, Inequitable Arm of the Law: 86 Years of Asian Exclusion

Asians, beginning with the Chinese immigrants to the United States or its then-territory of Hawaii in the 1840s, as well as those native-born to the United States, constantly had their Americanness contested, restricted or denied. The U.S. Naturalization Law of 1790 was explicitly racist, confining naturalized citizenship to White immigrants—a law that applied, regardless of the many times it would be modified, toward Asian immigrants until 1952 (Takaki, 1989). It originally stated that any alien, being a free White person, who shall have resided within the limits and under the jurisdiction of the United States for the term of two years, may be admitted to become a citizen thereof, on application to any common law court of record, in any one of the States wherein he shall have resided for the term of one year at least, and making proof to the satisfaction of such court, that he is a person of good character, and taking the oath or affirmation prescribed by law, to support the Constitution of the United States.... (p.14)

The universalistic idealism embodied in the American rhetoric remained in the 19th century far afield from the particularistic reality of its mainstream practice. This same multi-tiered, now selective-now restrictive, immigrant model depicted official and popular behavior. The model was highly selective toward English-speaking, Protestant, White groups; it was applied in a moderately-to-highly restrictive form toward other Whites from the 1830s to 1850s (Daniels, 1991, p. 265), and to Asian immigrants in a highly restrictive manner beginning in the 1870s and culminating in 1882 with the Chinese Exclusion Act, although still baring its exclusionary teeth against Japanese and Filipino immigrants. Daniels also points out that "...anti-Catholic legislation...at one time or another existed on the statute books of every colony," even in Maryland, where, along with Pennsylvania, most Catholics resided (p. 109), and that anti-Catholic sentiment, as anti-Asian sentiment in the latter part of the 19th century, have "never really died out," even as exclusionary policies that were "anti-*all* immigrants" [original italics] prevailed with the passage of the Immigration Act in 1924 (p. 265; see also Desmond, 1907, regarding the American Protective Association).

The immigrant model remained highly exclusionary, still, toward Native American (although they were not immigrants) and Black groups. As Daniels (2008) makes clear, for other groups, such as Chinese, Asian Indian and Japanese, it was not that they did not attempt to integrate and apply American models of behavior, including those that contradicted the stereotype that they were "'unable to acculturate to American ways'"—for each group did—especially in their respective use of legal means ("litigation, diplomatic pressure, lobbying, and coalition politics") to challenge the injustices to which they were each subjected. To take but one example, that of the Chinese in California, in criminal cases, the odds were definitely against this group. California laws were such that Chinese could not win, as White juries would not convict Whites who had been accused of unlawful activities against Chinese and Chinese could not testify against a White until 1872 (Daniels, 2008). In civil cases, which included property rights, the odds improved for Chinese immigrant[2] groups, where working with White lawyers was virtually required due to citizenship requirements relative to practicing law, and thus the *modus operandi* for Chinese groups, as Daniels (2008) illustrates:

> Basing their arguments on federal supremacy in matters of immigration, treaty rights, and, eventually, the Fourteenth Amendment, the various attorneys for Chinese achieved a high degree of success. Initially much of the defense of Chinese was sponsored by what can be called immigrant protection societies, ranging from the mercantile elite Six Chinese Companies to shoemakers' and laundrymen's guilds which served functions later assumed by civil rights organizations. After 1878 many of these functions were assumed by the American attorneys who served as co-consular representatives for the Chinese in San Francisco....Chinese and their attorneys won a number of individual cases—and, in the process helped to establish important legal precedents that protected other immigrant groups.

Nativist (anti-immigrant/anti-immigration) behavior extended toward Asians in general in the last half of the 19th century as they immigrated to the United States to participate in the mining endeavors associated with the 1849 California Gold Rush and to work in other areas as laborers, agriculture workers, manufacturing workers, domestic servants, and laundry workers—and, still later, as railroad construction workers (Daniels, 1991, p. 243). The Chinese Exclusion Act (May 6, 1882) prohibited new *laborers* (i.e., miners; skilled labor; unskilled labor) from immigrating to the United States for a period of ten years, except those who met the criterion of immigrating within the first 90 days of the Act or who entered prior to November 17, 1880 (National Archives, n.d.). Due to the Naturalization Act of 1870, from 1870 to 1943, Chinese (and other later Asian immigrant groups) were "ineligible for citizenship...some until 1952" (Daniels, 1991, p. 246). In 1888, President Grover Cleveland, upon signing the bill that canceled all certificates permitting legal Chinese immigrants residing in the U.S. to return to the United States if they left its shores, stated that the (Daniels, 1991):

> Experiment of blending the social habits and mutual race idiosyncrasies of the Chinese laboring classes with those of the great body of the United States...[has been] proved...in every sense unwise, impolitic, and injurious to both nations. (p. 272)

Later, laws in 1922, 1923, 1924 and 1934 imposed further restrictions on Asians, including loss of American citizenship by women if married to an Asian, prohibition of naturalized American citizenship to Indians of the Asian subcontinent, the right to American citizenship if born abroad to an American parent, and the loss by Filipinos of "American nationals" status and virtual loss of immigration rights (50 per year) (Mintz, 2007). These and other restrictive laws and policies—under the McCarran-Walter Act of 1952, for example, the quotas for European immigrants were set at 149,667, for Asian immigrants at 2,990, and for Africans at 1,400)—remained until the Immigration Act of 1965 became law on July 1, 1968, and eliminated U.S. immigration discrimination based on race, place of birth, sex and residence, including toward Asian countries.

The Dignity of Struggle within the Context of Exclusion

The confounding and conflation of race with ethnicity and color occurred in tandem with exclusionary laws and practices that identified Whites as the referent group for being American and situated all other groups in terms of their perceived degree of proximity or distance from this narrow, race-based standard. When applied to humans, race is, of course, a biological illusion that has been given scientific and popular currency mainly through surface feature distinctions purportedly unique to specific groups of people and used to differentiate groups from one another, particularly by color and selected facial features. Surface features, moreover, were early on linked to differential propensities and abilities to develop cognitive, moral, cultural and other qualities associated with civilization and being civilized, as opposed to being inferior or savage.

We have acted, perennially, in accordance with and, simultaneously, in defiance of Aristotle's understanding that "the nature of the equitable [is] a correction of law where it is defective" (Aristotle, *Nicomachean Ethics*, trans. 1925) and, its corollary axiom, "[if] liberty and equality, as is thought by some are chiefly to be found in democracy, they will be best attained when all persons alike share in the government to the utmost" (Aristotle, *Politics*, trans. 1885/2009). At the same time, we have justified and attacked a persistent particularism in the form of White American group dominance, especially, but not limited to, males, over subordinated American groups racialized as non-White or accorded other labels justifying their exclusion. Jackman (1994, p. 7) refers to this type of complex socio-economic circumstance between a dominant group and subordinate others as "long-term relations of social inequality." This circumstance is one in which the dominant group "expropriates" resources, particularly in the form of labor (to include skills, talents and creativity), from subordinate groups, who, by their labor, produce, increase and sustain the wealth, rights and privileges— power, in a word—of the dominant group.

In analyzing our national phenomenon of purposely structuring a post-slavery caste system, where particular groups are restricted to subordinate status while a dominant group is accorded full civil rights and privileges, Caldas and Bankston (2005) demonstrate that decades-long struggles for inclusion by African Americans were attempts to return to the civil rights status accorded them during Reconstruction and from which the Federal Government had retreated, particularly, but not solely, in the form of Supreme Court decisions, beginning in 1877 and lasting until 1954, and which the South had not only never accepted, but always fought to deny, legally and through vigilantism. The issue, then, of states' rights versus intrusion by the federal government—particularly how the latter has complemented or contradicted the former—has been at the core of our national approach toward civil rights since the end of the Civil War. Federal government actions have been required to guarantee adherence to our Constitution with respect to civil rights where state or local government actions in this arena have been questioned, but different Supreme Court decisions have demonstrated ambivalence in how adherence is viewed and ruled upon.

In 1866, Congress passed the Civil Rights Act, declaring "Black Americans to be citizens and to have equal right with all other citizens" (Caldas and Bankston, 2005, p. 15), which ushered in the modern era of federally initiated political authority and, concomitantly, the perennial national issue regarding the degree to which such authority is warranted. Although two more Civil Rights Act were passed, in 1871 and 1875, granting, respectively, African American rights to vote and access to public places, there was a lack of enforcement, and, when Reconstruction ended in 1877, Congress and the judiciary "began to acquiesce" to the South's caste system model, where "Blacks were largely consigned to a state of serfdom" (Caldas and Bankston, 2005, p. 17). The ensuing court decisions of 1883, which ruled that the Civil Rights Act of 1875 was unconstitutional, and 1896, where, through *Plessy v. Ferguson*, separate but equal—that is legal segregation by race, a definite form of apartheid—was declared constitutional and remained the law of land until 1954. Thus, the federal courts have demonstrated a clear ambivalence toward minority group civil rights, supporting in some cases the principle of inclusion, and in others, that of exclusion. This long-term advance-and-retreat oscillation neutralizes substantive gains that would enable the transformation of our society from its once *de jure*-now *de facto* segregated reality to that of unquestioned, unfettered equitable inclusion, the natural state of all Americans and the foundational glue of our nation's envisioned cohesiveness.

The centuries-long phenomenon of social inequality in the United States foments long-term *division* rather than unity, and legally mandated segregation was but the physical manifestation of the spiritual and emotional divide instigated by the White society and driven by its collective belief that the White group, particularly the Anglo-Saxon, was *inherently* superior to other groups, and was so by design. It is not that we, as a nation or people, have ever been united, for we have always been divided; thus, fragmentation has been our constant practice as the struggle for unity has been our constant conflict.

If there is a unity, it is in the dream of fulfilling America's principles by those who have least been privileged by law or practice to live it. President Obama recently marked his racial identity as belonging to the Census 2010 category "Black, African American or Negro," acknowledging, according to Harris-Lacewell (2010, p. 10), his Blackness "with all its disprivilege, tumultuous history and disquieting symbolism." Why? President Obama, whose mother was White, recognizes and embraces his shared circumstance—that of hypodescent—with all whose race has been and continues to be measured by the "one-drop" rule of our biologically unsustainable and culturally warped yardstick. Simply stated, President Obama understands full well that today, as it has always been within our nation (Harris-Lacewell, 2010, p. 10): "for those who also have African heritage, having a White parent has never meant becoming White."

Chapter 3

Constructing Racism: The Triumvirate of Entertainment, Science and Academia

Dehumanizing the Other: Racism in the Guise of Entertainment and Science

During the early 19th century, the United States began its relentless, and ultimately successful, attempt to quench its seemingly insatiable thirst for land. As a result, between 1800 and 1900, our national profile was transformed: our nation's land mass expanded from nearly 1 million square miles to about 300 million square miles, our "stock of productive land" multiplied by 14, our population distribution shifted from 7 percent in the West to 60 percent, and, from 1840 to 1900, the geographic distribution of total personal income shifted its concentration, as the West's proportion increased from less than 30 percent to 54 percent (Vandenbroucke, 2006). There were a number of factors that spurred the expansion: (a) the popularly and aggressively held general belief in the nation's right to view "Almost from the day when independence was declared...all the territory from the Mississippi to the Pacific as their property" (Beard & Beard, 1941, p. 586)—their manifest destiny, as it was to become known, (b) lower human and goods transportation costs, (c) high population growth through migration and births, and (d) an increase in technological innovations (e.g., timber cutting/clearing devices, plows, and wire fencing) that translated into land improvement and labor-saving efficiencies (Vandenbroucke, 2006). Thus, natives and immigrants could migrate with greater ease and expectations to the West, goods could be transported to and from each coast, and investments justified and made in improving productive land (Vandenbroucke, 2006).

The westward organized push involving diverse economic and political interests and military engagements resulted in rapidly achieving the vast territorial expansion envisioned, peaceful and otherwise. This period included the Louisiana Purchase in December 1803, but also a war with Mexico from 1846 to 1848 that added nearly 500,000 square miles, even as we continued our cultural war in Texas against the Indians residing there and who "stood in the way of the 'expansion of the White population'" (Neighbors, 1846, quoted in Sager, 2010). During the 1860s, Francis Galton espoused the belief in inheritable and hierarchical human group traits, which led to eugenics (coined by Galton in 1883) movements in England and the United States (Kevles, 1979). The eugenics model of racial superiority quickly spread through the two national populations, particularly among the U.S. middle class, who were positioned between the wealthy ("whom they resented") and the immigrant poor ("whom they feared") (Kevles, 1979). The mainstream professional and popular reportage at this time demonstrated the continuing multifaceted antipathy toward cultures, languages, and people outside the mythopoeic, self-aggrandizing, and self-flattering Anglo-American racial model, as Kevles (1979) points out:

> Further to advance the eugenic case, British eugenicists published the Eugenics Review and Americans contributed to the Journal of Heredity. In addition, eugenic advocates contributed numerous articles on the subject to popular journals and magazines. In 1914, American journals carried more articles on eugenics than on the three questions of slums, tenements, and living standards combined. (p. 5)

In the case of Texas and the Southwest, this journalistic racially imbued antipathy was particularly evident toward Mexico and Mexicans (Sánchez, 1989), whose population had increased from around 100,000 in 1910 to 1.5 million in 1930 (Romo, 1975/1994). Gutierrez (2004) writes:

> American writers were largely responsible for creating the types and stereotypes of the Mexican that would be etched into the minds of militant jingoists, politicians, and patriots as they articulated the God-ordained providential mission of the United States territorial expansion. (p. 262)

In the mid-1920s and continuing to mid-century, academicians such as Roy L. Garis of Vanderbilt University wrote vitriolic racist passages regarding Mexicans, under the guise of immigration scholarship, which were published in official government documents as well as in the popular media. Gutiérrez (n.d.) quotes a 1930 passage from Garis:

> Their minds run to nothing higher than animal functions—eat, sleep, and sexual debauchery. In every huddle of Mexican shacks one meets the same idleness, hoards of hungry dogs, and filthy children with faces plastered with flies, disease, lice, human filth, stench, promiscuous fornication, bastardy, lounging, apathetic peons and lazy squaws, beans and dried chili, liquor, general squalor, and envy and hatred of the gringo....Yet there are Americans clamoring for more of this human swine to be brought over from Mexico. (Mexicans as Immigrants, 1880–2005, para. 6)

Garis published five articles in *The Saturday Evening Post* between October 10, 1925 and April 19, 1930, whose titles continued the inflammatory rhetoric toward restricting immigration of Mexicans due to their undesirable character: Lest Immigration Fail (1925), It's Time to Clean House (1926), We Must be on Our Guard (1929), The Mexicanization of American Business (1930), and The Mexican Invasion (1930) (Fiction Mags Index, n.d.). Garis was far from being a lone example, as there were a variety of scholars who shared his views on race and immigration restrictions during this period. Hodgson (1991) describes the diverse sorts of academicians and professionals, as well as the views they tended to share:

> Individuals considering themselves population specialists included biologists, public health officials, geographers, historians, sociologists, economists, statisticians, lawyers, political activists, and politicians. They were concerned about overpopulation, de-population, uncontrolled fertility, excessively controlled fertility, unrestricted immigration, race suicide, and race degradation. (p. 1)

As the period of intense and ever-broadening restrictions on racially-based (ethnicity is here collapsed into the construct of race) immigration continued, negative public and official sentiment and action together also intensified relative to Mexicans and Mexican immigration. A double standard in civility was initiated in which U.S. Border Patrol agents (Ngai, 2003) were trained to act with civility, courtesy, and formality when dealing with Anglo citizens, ranch owners, immigrants arriving from Europe, and "high class tourists" from Canada [but] functioned within an environment of increased racial hostility against Mexicans. (The Border and Border Control, para. 16)

The official double standard of civility along the U.S. borders, in tandem with racially based bifurcated public sentiment relative to deportation, led to a wider policy of selective inclusion for illegal European immigrants that "contributed to a broader reformation of racial identity, a process that reconstructed the 'lower races of Europe' into White ethnic Americans," while concurrently maintaining "the notion that Mexicans had no rightful presence on United States territory, no rightful claim of belonging" (Ngai, 2003, Conclusion, paras. 3–4).

As the Mexican presence became more numerous and visible in the early decades of the 20th century, they—along with Eastern European immigrants—were increasingly subjected to negative stereotypes regarding their perceived innate lack of intelligence (Gutierrez, 2004, p. 271), as were Southern European immigrants, African Americans and Appalachian children—generally the result of having been measured on biased intelligence tests (see, for example, Autism National Committee, n.d.; Molnar, 1998, chapter 7; Schultz, 2006). The eugenics perspective—introduced by Francis Galton in 1883—advocated that only the healthiest and ablest of a society should have children or, in its negative proposition, that the "least able" should be prevented from having children (Carlsen, n.d.), was sufficiently strong in the U.S., that, as Eugenics in Encyclopedia (2009) reports

In 1907 Indiana became the first of more than thirty states to adopt legislation aimed at compulsory sterilization of certain individuals. Although the law was overturned by the Indiana Supreme Court in 1921, the U.S. Supreme Court upheld the constitutionality of a Virginia law allowing for the compulsory sterilization of patients of state mental institutions in 1927. (para. 35)

Our nation's *cultural reproduction of intergenerational naïveté*—that is, in a perpetual state characterized as foolishly credulous—is a socialization phenomenon that has historically plagued our schools, media and societal discourse in general. Through its transmission and practice, the construct, experience, and historical persistence and current effects of racism are ignored, viewed as non-existent, or trivialized as archaic remnants of a past, less-just society. Or they are forgotten—a convenient, short-term approach to seemingly moving on. The downside of both societal approaches is that we accept as resolved an issue that in fact is not, and which remains not only present but continues to fester. As this feature (in the form of "We didn't know" or "We forgot") appears to be a continuing phenomenon within our cultural framework, we are prone to repeat mistakes, so much so that Younge (2010, p. 10) remarks that "at times amnesia seems to be America's only renewable resource." The phenomenon also serves to uphold the status quo of racial differentiation and racial privilege. In its reproduction cycles across different eras, this static and harmful cultural reproduction strategy has exhibited a broad range of ways to consistently reinforce negative stereotypes and, by extension, the sense that exclusion is justified for particular groups.

Racism in the Media

Popular media, art and entertainment, as well as academia, with respect to African Americans and Hispanic Americans, have consistently participated in our national cultural reproduction of intergenerational naïveté. Explicitly racist language and images, including drawings, paintings, and film were prominent from the beginning of the 20th century. D. W. Griffith's film, *The Birth of a Nation*, released in 1915, was based on the 1905 novel *Clansman*, by Reverend Tom Dixon (Leiter, 2004). The exaltation of the Ku Klux Klan as saviors and protectors and the denigration of African Americans as clowns and sexual deviants seeking White women reflected Griffith's personal interpretation of the novel and was met with great audience success, not only when it opened in 1915, but when it was re-distributed in 1922. The film served to reinforce the popular notion, validated as we have seen by many within the scientific community, of inherent White racial superiority and African American inferiority, as Graham (2009) points out:

The storyline is not as important as are the film's implications and assumptions about Southern society: the Ku Klux Klan is portrayed in a sympathetic light as it defends chaste Southern ladies from marauding and raping Black freemen. *Birth of a Nation* seems exaggerated and impossible for modern audiences to believe, but [Karen] Ross points out that this stretching of the truth was common in early film and that the practice had specific purposes, but not just by displaying Black characters as violent. *Birth* is a rare film, for Black characters in cinema tended to be buffoons, not realistic threats. "The differentness of Black people," she writes, "was deliberately exaggerated to demonstrate their essential dissimilarity with White people, their lack of sophistication exemplified by their enjoyment of singing and dancing which further reinforced assumptions about their primitive and uncivilized natures." (para. 3)

Popular art manifestations included music and theatre acts that included the blackface/minstrelsy acts by White performers that began in the first quarter of the 19th century and persisted into the mid-20th century by entertainers of note such as Al Jolson (Kenrick, 2003) and the original White actors (Freeman Gosden and Charles Correll) who portrayed *Amos 'n' Andy* (and before, under the title *Sam and Henry*) on radio in the late 1920s (Widner, 2003), which lasted in radio format until 1960 (Ingram, n.d.). The minstrel songs of Stephen Foster and others, that produced *Swanee River, Old Black Joe*, and countless others (Tubb, 2009) from the mid- to late 1800s, and the still-earlier advent of blackface performers, popularized by Thomas D. Rice's (1808–1860) Jim Crow personage (NNDB, 2009), both presaged and originated this widely popular theatrical and later broader radio and television phenomenon. The minstrelsy phenomenon played to the expectations of the White stereotype— negative toward those perceived as non-White, positive toward their own group. The White stereotype, in turn, embodied a complex alchemy of fool's gold consisting of shared beliefs, attitudes, and practices that justified "oppression, genocide, slavery, colonization and/or conquest" (Bernal, Trimble, Burlew, & Leong, 2003, p. 9) of those groups designated or perceived as racially, and later, ethnically, inferior or otherwise wanting when compared to the White cultural imperative, in whole or in part.

The Retreat from U.S. Scientific Racism:
The Influence of WWII

The term *race* was popularly, and even academically, applied to represent also the phenomenon of *ethnic* group, although the latter term was used distinctly by a few specialists in the late 19th and early 20th centuries (Boas, 1966). By 1950, the United Nations Educational, Scientific and Cultural Organization (UNESCO) felt compelled to publish a declaration on the construct of race (Little, 1952) as these two terms had been routinely used in arbitrary, non-rigorous and overlapping ways by specialists and non-specialists alike. The statement itself was the concrete expression of an increasingly visible moral imperative, propelled particularly by members of the scientific community who were themselves designated as belonging to a minority group. The critical mass and shift in the race paradigm among scientists crystallized in part due to the mass targeting of particular "racial" groups for segregation and discrimination by Nazi Germany immediately prior to WWII and the establishment of concentration camps and extermination practices during the same war (UNESCO, 1969). The targeted groups included, above all, Jews, but also "Roma (Gypsies), people with disabilities, Poles, Soviet prisoners of war, ... Afro-Germans... political dissidents, Jehovah's Witnesses, homosexuals, and so-called asocials"; in this hyper-racist model, the Aryan "race" was superior to all others (United States Historical Memorial Museum, 2009). Ironically, there is no evidence of an Aryan group of people except in the minds of the race-based (or, as in the case of Gobineau, caste-based) adherents who created it. The absurd levels to which the Aryan-Teutonic-Celtic myth-based racist framework extended is particularly evident in the late 19th century-to-post-World War I period writings of the German school of social anthropology (*Sozialanthropologie*), whose authors, of course, claimed that their works were based on sound, even irrefutable, scientific or aesthetic principles, when, in fact, they were as absurd and unsustainable then as they are now. The lengths to which these adherents of Aryanism went to deny that greatness could exist outside the Aryan race are well illustrated in the works of Ludwig Woltmann (1871–1907), whom Comas (1951/1969) quotes on the heritage of Jesus:

> There is not the slightest proof that his parents were of Jewish descent;
> there is no doubt that the Galileans had a proportion of Aryan blood;
> moreover, Christ's Aryanism is obvious in his Message....Joseph was not his
> father, because Jesus had no father. (p. 42)

Although they later formed a "common bond," the German school of social anthropology was not identical to the German eugenics school, whose particular momentum was set in motion with the treatise published in 1891 by Wilhelm Schallmayer (1857–1919). In 1904, Schallmayer and Alfred Ploetz (1860–1940) co-founded German eugenics, whose explicit focus was originally not race, as Weiss (1984) points out, but centered on the notion of *race hygiene* as a means to enduring *cultural and physical superiority* through "direct control over the differential birth rates of various national groups or classes in the interest of national efficiency" (p. 43). In the proposed eugenics world of Schallmayer, the German state would determine the health status of individuals, and based on the results of their health and disease-free status—their racial hygiene—decide who was fit to marry and therefore reproduce, and who was not.

During this period, of course, it was extremely difficult for us in the United States to differentiate our practices from those of our enemies. We, in the United States, adhered to a legislated separate-but-equal, race-based national practice, instituted in 1896, even before Nazi Germany instituted its discriminatory race-based policies and practices against Jews and other groups in 1935. Japan invaded and occupied China from 1931 to 1945, committing still-infamous atrocities upon hundreds of thousands resident of Nanjing in a six-week period in 1938–39, and our national practice, particularly in the South, although not limited to it, inflicted inhumane cruelties upon African Americans, including "endemic" lynching, which began in the 1870s, and was practiced still in the mid-1930s, even outside the South (Carr, 2006, pp. 50–52). The practice was so embedded in the United States South that President Truman, in his February 2, 1948 Special Message to Congress on Civil Rights, recommended "Federal protection against lynching" (Truman, 1948). Italy, during this time, invaded East Africa (Ethiopia, Italian Somaliland, and Eritrea) in 1934. Germany and Italy practiced explicit discriminatory race-based policies: Germany, extermination of Jews and other targeted groups;

Italy, racial segregation and laws against miscegenation in Northeast (Libya) and East Africa (Robertson, 1988), while we in the United States maintained racial segregation and miscegenation laws as well.

There were tensions that sprang from the parallels of our nationally- and state-sanctioned explicit racism with the race- and ethnic-based atrocities committed by Germany, Italy and Japan. These tensions were a product of the obvious contradiction of our national railing against foreign tyranny that was, in part, race- and ethnic-based, which we ourselves practiced on the home front. Within this contradictory context of actual shared experience with the enemy co-existing with differentiated national rhetoric that extolled democracy and its universal benefits, the United States maintained its isolationism and neutrality from 1935 to 1941. We declared war on Japan the day after the Japanese attack on Pearl Harbor on December 7, 1941, which prompted Germany and Italy to declare war on the United States.

As early as 1933 in the United States, as Hitler ascended to national power in Germany, more consciously moderate stances toward biological determinism were evident among eugenicists, and, by 1935, "Race enthusiasm no longer enjoyed respectability" (Barkan, 1992, p. 275). *Plessy v. Ferguson*, the law that legally segregated the races in the United States, would still be in place until 1954, and it would not be until 1943 that our nation would repeal the Chinese Exclusion Act, first enacted in 1882 and made permanent in 1902 (Daniels & Kitano, 1970, p. 44). These types of national conciliatory actions were a function of the war and served to expediently promote the image of the United States as a representative democracy rather than having been a result of any evolutionary movement of our national social or scientific consciousness. Our U.S. Department of State (n.d.) acknowledges on its official Web site that wartime conditions determined the repeal of the Chinese Exclusion Act in 1943 rather than an evolved sense of justice:

> The repeal of this act was a decision *almost wholly grounded* [italics added] in the exigencies of World War II, as Japanese propaganda made repeated reference to Chinese exclusion from the United States in order to weaken the ties between the United States and its ally, the Republic of China. (para. 1)

In any event, it was during the period from the 1930s to the mid-1940s, that the topic of eugenics, of Aryan or Teutonic or White racial superiority, became a national and global political liability, although the general racist sentiments and practices of Whites, and our racist laws, remained in common practice.

The degree of agreement among the scientists who generated and read the first (1950) and subsequent (1951, 1967) iterations of the Statement on Race, was high at the general level and lower at the specific level. Generally, scientists could agree that race was a social construct more than a biological one, as, biologically, all human groups are of a single species, *Homo sapiens*, and from a "common stock" (UNESCO, 1969, p. 502). Specifically, however, there were "different theories or divergent points" as the research addressing scientific questions of race remained inconclusive and were not reconciled insofar as explaining particular differential performance phenomena across groups (UNESCO, 1969, Appendix).

Labeling Minority Groups: The Construction of a Vocabulary of Exclusion

As the construct of race, among humans, became seriously weakened in scientific contexts, the related term *minority group* came into vogue immediately following the Second World War. The latter term, in its popular sense, has a conceptual kinship to the terms *race* and *ethnicity* as used in the United States and has served as a euphemism to refer to groups targeted for exclusion and discrimination based on trumped-up charges of inferiority or unsuitability—racial, ethnic, cultural, linguistic, or otherwise. As such, minority groups were not to be accorded, by law or fiat, the full rights and privileges accorded to Americans within the dominant group, or of being accepted as American. Calhoun's (2002) definition of minority group illustrates this exclusionary perspective:

> A social group or category of people who are stigmatized and/or discriminated against on the basis of that identity.... [Refers] to situations in which such groups are numerical minorities with respect to dominant cultural or ethnic majorities. Yet it sometimes includes all groups that suffer from disparities of power or unequal treatment, such as women, who constitute a numerical majority in the United States. (p. 312)

The relegation to second-class group membership status has had a deleterious effect on the cultural development and image of the excluded groups, and on our nation in general. The full range of development possibilities of our nation has been thwarted by the laws and practices that have precluded targeted groups the right to engage meaningfully and comprehensively in our nation's dynamic and complex structures and processes. The denial of opportunities has limited the development and maturation of the targeted groups in all ways, from academic to economic to political. Importantly, their collectively denied voice until very recently has limited their ability to participate in the negotiation process—the *civitas*—that ultimately drives the type and direction of our nation's democratic trajectory. It is precisely this nuanced, negotiated balance of the public and private, of the individual and collective, which each generation directly negotiates for itself and for successive generations to determine and secure America's overall well-being and prosperity.

Doctrines of exclusion went beyond race, ethnicity and minority groups, and included paternalism (Christman, 2009)—which was particularly salient in the case of our nation's treatment of Native American groups and may be seen as a variant of racism. Paternalism operates on the distorted belief that a dominant group can think, speak and act for a subordinate group or set of groups, thereby restricting the subordinated group's autonomy *for its own good*; in actuality, of course, the dominant group's actions serve to justify *to itself* the very exclusion of the subordinate group and the dominant group's deleterious differential treatment toward it. Paternalism also curtails, if not prohibits, a subordinated group's substantive collective development (for example, its language, its mores) even as it prohibits the minority group's integrated democratic participation within the larger society as prescribed by our Constitutional rhetoric.

John Dewey's perspective (1919–1921) on the ills of oppression and social conflict in the United States remains relevant as a guiding principle as we attempt to understand our culturally fragmented nation and move toward cohesion:

> [Social conflict is fundamentally] conflict between classes, occupational groups, or groups constructed along ideational, or perhaps even ethnic lines.... Social conflict occurs not because interests of the individual are

incompatible with those of his society, but because the interests of some groups are gained at a disadvantage of, or even by the oppression, of the interests of other groups.... We must devise means for bringing the interests of all the groups of a society into adjustment, providing all of them with the opportunity to develop, so that each can help the other instead of being in conflict with them. We must teach ourselves one inescapable fact: any real advantage to one group is shared by all groups; and when one group suffers disadvantage, all are hurt. (Dewey, 1919–1921, quoted in DeVillar, 2000, p. 331)

Thus, the fact that the scientific community in the United States changed course and distanced itself from scientific racism during WWII, more as a matter of political expediency than belief, did not necessarily transfer to the general public or cultural context of the United States. Franz Boas, writing in 1931, acknowledged that scientific knowledge does not necessarily lead to enlightened social practice as, in the specific case of the United States immediately prior to World War II, "No matter how weak the case for racial purity may be, we understand its social appeal in our society"; the twofold corollary to this state of affairs was that racial stratification always leads to racial discrimination, and that our nation "shall pay the penalty in the form of interracial struggle" (Boas, 1966, pp. 16–17).

Surface Inclusion, Deeply Rooted Exclusion

Interracial struggle, to be sure, is predictable and righteous in the face of racism and discrimination, as we have witnessed from our own Civil War to our civil rights movement. But exclusion has negative consequences far beyond struggle, however righteous. Exclusion also decreases the amount and forms of our nation's capital generation— human, social, intellectual, political and otherwise—and, more serious and threatening, our sense of peoplehood, our *unum*, that is, the *oneness* that is the founding core feature and value of our national identity. The struggle to which Boas alludes in 1931, therefore, is best seen as a means, not an end. Thus, the severe penalty for indulging in and willfully defending our long-term transgression comprised of racism, exclusion and discrimination is a weakened nation along many fronts, domestically and globally. We find ourselves, at present, unable to effectively address, much less fulfill, the educational, economic, health and security needs of whole swaths of the American public. One striking and highly threatening result of our policies of exclusion is the persistent differential performance outcomes and completion rates in schooling across racial and ethnic groups, and now males and females. Another is our waning ability to meet the commitment to entitlements relating to Social Security, Medicare, and Medicaid. At each end of our cultural spectrum, our future possibilities appear bleak, outside of our control. The fragmentation reflected in our larger political self is witnessed in the hyperbolic rants by political figures, media commentators and journalists, and members of the public over immigration, documented and undocumented. Our weakened state translates into diminished international credibility as a global leader, and impaired viability as a world-class competitor.

The contradiction of our nation's foundational rhetoric being egalitarian when, in actuality, the rhetoric was to be controlled and applied by a single group—at first by law and then in practice—has created civil discord, struggle and suffering, but also a marked cultural deficit in our American character. Our national arc of racism includes "the racism of many White feminists" both nationally and globally, as Nussbaum (2010) states in her review of Christine Stansell's history of the feminist movement (*The Feminist Promise, 1792 to the Present*), whose own promising title of a global history is, save one chapter, for all practical purposes a history of the feminist movement in the United States. White feminists during the post-Civil War period and first two decades of the 20th century, regularly argued that "it was absurd to give African-American men the vote but to deny it to women, so much more intelligent and cultivated" and that supporting the vote for suffrage of African American men and women, ultimately would result in the denial of the vote for all women, Black or White—which motivated African-American feminists to "typically [hold] themselves aloof from White feminists" (Nussbaum, 2010, p. 28). Kwok (1992) engages in a cogent examination of Christianity and women in China, and, in extending her analysis to Christian women within the Third World, which includes "Africans, Asians, Afro-Americans, and Latin Americans," succinctly points to a critical difference in feminist Christian frameworks and purposes relating to First World and Third World contexts:

> Third World feminists consistently challenge Western feminist theologians to construct a kind of theology that does not work simply toward the self-aggrandizement of White women but takes into consideration the plight of women in the Third World. (p. 192)

Kwok (2005, pp. 4–5) further lifts the veil covering the face of Christianity's missionary-led encroachment into Third World contexts and the collusive role White women played in its development, contributing as agents to the "narratives of empire" through the "fields of biblical studies, religion, and theology." White women also upheld the religiocentric belief and practice that the superiority of Christianity would rightfully replace the inferior spiritual belief systems by practiced by non-Westerners. As Kwok (2005) notes, White women were both useful in promoting this White male-dominated colonial expansionism and successful in terms of the developing women's movement:

> Because of the difficulties in reaching women due to the segregation of the sexes in some societies, Christian missions sent missionary wives and single women to labor in the field. Although with good intentions to save souls of "heathen" women, these women missionaries participated in "colonial feminism" both discursively and institutionally, by propagating the impression that native women were illiterate, oppressed, and waiting for the White women to bring light to them. Judging from the magnitude of women's participation in mission and the amount of money raised to support such activities, the women's missionary movement must be regarded as the largest women's movement in the nineteenth and early twentieth centuries. (pp. 17–18)

The collusive role of White women in slavery and colonialism—which sought to replace the very core of a people's spiritual beliefs and practices with Christianity while constructing and institutionalizing their economic and political dependency on the encroaching Western nation—was not generally acknowledged in the "second wave" of the feminist movement in the late 1960s (Kwok, 2005, p. 18). As such, according to Kwok's (2005) analysis,

> Some feminist theologians, like the rest of the feminist scholars, reproduced some of the colonialist assumptions in religious discourse....Feminist scholars [homogenized] non-Western women, while maintaining the superior position of Western women above the rest. (p. 18)

Today, we are perhaps less certain that we are in a post-racist era than was reportedly the case in November 2008 at the point of Barack Obama's election as President. As we continue our action-oriented discourse on the ongoing existence and effects of racism as a societal phenomenon in our nation, what should be more certain, as Kwok (2005) eloquently indicates, is that we "need to be vigilant about the deep-seated layers of colonialist patterns of thinking in the archaeological excavations of [our] minds" (p. 3).

In our essence, at the *deep structural level*—that is, from a perspective of power and equity—as a nation we are not who we say we are. From the perspective of taking advantage of the *surface features* of the diverse cultures that comprise our population, we do that well through our food, arts, and entertainment sectors, as well as through the flexibility of our American English dialect to absorb, modify, integrate, and even appropriate words from other languages. Genius and relevance, for example, have sprung from adversity and exclusion experienced by particular groups due to U.S. laws and practices of racism and segregation in the form of musical genres that span our nation's historical development through the mid-20th century and virtually define the notion of American, here and abroad, and America: spirituals, gospel, jazz, rhythm and blues, rock and roll, as well as popular standards ("White Christmas," 1942; "Over the Rainbow," 1939), national hymns ("God Bless America," 1938) and musicals (*Show Boat*, 1927; *Porgy and Bess*, 1935). The composers and interpreters are too many to name, but Thomas Dorsey's innumerable gospel compositions ("Peace in the Valley"; "Take My Hand, Precious Lord"); George Gershwin's popular, symphonic, operetta and opera compositions ("Summertime," *Rhapsody in Blue*); the popular and musical theater compositions of the teams of Richard Rogers and Lorenz Hart and of Jerome Kern and Oscar Hammerstein II; Duke Ellington's big band compositions; Louis Armstrong's revolutionary and all-defining trumpet interpretations in jazz and the innovative clarinet compositions and interpretations of Artie Shaw; as well as the vocal interpretations of Paul Robeson, Marian Anderson, Mahalia Jackson, Ella Fitzgerald, Bessie Smith, Billie Holiday, and Mel Tormé, among countless others, were either Jewish Americans or African Americans. The culturally seismic, far-reaching and embedded contributions by African Americans and Jewish Americans—who at junctures were intertwined, at others, were in competition or independent (Lehman, 2009)—have at once substantively influenced the mainstream and at the same time have not been immune to appropriation or exploitation, or chastisement, by it.

Despite defining cultural contributions by minority group members, maintaining our status quo continuity—that is, the fundamental narrowness of selective group inclusion coupled with targeted group exclusion reinforced by discrimination—has been our default legacy. All challenges and changes to broaden the borders of power and equity—to live up to and to live the American principles set forth by our core documents generated by the Founders of our nation—have come through struggle rather than collective civic enlightenment. Thus, the structures we have produced are severely wanting in all aspects and dimensions. Our public schools that continue to house, rather than serve, ever-increasing numbers of segregated, underperforming, at-risk students are the clearest illustration of our nation's lack of resolve toward cohesiveness, integration and development. As a nation, we need to adopt, advocate and live a conscious, wide-spread policy of inclusion that reflects our deep structure. We need to foster change through inclusive civic discourse and action, without the interracial or inter-ethnic struggle as has been our wont. It is incumbent upon us to understand that *wont* is by choice, not destined. Foods, entertainment, holidays, fashions and the like are vestiges and adaptations of imagined or remembered cultures, however imaginative or popular the creations and fusions that result. Thus, we must understand that surface features associated with racial and ethnic groups do not impact movement away from the status quo—indeed, they might reinforce it as they can generate a false sense of change.

Academia as a Platform for Exclusion and Maintenance of the Status Quo

Samuel Huntington's (2004) screed entitled "The Hispanic Challenge," published in *Foreign Policy* (a magazine he co-founded), embodies this status quo perspective and extends it to the present. His fear-inducing, nativist perspectives archaically warn of the cultural contamination, dilution, and endangerment brought on by Hispanic immigrants and their practices that threaten the primacy (one might also add, purity) of Anglo Protestant values and our very (Anglo-centric) nation. Huntington's framework is clearly reminiscent of the German schools of social anthropology and eugenics mentioned earlier. The threats with which Hispanics endanger "America" include, for Huntington, Catholicism, Spanish, and economic and cultural independence from mainstream culture—all of which are seen by Huntington as antithetical to the unity and prosperity of the nation:

> The persistent inflow of Hispanic immigrants threatens to divide the United States into two peoples, two cultures, and two languages. Unlike past immigrant groups, Mexicans and other Latinos have not assimilated into mainstream U.S. culture, forming instead their own political and linguistic enclaves—from Los Angeles to Miami—and rejecting the Anglo-Protestant values that built the American dream. The United States ignores this challenge at its peril....The United States' national identity, like that of other nation-states, is challenged by the forces of globalization as well as the needs that globalization produces among people for smaller and more meaningful "blood and belief" identities. In this new era, the single most immediate and most serious challenge to America's traditional identity comes from the immense and continuing immigration from Latin America, especially from Mexico, and the fertility rates of these immigrants compared to Black and White American natives....This reality poses a fundamental question: Will the United States remain a country with a single national language and a core Anglo-Protestant culture? By ignoring this question, Americans acquiesce to their eventual transformation into two peoples with two cultures (Anglo and Hispanic) and two languages (English and Spanish). (paras.1, 6, 7)

Through his "Hispanic Challenge" argument, Huntington attempts also to foster misunderstanding toward Hispanic Americans by African Americans and promote inter-minority group division and conflict, claiming that Hispanics, as bilinguals, would obtain employment at the expense of African Americans:

> For the first time in U.S. history, increasing numbers of Americans (particularly Black Americans) will not be able to receive the jobs or the pay they would otherwise receive because they can speak to their fellow citizens only in English. (Hispanic Challenge, online version, p. 5, para. 5)

The stereotype that Huntington applies is fallacious on at least three counts. It is a fallacy to posit that one's heritage culture determines one's bilingualism; it is also fallacious to posit that if one's heritage culture (in this case, African American) is monolingual, one cannot become bilingual. A third fallacy is that if one's heritage is African American, one's native language is only English. Hundreds of thousands of African-origin individuals, mainly slaves, were forcibly sent to Spain and Spanish America beginning in the mid-fifteenth century, and not only learned Spanish, but also influenced the Spanish language, as Lipski's (2005) research succinctly demonstrates:

> From the second half of the fifteenth century through the end of the nineteenth century, hundreds of thousands of sub-Saharan Africans traveled first to Spain, then to Spanish America. Most were slaves, taken as part of the Atlantic slave trade, which displaced millions of Africans to Europe's New World colonies.... In Spanish America, Africans were found in every colony, from the highland mines of Bolivia, Peru, Colombia, and Honduras, to the Argentine pampas, the docks of El Callao, the port attached to Lima, Peru, and the streets of Mexico City.... [The] last wave of slave arrivals touched shore—in the Caribbean Islands, and along the Caribbean and upper Pacific coasts of South America.... Although living in the most humbling conditions, often physically outside the pale of mainstream Spanish society, Black Africans made a lasting impression on the language and culture of the entire Spanish-speaking world. Their use of Spanish was depicted—never flatteringly and often with much exaggeration—from the early sixteenth century to the middle of the twentieth century. (p. 1)

Humans who were slaves, of course, learned other languages within the contexts to which they were forcibly sent, including Portuguese and French.

Huntington's cavalier dominant-group perspective is further in evidence as he ends his warning of an imminent Hispanic invasion with the following quote he attributes to a bumper sticker:

> "Will the last American to leave Miami, please bring the flag." (Hispanic Challenge, online version, p. 7, para. 5)

Thus, Hispanics are, yet again, deemed not American and unpatriotic. In his Hispano-phobic portrait, Huntington (2004) includes African Americans, literally parenthetically (a punctuation device used, apparently, without irony), as victims of Hispanic success, real or imagined, and, by doing so, he continues to promote inter-minority group division and conflict and reinforce the status quo:

> The Cuban and Hispanic dominance of Miami left Anglos (as well as Blacks) as outside minorities that could often be ignored. Unable to communicate with government bureaucrats and discriminated against by store clerks, the Anglos came to realize, as one of them put it, "My God, this is what it's like to be the minority." (Hispanic Challenge, online version, p. 7, para. 5)

Huntington's outrage seems to be along the lines of "This should not be happening to me or us! We're the ones who are supposed to be on top!" It is a long way from producing scholarship that addresses the foibles of racially and ethnically-based win-lose models of national identity and the destructive contradiction they pose relative to fulfilling our founding egalitarian and democratic principles. His line of thought—"Let's band together, even with Blacks, to rid ourselves of this non-WASP menace to ensure our continued rightful place in America"—is yet another example of blind White privilege attempting to selectively use one minority group against another one to maintain inter-generational goals of hierarchy that will re-assert, maintain or extend that which it considers, however erroneously and misguidedly, the foundational status quo.

Huntington (2004) does not write from a position of scholarly strength or objectivity. Rather, he expresses a traditional insensitivity and condescension common to members of the dominant group toward the actual and persistent denigrated status of minority groups, while bewailing hypocritically its injustice and egregiousness when daring to be applied to him or other members of the dominant group, and thereby upsetting or threatening the status quo. His lack of scholarly preparation and intellectual intuition in this academic area is so great that one is left bereft of objective reasons as to the rationale for its publication, much less the attention it garnered.

Huntington, however, is not alone. There are many such scholars who are otherwise competent, even renown, in their areas of specialization but become academically wayward and woefully incompetent upon crossing into the terrain of race and ethnicity to explain group performance differentials and justify group exclusion in

America. Lloyd Dunn, the senior author of the *Peabody Picture Vocabulary Test Series*, for example, produced a monograph in 1987 in which he asserted that Puerto Rican and Mexican-American children in the United States performed poorly in school due to "inferior Spanish language skills" and that their performance was related to deficits attributable to their group (Dunn, 1987, quoted in DeVillar, 1994):

> Because of their lack of intellectual, scholastic, and language aptitude, but also for many other reasons...it is clear that these children are not, as a group, able to cope with the confusion of two languages. (p. 33)

Dunn continues his deficit-based, and scientifically baseless, assertions regarding the role of race and race mixture in the group's poor academic performance (Dunn, 1987, quoted in DeVillar, 1994):

> Race, as a contributing factor, cannot be ignored. It is recalled ... that most Mexican immigrants to the U.S. are brown-skinned people, a mix of American Indian and Spanish blood, while many Puerto Ricans are dark-skinned, a mix of Spanish, Black, and some Indian. Blacks and American Indians have repeatedly scored about 15 points behind Anglos and Orientals on individual tests of intelligence. (p. 33)

Dunn adds more blame to Hispanic students and their parents for having "failed the schools and society, because they have not been motivated and dedicated enough to make the system work for them" and valuing education "is a tradition that Hispanics in general do not appear to have." Walker (1987; cited in DeVillar, 1994, p. 34) characterizes the genetic deficiency position of Jensen (1971), the language-deficit perspective of Deutsch (1963), the dysfunctional family and cultural systems paradigm of Moynihan (1967), the field-sensitive learning style orientation of Ramírez and Castañeda (1974), and the low self-concept model articulated by various researchers as earlier examples of studies that attributed major, if not sole, responsibility for school performance to putative deficits attributable to minority students, their families, and their perceived cultural orientations.

Current Racial Conflict and the Persistence of Exclusion

Our national ability to maintain a contradictory commitment to the status quo—that is, a hierarchically fragmented society based on racial advantage—while appearing and claiming to achieve substantive change continues. The recent popular mandate, for example, to transform "a center-right country into a center-left one" (Smith, 2010, p. 22) through having elected Barack Obama President was quickly abandoned, and President Obama "found himself shouting into the wind," leading Smith to conclude with two points: "the easy history has been made, and it's simpler to change our leaders than ourselves." President Obama himself well understands the surface-substance distinction and his position in the long struggle for minority group civil rights in our nation (Obama, quoted in Remnick, 2010):

> I am a direct beneficiary of [civil-rights leaders'] sacrifice and their effort—my entire generation is....There is a certain awe that I continue to hold when I consider the courage, tenacity, audacity of the civil-rights leaders of that time.... There is a voice that is best captured by [Martin Luther] King, which says that we, as African-Americans, are American, and that our story is America's story, and that by perfecting our rights we perfect the Union [and] through the deliverance of the least of these, the society as a whole is transformed for the better. And, in that sense, what I was trying to communicate [in my Inaugural Ceremony] is: we didn't quite get there, but that journey continues. (p. 97)

Barkan's (1992, pp. 4, 8) profusely documented narrative in *The Retreat from Scientific Racism* centers on the thesis that the "discrediting of race prejudice [in the United States] was a result of the conscious efforts and commitment of a minority of scientists who ... remained social and political outsiders [, such as] Jews and women in Anthropology." Thus, at the dawn of the World War II, a shift was realized in which scientific support ceased in the United States for the biological notion of a distinct typology of races, leaving still intact the legally supported, socially and politically motivated barriers to inclusion into our mainstream culture. Despite the subsequent legal shifts of which President Obama speaks, and the explicit statements by scientists at the beginning of the 1950s, our current 21st century national (and general Western) climate—governmental, academic and popular—with respect to the construct and role of racial integration and its relationship to national unity remains turbulent, and our everyday societal discourse rages with conflict and division, particularly in the face of transgenerational ignorance and embedded stereotypes—positive toward the mainstream, negative toward the "other."

A contemporary form of the eugenics perspective, for example, remains prevalent among particular groups of scholars and internet groups, who conflate race, ethnicity, language and culture into a single category of *race*. They continue to vehemently protest multiculturalism in the United States and other countries, and believe that genetic (inheritable) differences account, in part, for persistent tested differences across ethnic and racial groups (American Renaissance.com, 2006). On April 2, 2006, the *Sunday Times* of London published a comment on racial IQ research in which eight professors from the U.S., Canada, Denmark, Ireland and Scotland signed a statement—including Arthur Jensen—protesting disciplinary action against an academic colleague who engaged in such research, which, in part, read (Racial IQ Research, 2006):

> Dr Frank Ellis [has presented] research, published in peer-reviewed academic journals and scholarly books which demonstrates that Blacks have, on average, lower IQ scores and poorer academic achievement than do Whites .... Much solid research also makes it more likely than not that there is a genetic contribution to this (and other) group IQ differences. Dr Ellis, then, has done no more than restate what has been said for half century by a number of eminent psychologists and anthropologists at leading universities....There is an important and legitimate debate going on in intelligence and genetics. (paras. 1–3)

Current racial conflict and nativist exclusionary rhetoric internal to our nation are reported in media outlets outside the United States, and associated with the Tea Party movement. The Tea Party movement—heavily financed by Charles and David Koch, billionaire brothers who own Koch Industries and who collectively are only behind Bill Gates and Warren Buffet in wealth (Mayer, 2010)—and those media-savvy personages associated with it (e.g., Glenn Beck, Sarah Palin, and Tom Tancredo) are characterized by terms such as "ultraconservative wave," "far-right television personality," "penchant for conspiracy theories." But at its center, as one reporter writes:

"Ultimately, this movement is about race. The Tea Partiers say they want to 'take America back for Americans'—but what they mean is White, native-born Americans" (How they see us: Is the Tea Party a real threat?, 2010, p. 14). The latter journalist's experience at a Tea Party convention highlights the connection between Tea Party affiliation and its racist underpinnings (How they see us: Is the Tea Party a real threat?, 2010):

> One of the main speakers, former Republican Rep. Tom Tancredo, is famous for trying to amend the U.S. Constitution to establish English as the sole national language. He railed against immigrants and poor Blacks, saying that Barack "Hussein" Obama came to power only because the U.S. allows people to vote "who can't even spell 'vote' or say it in English." His plea for "a return to the literacy tests that were used during segregation to keep Blacks from voting" registered with the Tea Partiers, who are mostly "Whites in a panic over the arrival of a Black in the White House." (p. 14)

Such Tea Party fringe-group rhetoric does not reflect or respect our current national laws regarding language or voting. Its archaic rhetoric harks back to our nativist-segregative historical practice and apparently still strikes a chord, however dissonant to those who value inclusion, among those who believe that a White Anglo Saxon Protestant (WASP), monolingual English-speaking America is the only real America.

The Effects of Systemic Vacillation and Naïveté on Cohesion and Competitiveness

As a nation, we continue to be consistent in our inconsistency with respect to either universally applying our official rhetoric and practice to all groups or passively accepting the racialized status quo model. This prickly oscillation has been present regardless of the historical period or relative degree of tension or threat between these fundamentally oppositional nationhood perspectives. Some cultural analysts attribute the give and take in these areas of American discord to our system of *checks and balances*. This system, in the words of Pulitzer Prize-winning journalist Anna Quindlen (2009), ironically serves to stall or deform issues of national transformative concern rather than push them forward to implementation for the common good:

This is a country that often has transformational ambitions but is saddled with an incremental system [of checks and balances], a nation built on revolution, then engineered so the revolution can rarely take hold....The small steps an incremental system guarantees become even smaller in the face of pitched partisan rancor, until eventually nothing moves at all....Many abolitionists decried Lincoln's executive order, which freed few slaves and failed to make the buying and selling of humans illegal, while conservatives thought it was radical and unwise. (pp. 32, 34)

Our national cultural contradiction of particularistic cohesion and universalistic exclusion co-exists to differing degrees of tension depending on the era with a corollary principle that is self-serving, self-deceiving, and, ultimately, self-destructive: freedom reigns for all who are in the United States. Thus, any group who has not availed itself of the opportunities and benefits must be due to the group itself, whether by nature (i.e., inherent traits) or nurture (i.e., of the group's own making). This peoplehood-destroying contradiction and accompanying corollary continue to operate in the present—their pretense to righteousness fueled periodically by race-based, faux-academic literature that too-easily worms itself into the popular and professional press and discourse—and reinforce our national race-based ethos, as if it were substantive and worthy of serious consideration.

Eugenics, including its noxious presence by any other name, is clothed in pseudo-scientific garb, even by modern-day scientists, to justify biological exclusion, not mere social exclusion, and promotes sterilization, abortion, and other reproductive-restricting tactics to ensure ultimate disappearance. There are strong and weak versions of this strategy, but genetic-deficit based on race (in its expanded sense as used popularly and erroneously by the general public and professionals, alike) is at its core (see, for example, Jensen, 1969; Shockley, 1963, 1965 [speeches at Gustavus Adolphus College, 1963, 1965; see Shurkin, 2008]; Dunn, 1988; Herrnstein and Murray, 1994; and Huntington, 2004; among others).

Our negative attitudes toward perceived racial differences—to include the specific and general meanings of the term—and self-justified, self-serving exclusionary practices, coupled with our refusal to repudiate them, will continue to generate dire consequences for our nation. Dinesh D'Souza, a native of Mumbai, India, self-proclaimed conservative, writer and "public intellectual" associated with the conservative Hoover Institution and current president of The King's College in New York City, interweaves and spreads crude racist remarks, at times quoting others but also generating his own, against African Americans in his books, including:

> 'A mind is a terrible thing to waste—especially on a nigger.' (D'Souza, *Illiberal Education*, 1991, p. 1)

> "In summary, the American slave *was* treated like property, which is to say, pretty well." (D'Souza, *The End of Racism*, 1995, p. 91)

In D'Souza's recent cover article in *Forbes* (2010), he casts suspicion on President Obama's degree of Americanness, stating, "Here is a man who spent his formative years—the first 17 years of his life—off the American mainland, in Hawaii, Indonesia and Pakistan, with multiple subsequent journeys to Africa," to then use his upbringing in the state of Hawaii, as well as residence and travel to other countries, as formative elements in the development of Obama's un-American cultural character, making him, in D'Souza's words, "the most antibusiness president in a generation, perhaps in American history." In the article, D'Souza continues to build his psychoanalytic-like framework, explicating Obama's anti-business/anti-American actions from having appropriated his father's "dream"—used in Obama's autobiographical work entitled *Dreams from My Father* (1995/2004): to destroy neocolonialism—the last vestige being the United States— through government actions that control business, or, in D'Souza's words, "to wring the neocolonialism out of America and the West." To cherish and live Obama's father dream is an odd personal, much less political, goal, as Obama's father was, D'Souza writes disparagingly, a polygamist who not only had, at different points in his life, four wives and eight children, but who was accused of "abuse and wife-beating," and who was a "regular drunk driver," who killed one person and, later, killed himself in a driving accident. Yet, from him, President Obama, according to D'Souza,

> learned to see America as a force for global domination and destruction [and] America's military as an instrument of neocolonial occupation. He adopted his father's position that capitalism and free markets are code words

for economic plunder. Obama grew to perceive the rich as an oppressive class, power in the world is a measure of how selfishly it consumes the globe's resources and how ruthlessly it bullies and dominates the rest of the planet. (How Obama Thinks, online version, p. 3, para. 7)

D'Souza capitalizes on the anti-Muslim rants and perspectives of Glenn Beck (see chapter 7) by asserting that President Obama

supports the Ground Zero mosque because to him 9/11 is the event that unleashed the American bogey and pushed us into Iraq and Afghanistan. He views some of the Muslims who are fighting against America abroad as resisters of U.S. imperialism. (How Obama Thinks, online version, p. 1, para. 6)

The mainstream mantle of ignorance continues to be reproduced transgenerationally—formally through our schools and informally throughout our professional and social settings—veiling the immane effects of accumulated resistance on our aspirations toward national cohesion and our sustained development and global competitiveness. In our particular ideological case, United States democracy means representative rule by the whole without exercising tyranny toward any one group. While we may ideologically believe this, we have not voluntarily practiced it, as White racism, Anglo-Saxon ethnocentrism, and English language monolingualism have been our signature national policy and behavior. Our incremental movement toward universal inclusion is driven historically by official mandate rather than by mainstream moral consciousness or enlightened social practice.

We—the mainstream of the United States—are recalcitrant integrationists and, given our power and entitlement, we stave off integration in spite of official mandates through legal, economic and duplicitous means and see these tools as protective and righteous rather than as culturally reactionary, economically impoverishing, and a betrayal to the principles embedded in our democratic heritage and mandate. We, as a nation, as a people, must see our mainstream behavior as reactionary, impoverishing, and betraying in order to transform ourselves from our current operational belief that accepts as natural the socio-culturally vicious cycle of freedom for some and exclusion for others to a state of universal inclusion. We must view and reject the belief in the naturalness of selective freedom as an unsustainable contradiction that stifles and threatens the very survival of our democratic endeavor, national development, global competitiveness and American culture. If we do not do so, we will neither achieve our dream of transcendent national unity nor prevail as a vital cultural entity or model in the 21st century. The luster of our global preeminence will have faded, the power of our global energy, depleted.

Chapter 4

Life and Race in Emerging Suburbia: Redlining and the Selective Rise of the White American Middle Class

In the wake of war and depression, the GI Bill sent a generation to college and created the largest middle-class in history.

—President Barack Obama, Address to Joint Session of Congress, Tuesday, February 24, 2009

Between 1934 and 1962, the federal government backed $120 billion of home loans. More than 98% went to Whites. Of the 350,000 new homes built with federal support in northern California between 1946 and 1960, fewer than 100 went to African Americans.

—Larry Adelman, 2003

Increased Economic Inequality in the United States

The United States has become a nation that is increasingly characterized by division rather than unity. Our rhetoric of the 21st century is one that prizes conflict and self-righteousness across groups that seek to convince others of the justness of their particular cause and the dangers in adhering to alternative ones. Division occurs along many lines, but those within the political, religious and economic spheres have become increasingly salient and strident over the past three decades. The July 19–26, 2010 issue of *The Nation* dedicated a double issue to its cover story on inequality in America. Within its covers, specialists addressed ways in which increasing and disproportionate wealth-accumulation differences across classes and persistence of segregated neighborhoods continue to adversely affect the ability of schools to equitably serve and develop the socio-academic (DeVillar & Faltis, 1991; DeVillar, Faltis, & Cummins, 1994) needs and expectations of all America's students, but particularly those of our nation's poor and even middle-class students. Persistent and expanding differential schooling outcomes at the group level, whether by gender, race, ethnicity or income, stand in stark contrast, and dramatic misalignment with the egalitarian goals of our national rhetoric, and contribute to widening gaps and deficits between groups—and therefore the quality and extent of life chances, most ominously within the dimensions of career, economic and health.

The figures stated across the articles in *The Nation* are not necessarily new, but they do reflect a pattern that now forms part of our quotidian reality—a pattern that needs to be broken given that its direction and consequences are antithetical to the democratic rhetoric that characterizes us as a nation and the values that we supposedly hold and aspire to practice without prejudice. From the late 1970s to 2007, for example, the richest 1 percent of our nation received 23.5 percent of its total income, a figure not seen since 1928 when that same portion of our population received 23.9 percent of the total income (Reich, 2010). In fact, prior to the late 1970s, the richest 1 percent received "only 8 to 9 percent of America's total annual income" (Reich, 2010, p.13). Incomes within the financial sector have increased disproportionately as well. Even in 2009, as the United States remained devastated by the worst economic recession since the Great Depression, Madrick (2010) reveals that this sector continues its profligate behaviors in the face of national economic crisis characterized by "runaway incomes at the top of the earnings scale [amid] widespread income stagnation":

> But the true rub was when Wall Street paid [their people] $145 billion in 2009, a near record, when the rest of America was mired in the worst recession since the 1930s and one out of six Americans couldn't find a full-time job. (p. 21)

The top 20 percent of families fared well also, as their share of total income increased from 41.1 percent in 1973 to 47.3 percent in 2007, which means that the share of total income of the bottom 80 percent decreased (Madrick, 2010). At the individual level, Madrick and his colleague Nikolaos Papanikolaou found that median wages for the high school-educated and college-educated men with full-time jobs had virtually remained stagnated at 1969 levels. While incomes of women with full-time employment rose, they did not do so "robustly" and "remained below male levels;" thus, as hourly wages and benefits have virtually stagnated, the costs of services continue to increase, meaning that it takes more money for the middle class to receive the same services, including those relating to education and health (Madrick, 2010). Ironically, perhaps even bewilderingly, as Yglesias (2010) reminds us, in spite of the dire effects of our present recession in the United States, when seen from a broader perspective, the present context

> has been one of the greatest times to be alive in the history of mankind. The cause is the enormous improvement in living standards of the people in China, India, Brazil and other large developing nations. On the moral balance sheet, this betterment of some of the globe's poorest people more than outweighs the continued stagnation of middle-class wages in the United States. (p. 22)

Current official unemployment statistics at the general level for July 2010 hover around 9.5 percent, representing 14.6 million individuals (Bureau of Labor Statistics, August 6, 2010). African American unemployment, at 15.6 percent, is "nearly double that of Whites," while unemployment of workers between the ages of 16 and 24 is "roughly double that of all workers" (Newman & Pedulla, 2010, p. 18). Specifically, the BLS Employment Situation Summary for July 2010 noted:

> Among the major worker groups, the unemployment rate for adult men (9.7 percent), adult women (7.9 percent), teenagers (26.1 percent), Whites (8.6 percent), Blacks (15.6 percent), and Hispanics (12.1 percent) showed little or no change in July. The jobless rate for Asians was 8.2 percent, not seasonally adjusted. (para. 3)

Unemployment in May 2010 for Black teenagers, Patterson (2010) points out, "stands at a shocking 38 percent" (p. 18) and had increased to 40.6 percent by July 2010 (Bureau of Labor Statistics, 2010).

Beyond differential unemployment figures across racial, gender, age, and ethnic groups, Patterson (2010) notes that White median family wealth, at $100,000 in 2007, was 20 times that of Black median family wealth, which in 2007 was a paltry $5,000, having barely risen in the previous 23 year period (1984–2007). The Institute on Assets and Social Policy (IASP) report, "The Racial Wealth Gap Increases Fourfold," to which Patterson refers for his figures, was published in May 2010 and also reported that the average *middle-income White household* ($30,000 per year) had accumulated $74,000 in financial assets by 2007, whereas the average *high-income Black family* ($50,000 or more per year) had accumulated only $18,000 in the same period (Shapiro, Meschede, & Sullivan, 2010). The financial assets of the average *high-income White family*, from 1984 to 2007, had grown from about $53,000 to more than $240,000 (Shapiro et al., 2010).

Black median household income has decreased from $37,093 in 2000—the highest it has reached—to $34,218 in 2008; their relative proportions to White median household income were, respectively, 65 percent and 61.6 percent, which demonstrates that the median household income gap has increased over the past eight year period between African American and White households (Patterson, 2010). Our national sordid past of slavery and racism, which excluded millions of citizens and residents considered non-White from access to and participation in institutions and services reserved for White members of our nation, and which to varying degrees lasted officially until 1965, deprived them of the benefits that accrued to the White group—particularly education that ensured gainful employment and career development opportunities and wealth-building that could be transferred from one generation to the next.

The Active Role of Government in Residential Segregation

Home ownership was a critical factor in building and sustaining the middle-class family in America. Although our nation is currently mired in an economic recession of massive proportions and expanding social problems, both of which may well be long term rather than short term, home ownership in general has been a viable means to build wealth through appreciation and re-selling, and as a means to enter and maintain oneself within the American middle class. The National Housing Act of 1934 [Public–No. 479–73D Congress; H. R. 9620; Title I–Housing Renovation and Modernization] was enacted by Congress and authorized by President

Franklin Delano Roosevelt "To encourage improvement in housing standards and conditions, to provide a system of mutual mortgage insurance, and for other purposes" (p. 1). At the time of its enactment in 1934, race-based segregation continued as a legally mandated— *Plessy v. Ferguson (1896)* remained the law of the land until 1954— and societally-supported reality in the United States, including the North. This nationwide policy and practice allowed, even encouraged and enforced, a distorted yet universally applied reality that viewed and treated the African American as inferior and a perpetual trespasser, as W.E.B. DuBois (1934/1970) vividly recounts:

> No Black man, whatever his culture or ability, is today in America regarded as a man by any considerable number of White Americans. The difference between North and South in the matter of segregation is largely a difference of degree; of wide degree certainly, but still of degree. In the North, neither [George] Schuyler nor Kelly Miller[1] nor anyone with a visible admixture of Negro blood can frequent hotels or restaurants. They have difficulty in finding dwelling places in better class neighborhoods. They occupy "Lower 1" on Pullmans, and if they are wise, they do not go into dining cars when any large number of White people is there. Their children either go to colored schools or to schools nominally for both races, but actually attended almost exclusively by colored children. In other words, they are confined by unyielding public opinion to a Negro world. They earn a living on colored newspapers or in colored colleges, or other racial institutions. They treat colored patients and preach to colored pews. Not 1 of the 12 colored Ph.Ds of last year, trained by highest American and European standards, is going to get a job in any White university. Even when Negroes in the North work side by side with Whites, they are segregated, like the postal clerks, or refused by White unions or denied merited promotion....The higher the Negro climbs or tries to climb, the more pitiless and unyielding the color ban. Segregation may be just as evil today as it was in 1910, but it is more insistent, more prevalent and more unassailable by appeal or argument. (pp. 289–290)

Eileen Diaz McConnell and Faranak Miraftab (2009) offer a vivid, data-driven portrait regarding the effects of the *Plessy* decision on the extent of spatial segregation in U.S. residential patterns:

> Bolstered by the U.S. Supreme Court's 1896 *Plessy v. Ferguson* decision declaring that racial segregation was legal, for decades communities across America employed aggressive strategies to remain all-White. Such practices included violence, overt and covert threats of violence, and local ordinances

that excluded African Americans or sanctioned force to drive them out of town. Thus some communities practiced racial apartheid by becoming "sundown," places that used harassment, intimidation, economic and social ostracism, and local ordinances to keep African Americans, Mexicans, and other groups from living there (Loewen 2005). For example, between 1890 and 1930, the Black populations of several hundred counties declined by at least 50 percent within 10 years or less, perhaps entirely due to "racial cleansings" by local Whites that forced nearly all Blacks to flee the area (Jaspin 2007). As a result of these practices, perhaps a thousand U.S. localities—small towns, large metropolitan areas, and suburbs—were all White by design between 1890 and 1930 (Loewen 2005, p. 606).

Once again, the penetrating insights of W.E.B. DuBois (1903/ 1989), in his essay "Of Our Spiritual Strivings," serve to contextualize the effects of racism in the post-Civil War/Post-Reconstruction era, particularly on the consciousness of the African American male with respect to his circumstance. Racism, as in any century, was a dehumanization process that remained clearly in purposeful operation at the dawn of the Twentieth Century, and whose consequences, through "reflection and self-examination," were clearly and fully evident to the African American. More important, according to DuBois (1903/1989), its long-term consequences would have been projected to be even more disabling had not the African American male experienced that

> his own soul rose before him, and he saw himself,—darkly as through a veil; and yet he saw in himself some faint revelation of his power, of his mission. He began to have a dim feeling that, to attain his place in the world, he must be himself, and not another. (p. 9)

DuBois (1903/1989) presents in stark prose the details and circum-stances of which the African American male was conscious in 1903, a time squarely within the spatial segregation period described above by Diaz McConnell and Faranak Miraftab (2009):

> He felt his poverty; without a cent, without a home, without land, tools, or savings, he had entered into competition with rich, landed skilled neighbors. To be a poor man is hard, but to be a poor race in a land of dollars is the very bottom of hardships. He felt the weight of his ignorance,—not simply of letters, but of life, of business, of the humanities; the accumulated sloth and shirking and awkwardness of decade and centuries shackled his

hands and feet. Nor was his burden all poverty and ignorance. The red stain of bastardy, which two centuries of systematic legal defilement of Negro women had stamped upon his race, meant not only the loss of ancient African chastity, but also the hereditary weight of a mass of corruption from White adulterers, threatening almost the obliteration of the Negro home. (p. 9)

The National Housing Act of 1934 (NHA) was one of many Great Depression-related measures of the Roosevelt Administration (1933–1945) to get our derailed national economy back on track. But to what degree was this and other government actions a means to get our society on a non-racist track—that is, to generalize from the particular White group that historically was the sole beneficiary of opportunities to other American groups not designated or perceived as White? DuBois (1934/1970) was a realist relative to the Federal Government's role in extending rights and opportunities beyond the "Color Line" imposed and protected by White America:

> Segregation may be compulsory by law or it may be compulsory by economic or social condition, or it may be a matter of free choice. At any rate, it is the separation of human beings and separation despite the will to humanity. Such separation is evil....[In light of] the Depression and the New Deal[, the] government, national and state, is helping and guiding the individual. It has entered and entered for good into the social and economic organization of life. We could wish, we could pray, that this entrance could absolutely ignore lines of race and color, but we know perfectly well it does not and will not, and with the present American opinion, it cannot. (p. 292)

The Root of Wealth-Building Disparity: Redlining

The National Housing Act of 1934 confirmed the unjaundiced view of DuBois as it continued the practice of *redlining*, which was, as Massey and Denton (1993) point out, "initiated and institutionalized" by the prior year's Home Owners' Loan Corporation (HOLC) of 1933, whose intent was to provide

> funds for refinancing urban mortgages in danger of default and granted low-interest loans to former owners who had lost their homes through foreclosure to enable them to regain their properties. The HOLC was the first government-sponsored program to introduce, on a mass scale, the use of long-term, self-amortizing mortgages with uniform payments. (p. 53)

Redlining was based on a hierarchical 4-point rating scale to assess loan risks developed by the HOLC, where applicants within the first two categories would be granted loans and those within the next two would not—the fourth area was coded in red and reflected African American residential settlements.

The point, of course, is not that racial profiling and exclusion, coupled with persistent negative economic repercussions, in real estate as well as other sectors of our national economy was initiated in 1933 by the HOLC Act and continued by the National Housing Act of 1934, and specifically the Federal Housing Administration that the 1934 Act established. Real estate policies and practices followed our existing national racist laws, which were also reflected in the general employment, educational, health, recreational, religious and other everyday forms of American life that unfairly and inhumanely privileged only those who could be perceived as White. Rather, the point is that the HOLC Act and subsequent Acts expressed explicit federal government complicity and support in the midst of the Great Depression and the New Deal—and a decade later, the returning WWII veterans who were African American, Hispanic, Native American, Asian, Jewish, or who belonged to other "incompatible" groups—for the continued practice of segregating and devaluing African Americans and their property by redlining, as well as that of denying other ethnic groups considered "undesirable" or "inharmonious" the opportunity to save or own their homes by categorizing their residential areas as Category 3 or 4 risks and refusing them entry into the White residential areas (Massey & Denton, 1993, pp. 51–53). Thus, the federal government served as the prime model for maintaining the racist status quo and gave the green light, so to speak, for private agency lenders to continue or initiate their own redlining policies and practices.

Real Estate and Segregationist Policies: Market-Based Exclusion

A glaring example of how academic research influenced, supported and even solidified government policy-making and common private practice relative to lending that favored Whites and excluded African American and particular ethnic groups involved Homer Hoyt. Hoyt—a

Phi Beta Kappa graduate of the University of Kansas at 18 years old, who received his J.D. and Ph.D. at the University of Chicago, taught at various colleges, worked in real estate and later at MIT and Columbia—in 1933 published a hierarchical list of racial and ethnic groups relative to each group's influence on land values and in 1934 was hired by the federal government to "develop the first under-writing criteria—who is a good credit risk and who is not –for the new Federal Housing Administration (FHA)" (Dedman, 1988g). Simply stated, the policy and practice justified the continued exclusion of particular racial and ethnic groups, based on their perceived lack—and even tested lack, albeit through flawed instrumentation (see, for example, G. E. Allen, n.d.; Colvin & R. D. Allen, 1923; Cronbach, 1975; Darcy, 1963; Kroeber, 1948; Labov, 1972; Peal & Lambert, 1962; Pinter & Arsenian, 1937)—of ever meeting social, political or mental standards that would make them fit for inclusion in spaces that were meant for Whites of Northern European origins. The Hoyt market-based eugenicist model was present in the initial text of the American Institute of Real Estate Appraisers of 1933, "which warned appraisers of the harm to property values caused by the 'infiltration of inharmonious racial groups.' The list appeared in the bible of appraising, McMichael's Appraising Manual, as late as 1975," and, viral-like, infested the regulations, codes, handbooks and practices of banks and real estate agents until race-based exclusionary guidelines were universally purged as the result of a U.S. Department of Justice lawsuit settlement in 1977 (Dedman, 1988g). African Americans (9th place) and Mexicans (10th place), respectively, were the two lowest-ranking groups on the list, while Russians and "lower-class" Jews were tied for seventh place and "South Italians" were in eighth relative to "exerting the most detrimental effect" on land values in Chicago; English, Germans, Scotch, Irish, and Scandinavians, respectively, were all placed as first, given that representatives from each group exerted the "most favorable" effect on land values (Hoyt, 1933, p. 316).

Thus, the combination of Hoyt's analysis, hierarchical listing of racial and nationality groups, as well as his interpretations and recommendations, extended the extant policy and practice of racial and ethnic exclusion, and now buttressed it by the application of scientific methodology. Hoyt clearly understood that land values were influenced by class, race and ethnicity ("nationality groups") and that irrational prejudice played a part in determining their higher or lower land value. He understood as well that, due to forced or voluntary migratory shifts, the same neighborhood from which a valued group would leave would lose value once a lesser valued group entered. Writing in 1933, Hoyt states:

> Part of the attitude reflected in lower land values is due entirely to racial prejudice, which may have no reasonable basis. Nevertheless, if the entrance of a colored family into a White neighborhood causes a general exodus of the White people, such dislikes are reflected in property values. Except in the case of negroes [sic] and Mexicans, however, these racial and national barriers disappear when the individuals in the foreign nationality groups rise in the economic scale or conform to American standards of living. Hence, the classification given below applies only to members of the races mentioned who are living in colonies at standards of living below those to which most Americans are accustomed. While the ranking given below may be scientifically wrong from the standpoint of inherent racial characteristics, it registers an opinion or prejudice that is reflected in land values; it is the ranking of races and nationalities with respect to their beneficial effect upon land values. (p. 314)

Hoyt further understood, through his analysis of 100 years of land values in Chicago, that those Americans designated as Negroes or Mexicans were perceived and treated as constant pariahs—that is, as despised groups, as social outcasts, and as such the "racial and national barriers" *would not* disappear, regardless of their "rise in the economic scale or conform[ity] to American standards of living." *In all other cases*, regardless of a group's hierarchical placement on Hoyt's (1933) 10-category listing—in reverse order, beginning with number 8, "South Italians, Russian Jews of the lower class, Greeks, Lithuanians, Poles, Bohemians or Czechoslovakians, or North Italians"—group members could ultimately form part of the "harmonious" groups, the standard of which was, collectively, those listed in first place: "English, Germans, Scotch, Irish, [and] Scandinavians" (p. 316).

It is little wonder that in a racist society, where White is the prized color of reference for societal entry and acceptance, a society in which positive qualities of human exceptionality are attributed to the color White, and where all who have other skin colors are designated as lacking in positive qualities, that land values would follow whiteness, particularly those groups who were considered being most White. Nor is it surprising that African Americans, the lowest but for Mexicans on the hierarchical scale, and one of two groups who had never been associated with increased land values, would pay more rent for a less-desirable abode in a less-desirable area than would a White for a more-desirable abode in a more-desirable area, which was actually the case, at the turn of the 20th century as Hoyt's (1933) research demonstrates:

> The increase in immigration and the growth of the negro [*sic*] section was causing an expansion of some of these old areas. The ghetto was overflowing westward and a new ghetto was forming between Harrison and Fourteenth streets, Racine and Robey streets, by 1903. The colored belt had burst the boundaries that had prior to 1900 confined it between State and Federal streets from Twenty-second and Thirty-ninth streets where negroes had paid 8 per cent higher rents than were paid for far better houses east of State Street. (p. 216)

For Hoyt, and countless other participants in the "land game," whether as developers, sellers, buyers, landlords, real estate agents, appraisers, or bankers, race-/national group-based land value was an economic reality that transgressed national rhetoric (e.g., equality) yet complied with national law (i.e., enforced segregation of "races"). Essentially, segregation was specifically aimed at African Americans, but Asian Americans, Hispanic Americans and Native Americans, as well as Jews, were also groups who were considered undesirable and needing to be segregated; that is, they were to be excluded legally or by "gentleman's agreement" from the mainstream. Hoyt and others were able to view the situation of racist segregation monocellularly, from the single perspective of its effects on land values, and leave aside any mention, much less action, of a moral dimension. The era, after all, was clearly one of nationwide legal racism since the *Plessy v. Ferguson* Supreme Court decision in 1896, where Whites and whiteness reigned supreme.

The policies and practices regarding renting and selling in designated areas according to one's race or ethnicity—a "can't pass, won't sell" approach—were founded upon notions of racial differentiation that even in 1933 was difficult to scientifically justify. As we have seen, even Hoyt (1933) articulated that the practices could be labeled as prejudiced. Nevertheless, the rhetoric of equality in homeownership (and rental) opportunities, even within the era of the combined Depression and New Deal, continued to be trumped by a deference to racist attitudes and behaviors—and White members of a whole residential community could leave it to reside in another if encroachment, even by a single family or person of color, occurred.

In 1908, as new immigrants from less valued parts of Europe (south and east) and African Americans from the southern U.S. migrated to the North and Midwest United States, the segregated neighborhood boundaries, rarely fixed, began to expand. Hoyt (1933) describes the immediate effect on residents within one White neighborhood in Chicago in 1908 as the boundaries of the less-desirable neighborhood expanded:

> By 1908 the colored people had occupied Wabash Avenue solidly from Twenty-sixth to Thirty-ninth Street, had taken possession of many houses on Vernon and Calumet avenues in the same limits, and had placed thirty-two of their race on Groveland Avenue from Twenty-ninth to Thirty-third Street. An organization of White property owners endeavored to halt the advance east of Wabash Avenue by an agreement not to rent or sell to colored people. The effect of the appearance of the first colored family in a neighborhood was thus described: "The first colored man to move into a community of this character is compelled to pay higher rent but as soon as he is discovered, rents throughout the entire section go down, and it is with difficulty that any one is secured to occupy adjoining flats or houses." (p. 216)

Population increases among the diverse racial, immigrant and native-born groups in Chicago from 1830 to 1930 were dramatic. Prior to 1860, accurate data relative to foreign-born residents were unavailable and the increase in "colored population...was negligible" (Hoyt, 1933, p. 284). The increase in total population in Chicago, from 1830 to 1930, was 3,257,234. Of this total, the increase in foreign-born population comprised 787,633 (24%), that of the "colored" population, 248,697 (7.6%), and that of the White population from elsewhere in the United States, 1,111,433 (34%). Thus, the incoming White, foreign-born and "colored" populations accounted for more than 65 percent (65.6%) of the population increase in Chicago from 1830 to 1930, and for 68 percent of the total population increase in

Chicago from 1860 to 1930. The demand for housing, both rental and owned, increased as established residential communities were subjected to increasing flows of renters and buyers in need. The demand, together with the type of group in need of housing, sparked a shift in residential site preference and an opportunity for builders to construct new housing.

Landmark research by academicians such as Hoyt's in 1933 and landmark policies enacted by the federal government the following year relative to nationwide homeownership opportunities perpetrated the racial differentiation myth, effectively enabling the White group to prosper through government-secured loans while African Americans and other negatively marked groups were excluded and relegated to explicitly less desirable residential areas. This was a systemic approach to preserve and enhance land value, where the perceived need for banks to protect their loans was supported by federal government policy and practices, appraisers, and real estate agents, as well as many of the homeowners who were recipients of home mortgage loans, and thus indebted to a lending institution and the government. This systemic approach to wealth accumulation, at once selectively inclusive (Whites only) and exclusionary ("colored" populations, Jews), and its dire consequences for African Americans and other excluded groups, transpired in the North, as DuBois predicted all too well, and in the South and Midwest. This systemic economic racism prevailed across decades in our nation, including the West, as Adelman (2003) reports:

> Between 1934 and 1962, the federal government backed $120 billion of home loans. More than 98% went to Whites. Of the 350,000 new homes built with federal support in northern California between 1946 and 1960, fewer than 100 went to African Americans. (The Advantages Grow, Generation to Generation, para. 4)

As we shall see in the following section, the seed for what was to become the very model for the federally financed American suburb was planted in the North—three times, in fact: first in Levittown, New York, then in Levittown, Pennsylvania, and last in Levittown, New Jersey. And each and every time, the community was built for Whites only.

Redlining: Its Double-Edged Effects on
Minority Groups and Whites

Redlining had far-reaching detrimental social and economic effects for race relations in the United States, and for African Americans and ethnic (e.g., Hispanic Americans) and religious (e.g., Jews) minority groups in general. Bond and Williams (2007) poignantly characterize the long-term effects of redlining—that is, the dual-pronged government-supported policy and practice that, on the one hand, denied insurable home loans to African American and particular minority groups and, on the other hand, allowed White residential areas to expand in number and appreciate in value while channeling and relegating perceived non-White groups to segregated residential areas with little opportunity for wealth accumulation through home ownership or appreciation or social or geographic mobility:

> The racial segregation of U.S. cities today is inextricably linked with the government and private sector policies of the past. The Federal Housing Administration has insured 34 million properties since its inception in 1934, but critics contend that it has often fostered racial inequality in homeownership along the way. In its 1938 Underwriting Manual to banks' loan officers, the FHA explicitly contended that neighborhood stability depended on houses in an area not being "invaded" by "incompatible racial and social groups." The FHA ensured higher levels of racial segregation by color-coding maps to indicate areas" credit worthiness, "redlining" racially mixed—and thus less desirable—neighborhoods (Farley and Frey 1994)....
> Along with color-coding neighborhoods, the FHA further restricted Blacks in their housing options by financially backing residential projects that had restrictive covenants associated with them that prevented non-Whites from purchasing homes in White neighborhoods. This excluded Blacks from most suburban areas by preventing them from accessing federally insured mortgage markets. Between 1946 and 1959, "less than 2 percent of all the housing financed with the assistance of federal mortgage insurance was made available to Blacks" (Judd 1991:742). Coupled with the fact that the FHA insured very little inner-city housing (Judd 1991), the overt discrimination found in the housing market meant many Black families were left out of the post World War II home buying boom and prevented from moving from the city to the suburbs. (pp. 672–673)

The practice of redlining, then, gave Whites, particularly, but not solely, those of modest income means and net worth, a "jump start" relative to home ownership (and transferrable wealth accumulation), including a federally insured mortgage that presumably was accessible to all qualified veterans. Adelman (2003) reported on the differential in asset accumulation as a result of the race-based practice of providing federally insured loans to a virtually all-White clientele (98%):

> One result of the generations of preferential treatment for Whites is that a typical White family today has on average eight times the assets, or net worth, of a typical African American family, according to New York University economist Edward Wolff. Even when families of the same income are compared, White families have more than twice the wealth of Black families. Much of that wealth difference can be attributed to the value of one's home, and how much one inherited from parents. (Reaping the Rewards of Racial Preference, para. 1)

Even when anti-discrimination laws were on the books, redlining on the part of banks and real estate agents would still occur. Cunningham (1997) notes that it remained an ongoing practice as our nation approached the last decade of the twentieth century:

> Although the practice of redlining is illegal under the Fair Housing Act of 1968, suspicion that it continued led Congress to pass the Home Mortgage Disclosure Act (HMDA) in 1976 and amendments to the act in 1989. HMDA requires most mortgage-lending institutions to publicly disclose the geographic distribution of home mortgage and home improvement loans that they originate and purchase, as well as the race or national origin, gender and annual income of loan applicants and borrowers.... [In 1991,] regardless of income group, White applicants are more likely to have their mortgages approved and Black applicants to have theirs denied. (pp. 45–46)

Cunningham (1997) reports that investigations by the Department of Justice and the Federal Reserve Board of Boston found that Decatur Federal Savings and Loan Association in Atlanta, Georgia "rejected significantly more Black applicants than White applicants" (p. 46) and the percentage of loan denials to qualified African Americans among the 131 financial institutions investigated in Boston would have been 20 percent rather than the actual figure of 28 percent "if race had not been a factor" (p. 47).

In 1988, Bill Dedman of *The Atlanta Journal-Constitution* wrote a series of articles under the collective title "The Color of Money," regarding racial discrimination by mortgage lenders in middle-income neighborhoods, for which he won the Pulitzer Prize the following year. Dedman's study "tracked home-purchase and home-improvement loans made by every bank, savings and loan association, and large credit union in metro Atlanta from 1981 through 1986" within 64 middle-income neighborhoods, of which 14 were Black, 11 were integrated, and 39 were White (Dedman, 1988a). The relationship of race and class, and its impact on lending patterns, was facilitated by the fact that housing patterns in Atlanta were highly segregated in 1988 as they "almost always [followed] racial lines" and there was a "substantial and identifiable Black middle class" (Dedman, 1988a). A telling finding by Dedman (1998a) that indicated redlining was the substantive differential proportion in loans made to African American applicants when contrasted with White applicants:

> Banks and savings and loans made 4.0 times as many loans per 1,000 single-family structures in White neighborhoods as in comparable Black neighborhoods in 1984, 4.7 times as many in 1985, and 5.4 times in 1986.... Even lower-income White neighborhoods received more of their loans from banks than upper-middle-income Black neighborhoods. (Measuring Impact of Race, paras. 5–14)

Bank loans are a major method that homeowners maintain and improve their property, and in the absence of loans to appropriately maintain or improve residences, property values may well decline and the neighborhood become less desirable and marketable. As mentioned earlier, homeownership has been a significant means by which to accumulate wealth, for oneself and one's family, and to use the property to secure loans for the family's education, recreation and other perceived or actual needs. Given the government-, institutional- and professional community-supported policies and practices that generated the stark disparity in the possibility of homeownership, White net wealth has far outstripped that of African American families—2,000% in 2007 ($100,000 versus $5,000, respectively). In 1984, the percentage differential was 1,150%—$39,135 versus $3,397, respectively, which motivated Senator William Proxmire, a Democrat from Wisconsin and chair of the Senate Banking, Housing and Urban

Affairs Committee, to assess the status of redlining in the United States (quoted in Dedman, 1988a) in the following, blunt manner: "Let's face it: Redlining hasn't disappeared.... Neighborhoods are still starving for credit."

The G.I. Bill and Its Impact

The effects of the G.I. Bill (known originally as the Servicemen's Readjustment Act of 1944) on WWII veterans' home ownership continued the exclusionary policies and practices of the National Housing Act (1934) toward groups designated as non-White or otherwise undesirable and extending the franchise of White privilege and wealth-building. Yamashita (2008) concludes that from its inception in 1944 to 1980 the

> G.I. Bill had a significant impact on increasing homeownership of veterans compared to otherwise similar non-veterans among Whites, while its effects on African Americans were negligible. The G.I. Bill, thus, contributed to widening the racial gap in homeownership in the post-war period. (p. 1)

The G.I. Bill enabled veterans to obtain a government guaranteed loan on a house, with no down payment, and a 4 percent fixed loan over a 20 year period. In 1947, the first Levittown residential neighborhood was built by Levitt and Sons in New York, offering veterans (and non-veterans) rental homes. The project was so successful that by 1949, Levitt and Sons turned to building homes for purchase for under $8,000 ($7,990) and a $58 per month mortgage payment, particularly targeted at veterans. The homes, measuring 800 square feet of living space at less than $10 per square foot, offered an expandable attic, a General Electric stove and refrigerator, stainless steel sink and cabinets, Bendix washer, and a York oil burner (Levittown Historical Society, n.d.). Other features included Venetian blinds, legal fees, appraisal charges, a 19-foot glass wall, a lawn, garden and fruit trees, and a fireplace in the red brick kitchen (Levittown 1949 advertisement reproduced in Yamashita, 2008). The demand was immediate and non-stop, and Levittown houses were mass produced and sold at a parallel pace, which, by 1951, accorded Levitt and Sons the distinction of having produced the "largest housing development ever completed by a single builder" (Levittown

Historical Society, n.d.). William Levitt had gained a level of fame that led to his portrait on the July 3, 1950 cover of *Time* magazine. The Levittown houses and lawns, and neighborhood elementary schools, churches, swimming pools, each having purposeful, easy access to shopping centers, high schools, library and parks, was a "prototype of postwar suburbia" (Gans, 1967).

But Levitt's sentiments, policies and practices were steely clear regarding for whom these low-cost, well-appointed suburban homes were designed: Whites only. Sokolove (2008), ascribes a quote to William Levitt in his *New York Times Magazine* article, and describes him as a builder who

> weakly insisted that he would love to sell houses to Black families but had "come to know that if we sell one house to a Negro family, then 90 to 95 percent of our White customers will not buy into the community. That is their attitude, not ours." (para. 6)

Breaking the Segregationist Suburban Model

In any case, the Whites-only policy and practice prevailed until August 13, 1957, when the first African American family—Bill and Daisy Myers and their three young children, William III, Stephen and new-born Lynda—moved into Levittown, Pennsylvania,[2] a community of 60,000 Whites. The act of transgressing the segregated housing policy was met with controversy, demonstrations and violence.[3] Acts of aggression toward the Myers family also included Ku Klux Klan-inspired cross-burnings on lawns and schools, that ubiquitous symbol usurped by racist zealots, the Confederate flag in full view (Kushner, 2009) flying from car antennae, hanging on house windows and waving in residents' hands, and, unbelievably, the renting of a house, behind that of the Myers', that was named the Confederate House by its residents. A dog, maliciously named "Nigger" by his owner, was kept at the Confederate House, where its owner would have it roam the Myers' property line and, addressing it loudly by its racist name, give it commands to "come," "go" and the like. Music, such as "Old Man River," in which reference was made to African American workers by the same derogatory label would play from the Confederate House loud enough so the Myers could hear. Pro-segregation meetings were held at the Confederate House and activities to harass the Myers were plotted there and later executed. In addition to the above, the initials KKK were painted on an outside wall of the Wechsler family that faced the Myers home, racist epithets ("Nigger lovers") shouted or threatening notes sent ("Pull out while you can") to neighbors who demonstrated support for, or those who made deliveries to, the Myers, and anonymous phone calls made throughout the night to their home—all under the ostensible but ineffective watch of the local police (Kushner, 2009).

Local and nearby newspapers, such as the *Philadelphia Evening Bulletin, Philadelphia Tribune*, and the *Trenton Evening Times*, published editorials decrying the racist policy that Levitt assertively continued and that tarnished not only the character of Levitt but that of the Levittown, Pennsylvania community (Kushner, 2009, pp. 122–123):

> From the beginning all Negro applicants were turned down on the sole basis of color. The builder let it be known that he would not under any circumstances sell a single house to any Negro, regardless of his character or financial status. (*PEB*, p. 122)

> Levittown is a disgrace to America! The people responsible for this Jim Crow town in the Commonwealth of Pennsylvania are as prejudiced as the most anti-Negro bigot in the Deep South. (*PT*, p. 123)

> Levittown is a new and attractive community which so far in its brief history has had a creditable record of good neighborly relations and orderly behavior by its residents. It is in many respects a model town...[but] this demonstration of racial antagonism reveals an unseemly and repulsive aspect of life in a community whose people enjoy many superior advantages. Something better in the way of tolerance was to be expected of them....It is not conceivable that this demonstration of mob violence is representative of the spirit of Levittown as a whole." (*TET*, p. 123)

Less than a year later, in spring 1958, William Levitt again publicly affirmed that the new Levittown, New Jersey residential community would remain White and that houses would not be sold to African Americans, even in the face of the New Jersey law that made it illegal to practice discrimination in federally subsidized housing and mounting pressures from the state government and religious groups engaged in civil rights activities such as the Burlington County Quaker group, the Burlington County Human Relations Council, and the "national Jewish community" (Gans, 1967, pp. 371–373). Levitt stood firm and fought the suit brought against him by two African Americans who had been denied access to purchasing houses in a federally subsidized housing developing. Levitt believed that economic considerations overrode social ones and that as a builder he should not be singled out to shoulder the economic responsibility and risk of integration, which was, in his view, a national issue to address and resolve. Bressler (quoted in Gans, 1967) offered insight into Levitt's perspective:

> In defending his policy of racial exclusion, Levitt had often had occasion to assert that both as a Jew and a humane man he sympathized with the plight of struggling minorities, but that economic realities reluctantly compelled him to recognize that "most Whites prefer not to live in mixed communities ...the responsibility for this is society's...it is not reasonable to expect that any one builder could or should undertake to absorb the entire risk and burden of conducting such a vast social experiment." (p. 372)

Levitt's hard-held, self-serving but widely supported, both tacitly and explicitly, racist policy and practice that forbade selling housing in an all-White community was, after a decade, finally crumbling under the national wave of civil rights actions, community and religious organizations' leadership, federal support and intervention for upholding the law of the land regarding desegregation, and the establishment and enforcement, to a greater degree than any previous point in our nation's history, of state and national laws regarding equality of access.[4] Those in Levittown, Pennsylvania who colluded to oust the Myers and continue the all-White housing policy of Levitt and the Levittown suburban community also explicitly supported and promoted a "Back-to-Africa" plan and corresponded with the then imperial wizard of the Ku Klux Klan, E. L. Edwards, who resided in Georgia and planned to travel to the North to attend the Levittown Klan initiation ceremony once sufficient members were recruited (Kushner, 2009). In light of the harassment toward the Myers and Wechslers, two trials were held in the County Court of Common Pleas of Buck County, Pennsylvania. The first trial began on December 9, 1957, its objective being to seek a permanent injunction against the group (known as the Levittown 7) from harassing the Myers and those who befriended or supported them; the second, on January 31, 1958, was to determine the guilt or innocence of two of Levittown 7 regarding charges of harassment in the form of placing and burning a cross on the Wechsler's lawn, although the incident was one of various others they had undertaken. In both cases the decision found the perpetrators guilty. Judge Satterthwaite's ruling on August 14, 1958, found the perpetrators guilty of "unlawful conduct...and of an attempted violation of the [Myers'] rights 'and [those of] other peaceable residents of the area' [which] constituted an unlawful conspiracy" (Kushner, 2009, p. 188).

Desegregation in Levittown, New Jersey:
The Exception Proves the Rule

In April 1960, Levitt ultimately decided to voluntarily desegregate Levittown, New Jersey, although he had taken the case to the state Supreme Court, it was anticipated by Levitt and others that the case, once heard, would result in a decision favoring desegregation. Thus, by June 1960, exactly two years after Levittown, New Jersey had opened for sales as a Whites-only residential community, the first African American family moved into it. Levitt hired a consultant to defuse runaway emotions on either side of the segregation-desegregation issue, who designed and implemented an incremental desegregation project called Operation Hothead aimed at White Levittown residents, prospective White and African American Levittown buyers, and Levittown real estate agents. The one policy that Levitt enforced in 1960 in this otherwise non-discriminatory plan—at least for the era we are speaking of—was that "under no circumstances should two Negroes be permitted to buy adjoining houses" (Pooley, 2003).

The number of African American families went from zero in 1958, to 4 in 1960, to 50 by 1964, and, by the mid-1970s, "non-White" families comprised almost 20 percent of the Levittown, New Jersey development (Pooley, 2003). Through a nefarious mortgage-qualifying scheme that smacks of our nation's recent subprime lending scandal, real estate agents in Levittown, New Jersey secured insured mortgages for buyers who were purchasing home mortgages beyond their means; once the residents, primarily African American, defaulted, the banks would be repaid by the government and the real estate agents would again begin the cycle of targeting another family to qualify for a house it could not afford, and pocket the commission. This policy and practice affected the cosmetic appearance of the neighborhood, as foreclosed houses were not kept up and shuttered until made market-ready for resale, and was a factor in White families selling their homes, such that by the year 2000, the Levittown, New Jersey overall population had decreased by nearly 25 percent and 67 percent of the community was now African American—although the community's home values have not kept pace with the other Levittowns, or the national average or even that of New Jersey, the community is stable, attractive and middle-class, motivating Pooley (2003) to write of the misconceptions toward residential communities that are predominantly African American or minority, whether suburban or urban:

> That a place like Willingboro might be considered anything but thriving reveals a persistent problem. Many of America's minority communities—from Levitt's new suburban neighborhoods to downtown urban districts—have yet to escape the misperception of neighborhood decline. Willingboro, with its current energy and vitality, and its residents' strong sense of community and pride in their town, is successful by most standards. It is a beautiful town with housing in excellent condition, winding and quiet residential streets, nearby retail and commercial centers, and scores of neighborhood anchors (such as churches) that have been a part of the town for decades. Yet Willingboro is an undervalued community whose perceived degeneration has translated into real implications for its residents. Housing values trail those of its neighbors as well as its Levitt-built counterparts, and little new development—residential or commercial—has taken place within its borders....As faces change throughout the United States, and as more and more cities see their populations shift, the story of Willingboro should encourage us to rethink the assumptions we make about race and place. Anyone concerned about the future of our cities and neighborhoods should pay close attention—not just to the model of community building that Willingboro can offer, but to why it has been overlooked in the first place. (p. 11)

Notwithstanding the Levittown, New Jersey experience, segregation remained the order of the day with respect to Levittowns in general. In the year 2000 (Sokolove, 2008), Levittown, Pennsylvania was comprised of 2 percent African American, 2 percent Hispanic

American, and 96 percent White, while the White population of Levittown, New York made up 94 percent of the community (Pooley, 2003).

Poole's concern regarding how minority-dominant (that is, non-White) residential communities fare in perception and house-related appreciation is illustrated by a comparison of the three Levittowns (New York, Pennsylvania and New Jersey) relative to crime rates and housing appreciation rates. The crime rate in Willingboro (previously Levittown), New Jersey was 8.36 per 1000 residents, ranking its crime index at 76, meaning that Willingboro is "safer than 76% of the cities in the US" (Neighborhood Scout, 2010a), while the crime index of Levittown, New York was 65 (Neighborhood Scout, 2010b) and that of Levittown, Pennsylvania, 49 (Neighborhood Scout, 2010c). The violent crime rate was also appreciably lower in Willingboro (.84 per 1,000 residents) than in Levittown, New York (1.15 per 1,000 residents) or Levittown, Pennsylvania (1.83 per 1,000 residents).

Appreciation rates for homes until recently in the three communities was higher than the national average, equal to a 9.06% annual appreciation rate over the past decade (2000–2010) for Willingboro, and a median cost of homes of $225,314 ("some of the lowest in New Jersey"); a 12.23% annual appreciation rate over the same period for Levittown, New York, and a median cost of homes of $443,500; and a 9.79% annual appreciation rate over the same period for Levittown, Pennsylvania, and a median cost of homes of $254,571 (Neighborhood Scout, 2010a, 2010b, 2010c). The respective annualized appreciation rates of each community, based on the latest quarter reported (1st quarter 2010), were all negative, although to differing degrees: Willingboro, New Jersey, -5.52%; Levittown, Pennsylvania, -1.28%; and Levittown, New York, -0.16%.

The Three Levittowns: Comparative Educational Performance

Comparison of educational performance among the three communities (Neighborhood Scout, 2010a, 2010b, 2010c) demonstrates that Willingboro is at the bottom with a district rating of 1 out of 10, the lowest score possible and outperforming only 4.3% of other school districts in New Jersey and 16.7% of other school districts in the United States. Levittown, Pennsylvania's district rating was 2 out of 10, and outperformed 12.2% of other school districts in Pennsylvania and 44% better than other U.S. school districts. Levittown, New York's district rating was 9 out of 10, performing better than 81.7% of New York school districts and 85% better than other U.S. school districts.

Demographics within the three districts are quite diverse, as are their socio-economic status figures, and *did not* conform to stereotypic surface patterns in all cases regarding educational performance—that is, the expectation was not confirmed that the higher the percentage of "economically disadvantaged" students and the higher the percentage of enrolled minority group students, the lower the overall educational performance. Willingboro's White student population was 2.3%, as compared to 90.8% African American; its percentage of economically disadvantaged students was 40.5 percent. Levittown, Pennsylvania's White student population was 70.7%, as compared to 18.9% African American, 7.2% Hispanic and 2.6% Asian or Pacific Islander; its percentage of economically disadvantaged students was nominally higher at 41.7% than that of Willingboro, New Jersey. Levittown, New York's White student population was 85.6%, with African American students comprising 0.5% of students, and Hispanic (9.3%) and Asian or Pacific Islander (4.5%) students comprising the rest; its percentage of economically disadvantaged students was 6.3 percent.

The percentage of per pupil instructional expenditures to overall educational expenditures across the districts differed modestly: Willingboro, 58%; Levittown, Pennsylvania, 54%; and Levittown, New York, 61%; thus, the Willingboro district spent a greater percentage of its budget on instructional expenditures than did Levittown, Pennsylvania, but less than did the Levittown, New York district. The Willingboro school district spent proportionally more on student support (7.7%, or $1,172) than did either Levittown, Pennsylvania (3.6%, or $553) or Levittown, New York (5.2%, or $862). Class size was comparable, ranging from 12 in the case of New York to 14 in Pennsylvania, with Willingboro in the middle with an average class size of 13. When compared with each community's state average class size, Willingboro's average class size of 13 was larger than the state average of 12, while Levittown, Pennsylvania's average class size of 14 was one less than the state average of 15 and Levittown, New York's of 12 was one less than the state average of 13.

The average educational and income levels of the three Levitt-built community developments differ, but, again, do not conform to stereotypic perspectives regarding educational and income levels of a neighborhood and educational outcomes of their students. Nearly 19% (18.87%) of adults 25 years or older in the Willingboro community had earned at least a Bachelor's degree; this educational achievement level was higher than the 14.96% at the national level and the 13.41% of earned Bachelor's degrees in Levittown, Pennsylvania. Twenty-two percent (22.51%) of adults in Levittown, New York had earned at least a Bachelor's degree. The average family incomes of each community were $87,196 for Willingboro, $80,188 for Levittown, Pennsylvania, and $103,668 for Levittown, New York (Neighborhood Scout, 2010a, 2010b, 2010c). Thus, average educational and income levels are insufficient in this case to explain educational performance differences, as, overall, students in the Willingboro district were outperformed by students in districts where the average educational and income levels were lower (Levittown, Pennsylvania) and higher (Levittown, New York).

Perpetration of Redlining, Its Apologists and Residential Segregation

The redlining phenomenon, which began as a federal government-supported endeavor to exclude groups by race and ethnicity in the early 1930s, remained robustly intact in 1991, and despite acts by Congress in 1968 and 1976, and amendments to the latter act added as late as 1987—all mentioned earlier in this chapter and the previous one—to thwart and sanction the activity through regulation. The question is how has redlining persisted in the face of these federal government-instituted acts and the agencies established to ensure equitable loan distribution by banks and savings and loans associations? Each year the U.S. government grades America's 17,000 banks and savings and loans on Dedman (1988b) reports that the nation's 17,000 banks and savings and loans are graded by the federal government relative to "how fairly they serve their communities, including working-class and minority neighborhoods." The government grading system enabled 98 percent of all lenders to pass and 99 percent of lenders in the South to pass. As Dedman (1988b) states: "Supporters of working-class and minority neighborhoods suspect grade inflation."

The Community Reinvestment Act (CRA) of 1977 was enacted to end redlining but it, as historically has been the case regarding Supreme Court decisions addressing racial and language minorities, lacks sufficient follow-through relative to enforcement and is open to interpretation regarding criteria relative to meeting standards or even expectations as banks only have "an affirmative obligation" to serve communities across the diverse income groups. Insufficient resources and clout are not the only weakness in federal agencies' ability to effectively monitor lenders' practices, as the integrity of regulators has also been placed in question by some. Allen Fishbein, general counsel for the Center for Community Change in Washington, D.C. was quoted by Dedman (1988b) as stating that the ease with which virtually all lenders have passed inspections relates to the

> regulators being very close to the industry they regulate, being very reluctant to vigorously slap the wrist of people who violate the law. In many instances the regulators are defending the institutions more adequately than the lenders are defending themselves.... [The] number of examiner hours per year expended to check banks on compliance with consumer regulations *fell by 74 percent from 1981 to 1984* [italics added] at the Office of the Comptroller of the Currency, the Federal Deposit Insurance Corp., and the Federal Home Loan Bank Board, which regulate most of the banks and savings and loans. The Federal Reserve Board regulates only about 1,000 institutions. (paras. 18–21)

Bank executives, as well as executives of the Federal Reserve Bank, to include its then chair, Alan Greenspan, denied that lending patterns were sufficient evidence to prove discrimination—despite the enormous and persistent discrepancies in lending practices to members of the African American community when contrasted with Whites, regardless of a family's income, and despite findings reported in Dedman (1988c) that

> some banks had closed branches as areas changed from White to Black or integrated; kept offices open fewer hours in Black areas than in White areas;

accepted mortgage applications only in offices near White areas; enforced minimum loan amounts that lock out lower-income customers, many of whom are Black; chose not to offer VA and FHA loans that may be preferred by homebuyers with fewer assets, particularly Blacks; and made few of their Small Business Administration loans to minority-owned businesses. (Black Homebuyer Not Sought, para. 1)

And, finally, despite that this suspect lending pattern surfaced in an earlier 1983 study—never distributed—by the Federal Reserve itself, which accessed and analyzed records of every home loan by every bank and savings and loan association in 100 cities during 1981, and found that "race strongly affected lending patterns in many cities" (Dedman, 1988d).

The public statements by bank executives and employees of the regulating agencies in response to Dedman's 1988 study reported in *The Atlanta Journal-Constitution* ranged from arrogance—as evinced by Federal Reserve economist Glenn Canner's comment: "We've looked over the years at dozens of cities and dozens of cases. For us, the disparities are fairly well known. It might be news to the general public," quoted in Dedman, 1988d)—to mentally flaccid and ethically naïve comments such as that of Robert L. Clarke, comptroller of the currency: "We have no disagreement with some of the basic findings of the *Atlanta Constitution* series .... Some segments of the Atlanta community are probably not serviced by financial depository institutions as well as other segments are" and that of Alan Greenspan, then chair of the Federal Reserve (Dedman, 1988c):

> Institutions could be purposefully discriminating against home purchase loan applicants from minority neighborhoods....Detection of discrimination in lending is difficult, particularly since it rarely is done overtly....Therefore, one cannot conclude absolutely that no racial discrimination exists in residential lending in Atlanta. (para. 5)

Greenspan's statement resonates in its convoluted meaning to perhaps convey the opposite with the statement made on August 22, 2010, by Mitch McConnell, the Senate minority leader, as to whether he believed that President Barack Obama was of the Muslim or Christian faith: "The President says he's a Christian. I take him at his word," a response with the reported intention to "seed doubt" (Stein,

2010) within the nation rather than to affirm support, not only for believing a person with respect to a personal statement concerning his or her religious faith, but perhaps more importantly in the belief in and right to religious pluralism in our country, and in the separation of church and state. Reactions to Dedman's reporting also took the form of indignation—"The most painful thing was not reading the paper but hearing the vitriolic attacks from political people claiming deep-seated racism"—and denial, as did Raymond Riddle's, president of First Atlanta, response: "We do not redline" (Dedman, 1988e). Finally, there was distortion, as in the case of then Georgia Banking Commissioner Jack Dunn, who responded that the *AJC* study had included data "from only a very small number of banks" despite that the study has used and analyzed federal computer tapes that included "data from 88 institutions: every bank, savings and loan association and large credit union in the metro area. The data covered every home loan made by these institutions from 1981 to 1986" (Dedman, 1988f). Given our nation's financial institutions' (and related agencies involved in every step of real estate transactions) recent ill-advised and economically devastating spree into the realm of subprime housing loans, it is necessary to make clear that the point of groups, such as the Legislative Black Caucus, advocating for increased mortgage loans within historically redlined areas was never for banks to make bad loans or to give "charity;" rather, as Georgia State Representative Charles Walker stated (Dedman, 1988f): "We simply want fairness."

Of course, the continued lack of fairness in the equitable distribution of homeownership loans (economics) and access to suburbs built for Whites (segregation) resulted in the continuation of another fundamental group need that remains unmet: *equity in quality schooling*. Gene V. Glass, an eminent educational researcher and the developer (with M. L. Smith) of the groundbreaking quantitative research synthesis technique known as meta-analysis, offers his less-than-sanguine, but perhaps no less probable, prediction of national trends that serve as interrelated barriers to achieve equity in quality schooling, societal integration, or reduction of economic disparities in the near-term. These, according to Glass (2008), include (1) a greater disparity in income distribution that will erode our already fragile sense of civic responsibility; (2) a dual push for reduction in taxes and "private privileges for one's children and grandchildren at public expense" that will find their expression in alternate forms of education; (3) an increase in segregation; (4) the characterization of the traditional public school as the "province of the poor and minorities, particularly in metropolitan areas;" (5) state-subsidized home schooling, particularly subscribed to by the White, middle-class; (6) the rise of private-sector-led "virtual schools" in which poorer families would participate less; and (7) the misguided application of rhetoric-rich philanthropy that lacks "innovative or fruitful ideas" (pp. 237–240).

Chapter 5

Building toward Multicultural Education

The great Melting Post where all races... are melting and reforming! ... The real American has not yet arrived. He is only in the Crucible... will be the fusion of races, perhaps the coming superman...Ah, what a stirring and a seething! Celt and Latin, Slav and Teuton, Greek and Syrian,—Black and yellow—...the glory of America, where all races and nations come to labour and look forward!

—Israel Zangwill, 1916

The outstanding and all-inclusive effect of race prejudice on the Negro can be summed up in one word, *segregation.*

—Kelly Miller, 1925

African American Scholars' Discourse in 20th-Century Racist United States

The triple legacy of racism, *de jure* segregation, and disregard for the law of the land, which were instigated by White society in the late 19th to early 20th centuries, were addressed by African American scholars in their writings during this same period. The social scientific scholarship produced by W.E.B. DuBois in the years from 1894 to 1915 figured prominently among them (see Lange, 1983). Kelly Miller, a preeminent scholar who received his master's degree in mathematics from Johns Hopkins University—the first African American to do so—taught mathematics and sociology at Howard University, wrote in "Harvest of Race Prejudice" (The *Survey Graphic*) in March 1925:

Like a two-edged sword, race prejudice cuts both ways. It weakens the energies and paralyzes the moral muscle of the White race; it stultifies the conscience and frustrates the normal workings of democracy and Christianity. It fosters a double standard of ethics, and leads to lawlessness, lynching, and all manner of national disgrace....The Ku Klux Klan spreads its virus through our democracy; Nordicism carries it to the ends of the earth. Its effects are nationally and internationally threatening, and the American people and the Nordic civilization of which they are a part must stop to consider whether in this evil fruit they are not nurturing the fatal seeds of world dissension and catastrophe....The outstanding and all-inclusive effect of race prejudice on the Negro can be summed up in one word, *segregation*....This attitude of the White race has decreed residential segregation....In their too hasty zeal they over-rode the reaches of the Constitution and the law; Negroes, through the National Association for the Advancement of Colored People, contested the constitutionality of these ordinances and won a unanimous decision from the Supreme Court. Yet the legal victory merely modified the details of procedure; it had little effect upon the actual fact of segregation, which operates as effectively without the law as within it....The most gigantic instance of racial segregation is Harlem [where] we find 200,000 Negroes shut in segregated areas as sharply marked as the aisles of a church....We may then take Harlem as a fair specimen of race prejudice throughout the United States. (pp. 682–683)

In 1925, Alain Locke, "the most influential African American intellectual born between W.E.B. DuBois and Martin Luther King, Jr." (Harris & Molesworth, 2008, quoted in Romano, 2009), wrote elegantly and incisively on the ills of segregation and power of integration. Locke was addressing the transformation of African Americans from a phenomenon of condition to one of consciousness, made possible through their multiple manifestations of integration and expression within the context of Harlem (Locke, 1925, reprinted in Bracey, Meier, & Rudwick, 1970):

Hitherto, it must be admitted that American Negroes have been a race more in name than in fact, or to be exact, more in sentiment than in experience. The chief bond between them has been that of a common condition rather than a common consciousness; a problem in common rather than a life in common. (p. 338)

Locke's analysis is neither limited to African Americans nor to the first quarter of the 20th century, as it remains meaningful in its application to our general populous and time. His interpretive insight serves to pinpoint the perennial dilemma of our inability to surmount the self-imposed barrier of race (and its socially constructed derivatives that include ethnicity, gender, religion and class) even as we seek to achieve the promise of United States unity within the context of a democratic nation. We have long needed to sound the death knell on our founding, philosophically toxic cultural virus: the self-instigated and self-serving division of human groups based on a false and ultimately self-defeating construct of one group's superiority over all others, which migrated maliciously throughout our legal system and quotidian practice once our nation was formed.

Nevertheless, segregation within our nation remains a natural social phenomenon to us—ironically perceived as a matter of choice rather than legacy or class or design. Our national model of moving at an incremental, ambiguously interpreted pace toward integration masks a mainstream reluctance, even aversion, certainly a distrust, to engage in what would be perceived, at best, an uncomfortable, forced unity. Wollenberg (1978, pp. 1–2) declared that during the course of more than a century (1855–1975) "due to sustained efforts to exclude minorities from the public education system and to segregate them in the public schools...the courts have become the major field of battle in the struggle against school segregation." With respect to the second point, the Supreme Court's *Brown v. Board of Education 1954 (I) and 1955 (II)* ruling mandated that schools be desegregated "with all deliberate speed"—essentially resulting in a dictum that had no measurable time table attached to it or enforcement to actively support it by the three branches of our government, and which, by 1957, had led to the enactment of "at least 136 new laws and state constitutional amendments...to delay or prevent the process" (Salomone, 1986, pp. 45–46), as well as murders and other acts of public and clandestine violence, abuse and humiliation against African Americans and White supporters that persisted through 1965 (Williams, 1987).

White Privilege, Black Schools and Structural Subordination

From 1790 to 1952, immigrants who could be naturalized as American citizens would have to be designated as "White," a term that expands and contracts depending on historical context, as well as upon social mores and legal interpretation, but that has not included African Americans, Asians or Native Americans. Based on race, education became a selective privilege, as opposed to a universal privilege in our putative democratic nation, from 1896 to 1954, by virtue of *Plessy v. Ferguson*, in which our Supreme Court upheld states' rights to deny whole groups of Americans—African Americans, in this case— universal access to integrated schools. Access is the initial step in ensuring equity, but it is not sufficient unto itself, as students need also to participate meaningfully in the learning process to derive benefit from it; moreover, the conditions of integration, communication and cooperation within classrooms appear fundamental to guide, measure and achieve equity (DeVillar & Faltis, 1991; DeVillar, 1994; DeVillar & Faltis, 1994). Thus, African American students also were effectively denied participation in the very institutions from which they would derive benefit and thereby contribute as a group to our national development, both government-wise and economically, and to our competitive preeminence in ways associated with enhanced formal education and professional development.

How equal were these separate schools? The Slater Fund was established by the industrialist John F. Slater in 1882 "to help educate former slaves in the South," as well as generate reports of their development in the South (Library of Congress, 2003). In 1926, a Slater Fund Report described the typical African American teacher profile (Southern Education Foundation, n.d.):

> [I]t appears that the typical Negro teacher of the South is a woman of rural heritage about 27 years old. She has completed high school and had ten weeks in summer schools. She teaches 47 children through six grades for a term of six months, remaining about two years in the same school. Her annual salary is $360, or $1 a day, and she teaches for about five years. (para. 10)

African American teachers in 1910 were paid 20 percent of what a Southern White teacher made; fifteen years later, in 1924, they were paid 25 percent of a Southern White teacher's wage (Southern Education Foundation, n.d.). Following the same negative differential pattern between segregated schools and White schools in the South, African American schools operated on an academic year schedule of 144 days, in contrast to the 164-day schedule of White schools, and received less than 38 cents per student for every dollar of funding allocated to White schools per student—although in South Carolina, in 1931, the White student-African American student funding ratio was *less than* 10 to 1, which led "the South and nation for gross disparity in per child school expenditures" (Southern Education Foundation, n.d.).

In 1927, the denial of the privilege to attend school with White students was again reinforced by the Supreme Court in its ruling that native-born American children of Chinese descent were not entitled to attend school with Whites and should attend schools with another group of American-born students of African descent (*Gong Lum v. Rice, 275 U.S. 78* [1927]. Legislatively-driven school segregation of minority group members was common in the United States from the 1930s until 1954 [*Brown v. Board of Education, 347 U.S. 483* (1954) (USSC+)], as Alvarez (1986) succinctly reports:

> In 1954 there were 17 U.S. States all in the South or bordering the South, plus the District of Columbia which by law made segregated school mandatory. Four states (Arizona, Kansas, New Mexico and Wyoming) allowed varieties of local option in segregating and sixteen states prohibited segregation but enforcement was random. The eleven remaining states had no laws on segregation aimed at Blacks or [Hispanics] and most had no reported cases in the courts. California however, did by law exclude Native Americans making it legal to segregate people of Indian descent. (Notes, para. 2)

African Americans and the Great Migration to the North

Schools were far from the only institution in which particular groups of Americans were excluded from equal access in America to opportunities, and the goods and services, that the excluding class— the privileged group—shared with one another, in well-distributed *symbolic* form, if not in material, occupational, educational or political form. In any case, regardless of the actual intra-racial distributive divides among the White privileged group, the ideal, and to varying degrees the reality, was that these divides were permeable. This belief was not convertible to reality for those pertaining to excluded groups in America, although it was in highly exceptional, mainly individual, circumstances, and never generalizable to the members of the excluded group.

Restrictions were commonly and legally applied based on wealth, gender, race, and ethnicity, that prohibited or curtailed choice-based engagement in the democratic process across many critical dimensions, including self-government, gainful employment, voting, running for office, membership in social and private organizations, access to entertainment and accommodations, and intergroup social interaction. Life in the segregated American South was a period that, demographically, was a precursor to the six million people-strong African American Great Migration northward that was to transpire in successive waves beginning in 1915, continued during the First World War (1914–1918), through the 1920-decade that witnessed official prohibition, prosperity, widespread and diverse creativity, optimism, coupled with economic polarity and high-risk behaviors that culminated in the Great Depression and the hardship and gloom of the 1930s, through the Second World War and the Civil Rights Movement, subsiding, finally, in the 1970s. Lepore (2010) describes aspects of everyday segregated life in the South at the dawn of the 20th century:

> Georgia was the first state to demand separate seating for Whites and Blacks in streetcars, in 1891; five years later came *Plessy v. Ferguson*. By 1905, every Southern state had a streetcar law, and more: in courthouses, separate Bibles; in bars, separate sections; in post offices, separate windows; in libraries, separate branches. In Birmingham, it was a crime for Blacks and Whites to play checkers together in a public park. (p. 77)

Isabel Wilkerson (2010), author of *The Warmth of Other Suns: The Epic Story of America's Great Migration*, writes of another type of everyday occurrence in the life of African Americans in the post-Civil War/post-Reconstruction South, lynching and burnings:

> Across the South, someone was hanged or burned alive every four days from 1889 to 1929...for such alleged crimes as "stealing hogs, horse-stealing, poisoning mules, jumping labor contract, suspected of killing cattle, boastful remarks" or "trying to act like a White person." (p. 39)

The African American Great Migration was, in Lepore's words (2010):

> ...bigger than the Gold Rush....than the Dust Bowl Okies. Before the Great Migration, ninety per cent of all Blacks in the United States lived in the

South; after it, forty-seven per cent lived someplace else. Today, more African-Americans live in the city of Chicago than in the state of Mississippi....Isabel Wilkerson ... calls the exodus "the biggest underreported story of the twentieth century." (p. 77)

Segregation in the post-Civil War South, however, was not based on residential patterns per se. That is, while the type, quality and value of White residences far exceeded that of African American residences, these residences were not in separate areas geographically distant from one another. Rather, as Massey and Denton (1993, p. 26) observe: "Neighborhoods in many southern cities evolved a residential structure characterized by broad avenues interspersed with small streets and alleys." The Reconstruction period transformed the master-slave relation to one of "master and servant, or a paternalistic relationship between boss and worker" (Massey & Denton, 1993, p. 26). The African American ghetto was to be developed in the North.

African Americans migrated to the North for diverse, interrelated reasons: lack of jobs in the South due to severe reduction in agricultural and cotton production (devastated by the Mexican boll weevil), availability of jobs in the North due to industrialization, the stability of the African American worker when compared to the European immigrant whose local stability shifted with employment opportunities in Europe, and to escape the oppression of the Jim Crow South (Massey & Denton, 1993, pp. 26–29). These same four reasons were offered by DuBois in 1918 in a published article entitled "The Economics of the Negro Problem" (see Foner, 1970, pp. 268–269, for extracted parts of the article relating to the African American exodus from the South). Migration was intense, beginning in the 1890s and continuing through the Great Depression, by which time some 1,800,000 African Americans had left the push of the American South for the pull of the American North. The harsh but hopeful consequence of this massive geo-cultural shift was expressed by Langston Hughes in his poem The South, published in 1922 (Hughes, in Rampersad & Roessel, 1995, p. 26):

The South

The lazy, laughing South
With blood on its mouth.
The sunny-faced South,

Beast-strong,
Idiot-brained.
The child-minded South
Scratching in the dead fire's ashes
For a Negro's bones.
Cotton and the moon,
Warmth, earth, warmth,
The sky, the sun, the stars,
The magnolia-scented South.
Beautiful, like a woman,
Seductive as a dark-eyed whore,
Passionate, cruel,
Honey-lipped, syphilitic—
That is the South.
And I, who am black, would love her
But she spits in my face.
And I, who am black,
Would give her many rare gifts
But she turns her back upon me.
So now I seek the North—
The cold-faced North,
For she, they say,
Is a kinder mistress,
And in her house my children
May escape the spell of the South.

Whites in the North, however, did not tend to be kind to the African Americans and "viewed this rising tide of Black migration with increasing hostility and considerable alarm," quickly manifesting their perceived entitlement and superiority by dint of race through the racial epithets vocalized by White immigrants and mainstream newspapers, by White parents shunning schools that enrolled African American children, by African American professionals losing "White clients, associates and friends," by White-induced violence toward African Americans, and by Whites refusing to live in the same neighborhoods with African Americans, which ultimately relegated African Americans, regardless of profession or income, to segregated neighborhoods (Massey & Denton, 1993, pp. 29–30). Thus, "by World War II the foundations of the modern ghetto had been laid in virtually every northern city" (Massey & Denton, 1993, p. 31), a bitter extension and confirmation of the cruel but accurate 1934 depiction by DuBois of African American life in the segregated North and lamentable coda to Langston Hughes' hope that "in her house my children may escape the spell of the South."

As noted above, the restrictive policies and practices on individual and group choice extended even to where one could purchase land or housing or obtain a bank loan regardless of financial qualifications. In December 1946, President Harry Truman created the Committee on Civil Rights (CCR), which issued its report, *To Secure These Rights*, in October 1947, and described everyday segregation thusly (quoted in Kurland, 1963):

> Legally enforced segregation has been followed throughout the South since the close of the Reconstruction era. In these States it is generally illegal for Negroes to attend the same schools as Whites; attend theaters patronized by Whites; visit parks where Whites relax; eat, sleep or meet in hotels, restaurant or public halls frequented by Whites. This is only a partial enumeration—legally imposed separation of races has become highly refined. (p. 150)

Although not mentioned by President Truman, the practice of segregation, as we have documented, extended to the North. The CCR recommendations, which numbered thirty-four, were popularly and officially viewed in the South as heresy. President Truman, who, on February 2, 1948, forwarded a number of them for enactment by Congress only weeks after his inaugural address on January 7th, was stridently and generally damned by Southern political figures as having betrayed and threatened the South (Leuchtenburg, 1991). President Truman, a Southerner, whose parents and earlier family descendents were arch-racists and segregationists, was raised in the same vein and examples are on record of his explicit and crude references toward Americans of African descent during stages of his political career (Leuchtenburg, 1991). However, as President of the United States, Truman transcended personal and socially ingrained prejudices. He exemplified his ability to transcend prejudice in his Special Message to the Congress on Civil Rights, February 2, 1948, within which he addressed the noxious reality of discrimination in our nation and the insurmountable barrier it posed to achieving our national ideals. He specifically presented ten recommendations to our

U.S. Congress as a means to secure essential human rights in our nation (President Truman quoted in Woolley & Peters, 2006):

> Today, the American people enjoy more freedom and opportunity than ever before. Never in our history has there been better reason to hope for the complete realization of the ideals of liberty and equality. We shall not, however, finally achieve the ideals for which this Nation was founded so long as any American suffers discrimination as a result of his race, or religion, or color, or the land of origin of his forefathers. Unfortunately, there still are examples—flagrant examples—of discrimination which are utterly contrary to our ideals. Not all groups of our population are free from the fear of violence. Not all groups are free to live and work where they please or to improve their conditions of life by their own efforts. Not all groups enjoy the full privileges of citizenship and participation in the government under which they live. We cannot be satisfied until all our people have equal opportunities for jobs, for homes, for education, for health, and for political expression, and until all our people have equal protection under the law....We know that our democracy is not perfect. But we do know that it offers freer, happier life to our people than any totalitarian nation has ever offered. If we wish to inspire the peoples of the world whose freedom is in jeopardy, if we wish to restore hope to those who have already lost their civil liberties, if we wish to fulfill the promise that is ours, we must correct the remaining imperfections in our practice of democracy. We know the way. We need only the will. (paras. 9–12, 74)

The ten recommendations delineated by President Truman in early 1948 were (1) the establishment of a "permanent Commission on Civil Rights, a Joint Congressional Committee on Civil Rights, and a Civil Rights Division in the Department of Justice"; (2) "strengthening existing civil rights statutes"; (3) providing "Federal protection against lynching"; (4) "protecting more adequately the right to vote"; (5) establishment of a "Fair Employment Practice Commission to prevent unfair discrimination in employment"; (6) disallowing "discrimination in interstate transportation facilities"; (7) the provision of "home-rule and suffrage in Presidential elections for the residents of the District of Columbia"; (8) granting "Statehood for Hawaii and Alaska and a greater measure of self-government for our island possessions"; (9) making equal the "opportunities for residents of the United States to become naturalized citizens"; and (10) "settling the evacuation claims of Japanese-Americans" (from President

Truman's Special Message to the Congress on Civil Rights, Woolley & Peters, 2006, para. 19).

At mid-20th century, African Americans still needed Federal Government protection against being lynched and to exercise their right to vote and to use interstate transportation facilities. Howard Zinn (1980/2003) noted that no U.S. president, prior to and including President Truman, had issued executive orders to execute the Fourteenth and Fifteenth Amendments that would "wipe out" racial discrimination, although bound by the Constitution to do so. Even President Truman's request to Congress for legislation prohibiting discrimination in interstate transportation facilities was redundant, as "specific legislation in 1887 already barred discrimination in interstate transportation [yet] had never been enforced by executive action" (Zinn, 1980/2003, p. 450).

Thus, important legislation in civil rights—in *human* rights—that passed in earlier periods of U.S. history has been repeatedly sidestepped and otherwise ignored in favor of continuing the violations against a discriminated group, in this case African Americans. Passing critical human rights legislation and then not acting upon it in a manner that enables equitable inclusion has two important outcomes. First, the artifice of nationwide equality is maintained across generations, allowing mainstream society to live in the safety of segregated enclaves, perpetuating and reproducing through families and institutions, both private and public, the ignorance and intolerance that stubbornly, blindly and selfishly justifies injustice. Second, it denies the discriminated group the right to participate in a meaningful manner within the same institutions available to the mainstream—particularly quality schools—and keeps the group segregated and expending its resources, human and otherwise, to rectify an injustice that on paper has been declared surmounted. This dual-sided phenomenon occurred prior to the example by Zinn mentioned immediately above, specifically in the case of the Fifteenth Amendment (1870), which guaranteed the right to vote to all citizens regardless of race or previous condition of servitude. However, as Gillette (2001) observes, given the

> racist repression in the South, growing political indifference in the North, and federal inaction, [coupled with] the long retreat from egalitarian

principles after 1867, federal courts often interpreted the amendment narrowly to deny federal authority to prosecute violations of federal voting rights. (p. 264)

Thernstrom (1992, p. 900) elaborates upon the restrictive conditions imposed upon African Americans in the face of their "indisputable" right to vote:

From the late nineteenth century until 1965, most southern Blacks were disenfranchised by poll taxes, fraudulently administered literacy tests, White primaries, intimidation, and violence. The Supreme Court initially upheld literacy tests and poll taxes as constitutionally permissible means by which to maintain a responsible and informed electorate. (p. 900)

Thus, it is clear that African Americans were denied the right to vote, to exercise their vote, until the passage of the Voting Rights Act of 1965, a full 95 years after they were putatively granted the right to do so by the Fifteenth Amendment. It is also clear that in light of this breach of rule of law, they had to devote virtually a century of energy, of capital, human and otherwise, and other resources, both scarce and dear, to engage in a legal struggle within a national context of discrimination, danger and indifference, to actually gain access to the ballot box. It is this pernicious cycle of extended injustice, even as our laws from the highest court in the land state otherwise, that our self-righteous mainstream stance as a nation fundamentally dedicated to the rule of law is a strikingly hypocritical posture that can readily be viewed and assessed as selective and restrictive rather than universally inclusive, and as such, antithetical to our democratic principles and endeavors.

Transformative Legislation and Exclusion: Beyond Race

The period from 1920 to 1968 was transformative in terms of U.S. legislation, if not in our collective spirit or practice, as fundamental civil and human rights were granted, a collective phenomenon that resulted, not from enlightened social evolution of the dominant group, but through the organized struggles of the violated groups themselves working in tandem with supporters of all stripes. During this period, for example, women gained the right to vote (1920); Native Americans gained the right of citizenship (1924; their voting rights, however, were dependent on authorization by each state and still being contested as recently as 2004; see ACLU, 2004); African Americans won the hard-fought, landmark *Brown v Board of Education* (1954) desegregation ruling and meaningful voting rights (1965) along with rights of public access (1956); bans and quotas on Asian immigration were lifted (1943–1965) and rights extended to Asian immigrants and Asian American residents to become naturalized citizens (Campi, 2004); interracial marriage (1967) was allowed; and bilingual education (1968) was federally instituted.

Americans of Mexican descent were also legally segregated from using public facilities, such as public swimming pools, bathhouses, playgrounds, and park facilities, regardless of income, education, profession, or other descriptor—that is, they were barred from these public facilities solely on their ancestry. In California, this "No Mexicans Allowed" practice by the City of San Bernardino, California, was successfully challenged in 1943, in federal district court (Southern District), resulting in the *Lopez et al. v. Seccombe et al.* (1944) ruling in favor of the plaintiffs, who were all Americans of "Mexican or Latin" descent—and, by extension the Court noted, the "8,000 other persons of Mexican and Latin descent and extraction, all citizens of the United States of America, residing within said district" (Loislaw, 2010). In fact, the petitioners, who had all been denied access to the aforementioned public facilities, were a group of American citizens that included Reverend R. N. Nunez, a Catholic priest who presided over the San Bernardino Parish of the Guadalupe Church; Ignacio Lopez, a graduate of Pomona College and the University of Southern California, recent head of the Spanish Department in the Office of Foreign Language, Division of Office of War Information, and the Spanish speaking director of the Office of Coordinator of Inter-American affairs in Los Angeles, California; Eugenio Nogueros, a World War II veteran, originally from Puerto Rico, who was a college graduate, publisher and editor; and two students, Virginia Prado and Rafael Muñoz. The Court found (Loislaw, 2010)

> as true that for several years last past all persons of Mexican or Latin descent or extraction, though citizens of the United States of America have on repeated occasions been excluded, barred and precluded from using, enjoying or entering upon that portion of said park and playground

containing said swimming pool, plunge, bath house and facilities, by respondents, their servants, agents and employees....that petitioners and other persons of Mexican and Latin descent, all citizens of the United States, are denied the use and enjoyment of the facilities of said park as aforesaid notwithstanding that other persons and the public are allowed the use and enjoyment of said privileges at all times when such park and facilities are open to the public. *That by reason thereof, the injury to petitioners is continuous, great and irreparable, and is calculated to affect their health and rights as citizens of the United States of America, and of the State of California* [emphasis added]....That this action is brought on behalf of petitioners and some 8,000 other persons of Mexican and Latin descent and extraction all citizens of the United States of America, residing within said district. (paras. I–XVIII)

The Court (Loislaw, 2010) found, furthermore, the conduct of the mayor, City Council members, Superintendent of Parks, and Chief of Police:

illegal and ... in violation of petitioners' rights and privileges, as guaranteed by the Constitution of the United States of America, and as secured and guaranteed to them as citizens of the United States, by the Constitution of the United States of America, as particularly provided under the Fifth and Fourteenth Amendments. (para. XVI)

Americans of Mexican origin were also segregated relative to schools they attended in California. DeVillar (1994) elaborated upon this practice regarding the 1931 court case involving the Lemon Grove School District, an early example of administrative attempts to segregate Americans of Mexican origin, not by race—which was not legal in California—but due to putative language, academic and Americanization needs, which was legal:

Roberto Alvarez v. the Board of Trustees of the Lemon Grove School District (1931) successfully challenged the notion that Mexican-American students could be legally segregated from their Anglo-American peers and, in the same year, the Bliss Bill, which attempted to have Mexican-Americans designated as Indians and thereby subject to legal school segregation, was defeated (Trueba, 1988). In [1946 and] 1947, yet another court case in California, *Mendez v. Westminster*, ended the State's [unlawful] segregation of Mexican-Americans. (p. 32)

Moll (2010, p. 451) characterizes *Mendez* as the "first major and successful challenge to segregated schooling in California." State law in California authorized the segregation of Asian American and Native American students, while Mexican American and Mexican students were segregated in practice, if not by law. The case of *Mendez v. Westminster* (1946) successfully challenged the practice of segregating Mexican-origin students, who, along with their Spanish surnames, were considered "too dark-skinned," and thus "sufficiently undesirable" to attend the local Orange County, California school attended by White students (Moll, 2010, p. 451).

This racist perception and action in schooling mirrored the perception and actions of patterns in residential and home loan distribution initiated and officially supported by the Federal Government through the National Housing Act of 1934. The schooling practice was legally overturned by the U.S. District Court, which ruled that segregating Mexican American students "violated not only state law but also the equal protection clause of the Fourteenth Amendment," a ruling affirmed by the Ninth Circuit Court of Appeals (1947; Moll, 2010, p. 451). Moll (2010, p. 452ff.) elaborates upon a scholarly perspective—integrating and citing evidence by previous analysts—that *Mendez v. Westminster* served as a precursor to *Brown* in several ways. First, the use of social science research testimony to associate segregation with "harmful effects...on the development of Mexican American children." Second, the language used by the presiding judge, Judge Paul J. McCormick, which implicitly challenged our national practice of separate but equal, extant since the Supreme Court decision in *Plessy v. Ferguson* (1896), and anticipated the language used by the judges in *Brown*. A particularly relevant quote from the 1946 decision by Judge McCormick, cited earlier by Aguirre (2005), is presented by Moll (2010) to illustrate the constitutionally related thought and its expression into language that is similar across the two cases:

> The equal protection of the laws pertaining to the public school system in California is not provided by furnishing in separate schools the same technical facilities, text books and courses of instruction to students of Mexican ancestry that are available to the other public school children regardless of ancestry. A paramount requisite of the American system of

> public education is equality. It must be open to all children by unified school
> association regardless of lineage. (p. 451)

Third, at the appeal stage of the ruling, a number of amicus briefs—
American Civil Liberties Union, the American Jewish Congress, the
Japanese American Citizens League, the Attorney General of
California—were submitted, including one from the NAACP, that was
prepared by the same team—Robert Carter, Thurgood Marshall, and
Loren Miller—that later served as counsel for the plaintiffs in *Brown
v. Board of Education*, and "served as a model for *Brown*" (Moll,
2010, p. 452). Two months after the Ninth Circuit Court of Appeals
upheld the *Mendez* decision, on June 14, 1947, California's Governor
Earl Warren signed a bill repealing segregation—the same Earl
Warren "who as chief justice would write the celebrated unanimous
Supreme Court opinion in *Brown*" in 1954 (Moll, 2010, p. 452).

The *Mendez* case was also key in addressing the criteria for
segregating students of Mexican and Hispanic origin. Criteria that
were regularly applied to them *as a group* were based on negative
stereotypes and unwarranted, malicious assumptions. Moreover, all
members of the group were thought of monolithically, that is, there
was no thought to their differential generational or income status, or
to other factors. The common set of features attributable to them—
and there were 5,000 American students of "Mexican descent" in
Orange County, California, according to the Ninth District Circuit
Court of Appeals document (Google Scholar, 2010)—included having
special needs due to their poor level of hygiene and health, their
illnesses that could be transmitted, and their need for
Americanization. They were seen, in a phrase, as victims of a culture
characterized by a "tangle of pathologies that were alleged to plague
it" (Moll, 2010, pp. 452–453, quoting G. González, 1999). The Ninth
Circuit Court of Appeals ruling clearly states that these criteria were
part of the rationale used by the Westminster School District (Google
Scholar, 2010):

> The [earlier] court found that the segregation as alleged in the petition
> has been for several years past and is practiced under regulations, customs
> and usages adopted more or less as a common plan and enforced by
> respondent-appellants throughout the mentioned school districts; that
> *petitioners are citizens of the United States of Mexican ancestry of good*

moral habits, free from infectious disease or any other disability [emphasis added], and are fully qualified to attend and use the public school facilities....By enforcing the segregation of school children of Mexican descent against their will and contrary to the laws of California, respondents have violated the federal law as provided in the Fourteenth Amendment to the Federal Constitution by depriving them of liberty and property without due process of law and by denying to them the equal protection of the laws. (pp. 5–6)

This same racist set of group character-damning elements—a collection of pernicious stereotypes that reflected the impunity-saturated arrogance for misinterpreting federal law by the city administrators and elected officials of San Bernardino, California and the extent to which they could practice the misuse of civic power—had been applied earlier in *Lopez et al. v. Seccombe et al.*, with the same lack of success. Yet, the Court had to address the vacuous but humiliating accusation that Americans of Mexican descent, and those of Latin origin in general, were inherently less moral, less clean, less able, less healthy, and less intelligent than their White counterparts (Loislaw, 2010):

> This Court finds as true that all of your petitioners are of clean and moral habits not suffering any disability, infectious disease, nor have they any physical or mental defect, but in all other respects are persons proper and qualified to be admitted to and enjoy the use of said bathhouse, plunge, swimming pool, park, playground, and all facilities in connection therewith. That their admission to and the use of said bathhouse, pool, plunge and facilities within said park and playground is not inimical, harmful or detrimental to the health, welfare or safety of other users thereof. (p. X)

The Ninth Circuit Court of Appeals ruling also rejected the Orange County school district's "educational" rationale regarding placing all Mexican-descent students in segregated schools to teach them English (Google Scholar, 2010):

> This court judicially is aware that a century ago when California was taken over by the United States, the majority of its population was Mexican. Four generations of these people have been educated in English speaking schools. To these should be added the third and second generations of succeeding Mexican immigrants to California. A very large percentage of the present day school children descended from Mexican nationals is English

speaking. Many of those of older established families do not speak Spanish. All such children are discriminated against by the impaired facility of the teacher, occupied with teaching English to their classroom associates—as compared with those attending schools of English speaking pupils. (p. 785)

At the mid-Twentieth Century point, California, also geographically far from the South and from the North, was in parallel cultural kinship and mainstream practice with each region regarding what group was to have access to America's mainstream public institutions and those groups of Americans that were to be denied it.

The Pull of Exclusion, the Weight of Conscience

Our national sociocultural yardstick for measuring success in civil rights necessarily suffers from pervasive and complex irony. In the first place, all gains made on the exclusion-inclusion continuum generally have occurred as a result of intense, long-term and, at times, violent struggle, and, ultimately, law, to force "mainstream" America—a euphemism for, initially, Anglo American and, more recently, the regrettable, color-based appellation *White*—to act morally and abide by the universalistic principles of inclusion. These principles are not foreign to us as a people but embedded in our spirit, as they include those espoused by Christianity, to which vast numbers of Americans of all classes belong. More fundamentally, these principles of inclusion are clearly espoused in the language and spirit, and even design (if not originally, then in evolution) of our nation's core documents, which include the Declaration of Independence, Articles of Confederation, Constitution and its current 27 amendments, among others (see GPO Access, 2008). Nevertheless, our national long-term struggle for civil rights was ironically aided in its achievements by two geopolitical phenomena: (1) the racism embedded with Nazi Germany (discussed in chapter 3) and (2) the global strategy of Communism, promulgated particularly, although not exclusively, by the Soviet Union following WWII, which appealed to the anti-colonial movements within Third World contexts, themselves characterized in many cases by a preponderance of non-White populations.

Daniels (2008) offers an example of government action motivated by foreign policy, which aided the struggle-induced scenario of national change, stating that the "eventual repeal of the [Chinese] Exclusion Act [of 1882] in 1943 owed nothing to Chinese American activism, but was ...a side-bar to global diplomacy." Zinn (1980/2003) and, more recently, Minow (2010) have analyzed the federal push and tolerance for civil rights of segregated and otherwise subordinated groups in the United States during the post-WWII/Cold War era as a strategic move to gain the allegiance of populations within former colonial settings. Zinn (1980/2003) notes this phenomenon and relates the contradiction of racism within the United States with our twofold, interrelated need of presenting the United States as a democratic nation where equality was universal as a means to credibly countering Communism on a global scale:

> When the war ended, a new element entered the racial balance in the United States—the enormous, unprecedented upsurge of Black and Yellow people in Africa and Asia. President Harry Truman had to reckon with this, especially as the cold war rivalry with the Soviet Union began, and the dark-skinned revolt of former colonies all over the world threatened to take Marxist form. Action on the race question was needed, not just to calm a Black population at home emboldened by war promises, frustrated by the basic sameness of their condition, it was needed to present to the world a United States that could counter the continuous Communist thrust at the most flagrant failure of American society-the race question. What DuBois had said long ago, unnoticed, now loomed large in 1945: "The problem of the 20th century is the problem of the color line." (p. 448)

W.E.B. DuBois' prescient words were from his essay of 1903, "Of the Dawn of Freedom," in *The Souls of Black Folk* (DuBois, 1903)—words that clearly delineated the relationship between the festering problem of racism in America and the roiling quest for freedom and self-determination that was spreading across the globe:

> The problem of the twentieth century is the problem of the color-line,—the relation of the darker to the lighter races of men in Asia and Africa, in America and the islands of the sea. (p. 13)

In the administration that followed President Truman's, President Eisenhower (1953–1961), who, as Minow (2010) points out, was not favorably disposed to the decision in *Brown* and even suspected its supporters within the United Nations and "international economic and social rights" organizations to be of a socialist or even communist bent. Nevertheless, to bolster the global image of the United States, to combat the potential spread of Communism in the Third World, and to counteract the Soviet Union's critique of the "racial abuses tolerated by the U.S. system of government," the Eisenhower administration accepted the possibility of "ending official segregation, lynchings, and cross burnings" (Minow, 2010, pp. 169–170).

Thirty-five years after the end of WWII, which included the internment of Americans of Japanese descent in U.S. camps, the Commission on the Wartime Relocation and Internment of Civilians was established in late 1980 to determine if a "'wrong' had been done to Japanese Americans during the war" (Daniels, 2008). The Commission found that "'the broad historical causes' of the incarceration of Japanese Americans were 'race prejudice, war hysteria, and a failure of political leadership'" (Daniels, 2008), and made a number of recommendations, including a formal apology from Congress and financial reparations. The recommendations resulted in the Civil Liberties Act of 1988, whereby, beginning in 1990, "some 82,000 persons were compensated a direct cost of $1.64 billion" (Daniels, 2008), or $20,000 each.

The U.S. Congress, on August 10, 1988, by way of the Civil Liberties Act of 1988, apologized on behalf of the United States for its "fundamental violations of the basic civil liberties and constitutional rights of these individuals of Japanese ancestry" (Civics Online, n.d.). The Congressional apology was followed by a Presidential apology signed by President Clinton on October 1, 1993 (Children of the Camps Project, 1999). Daniels (2008) writes that the United States "has never formally apologized to Native Americans, to the descendants of slaves, or to anyone else;" thus, it was a unique occurrence that had implications within other national contexts where civil liberty violations had transpired, including pressures placed upon Japan for violations against China and Korean comfort women, and the formal apology by then Premier Tony Blair to the Irish for "the British government's failings during the famine years of the late 1840s" (Daniels, 1988). The same point made above warrants reiteration: It was due to the ceaseless efforts of activists within the Japanese American community that the apology and reparations materialized—including the release of the funds. The reparations, of course, could not compensate for the actual loss of assets, personal and business, as well as the humiliation and emotional and physical hardship endured, on the part of the American individuals and families of Japanese origin.

Thus, our national conflict has been based on the desire by restricted groups in America for "mainstream" America to open up to others what has been touted as available to all—the "what" referred to is, in fact, the cherished set of freedoms, rights and privileges particular to the mainstream and protected as such by law or practice. Moreover, as privilege prevailed, subordinate classes were created along divisions of wealth, gender, race, and ethnicity that were not entitled to those same rights and privileges. Within this dominant-subordinate cultural framework, the term *minority* (or any term whose label marked the *other* as a member of an excluded group, regardless of historical period or context) was created, literally, by our American democratic exclusionary political system and has been our *modus operandi-modus vivendi* for centuries.

Chapter 6

Contextualizing Multicultural Education in the Post-*Brown* – Post-Civil Rights Era

We the people of the United States, in order to form a more perfect union, establish justice, insure domestic tranquility, provide for the common defense, promote the general welfare, and secure the blessings of liberty to ourselves and our posterity, do ordain and establish this Constitution for the United States of America.

—United States Constitution, Preamble, 1787

This nation has still not come to grips with its racial past nor has it been willing to contemplate, in a truly meaningful way, the diverse future it is fated to have.... Perhaps the greatest strength of the United States is the diversity of its people and to truly understand this country one must have knowledge of its constituent parts. But an unstudied, not discussed and ultimately misunderstood diversity can become a divisive force.

—Attorney General Eric Holder, 2009

Goals of Multicultural Education

Multicultural Education (MCE) is a relatively new term that describes, and attempts to harness under a common rubric, a long tradition of academic interests, research, instruction, advocacy and action (Gay, 1994). These strands, to varying degrees, share frameworks and foci (Banks, 2004), and the same point of commonality: equitable inclusion for historically disenfranchised groups in the democratic enterprise within the United States. Common major categories and their constituent elements that scholars, teachers, and advocates, among others, identify for purposes of research, instruction or support include race, ethnicity, gender, class and language—other factors, such as exceptionality (Banks, 2004) and spirituality (Kwok Pui-lan, 2004), may also form part of the multicultural education elements. It is immediately clear that the operative word in the term Multicultural Education is *Education*.

It is a noteworthy irony that MCE originated in universities as a formal, academic institutional response by mainly minority group educators to a deeply embedded and general dominant group belief in racial hierarchy, driven by legitimized subjectivity (such as science and the law at the service of racism), and acted upon by the dominant group to perpetuate the behavior control and institutional exclusion of subordinate groups. Banks (2009) states that MCE developed "in the United States as a response to the civil rights movement," and operationally defines it as

> an approach to school reform designed to actualize educational equality for students from diverse racial, ethnic, cultural, social-class, and linguistic groups. It also promotes democracy and social justice. A major goal of multicultural education is to reform schools, colleges, and universities so that students from diverse groups will have equal opportunities to learn. In most nations around the world, schools reflect and reproduce the racial and class stratification within society.... The inequality that exists within society is reflected in the curriculum, textbooks, teacher attitudes and expectations, student-teacher interactions, languages and dialects spoken and sanctioned in the schools, and school culture....A major goal of multicultural education is to restructure schools so that all students acquire the knowledge, attitudes, and skills needed to function in ethnically and racially diverse communities and nations, and in the world. Multicultural education seeks to...facilitate [students'] participation as critical and reflective citizens in an inclusive national civic culture. (pp. 13–14)

Parenthetically, there are, of course, professional writers at major institutes—such as Thomas Sowell, Dinesh D'Souza, and Shelby Steele, all currently or formerly associated with the Hoover Institution on War, Revolution and Peace, at Stanford University—who are non-White (Sowell is African American) or who could be perceived as non-White (D'Souza is Asian Indian; Steele is biracial [African American father and White mother]), who are fervently conservative, ardently anti-multicultural education, and maintain high and credible visibility within the conservative and even popular media. D'Souza's blog and writings are available at http://www.dineshdsouza.com/; Sowell's

columns, on the Jewish World Review website at http://www.
jewishworldreview.com/cols/sowell1.asp; and Steele's op-ed pieces, at
the Hoover Institution's website, http://www.hoover.org/bios/steele.
html.

Banks' (2009) definition calls for reform, universal equality,
justice, bias-free curricula and textbooks, enlightened teacher
attitudes and expectations, meaningful teacher-student interactions,
appropriate and diverse language and dialect use, and restructuring of
schools in a way that enables students to function in their
communities, as well as in nations and the world, as they engage
critically and reflectively in their "national civic culture." One major
issue with such a comprehensive definition is that MCE is not a
person or a group or an institutional agency, but a construct
comprised of numerous and highly complex societal elements that, as
problems, are assumed to be at play and, as solutions, are to be played
out within our nation's preK–16+ schools. The multiple factors that
MCE attempts to embrace, or more accurately perhaps, harness, may
well be vast in scope and sensitive to integrate. As such, they may add
raw complexity and puzzlement rather than refined simplicity and
clarity to the range of definitional, methodological, and theoretical
parameters that delimit the term *multicultural education* (Ladson-
Billings, 2004, pp. 61–62).

As Grant et al. (2004, p. 198) determined in their review of
multicultural education research (1990–2001), sexuality and religion
are considered part of the multicultural education family, but have not
figured prominently in the actual research literature. Kwok Pui-lan,
for example, has worked for years developing, applying and
contributing research from the academic perspectives of the Asian
Christian feminist and postcolonial theology movements (see Kwok
Pui-lan, 2004). In like manner, the American Educational Research
Association (AERA) has a special interest group (SIG) dedicated to
"Queer Studies" (website: http://aeraqueerstudiessig.wetpaint.com/
page/AERA+2010). However, although both elements are theoretically included, there has been but a minor amount of multicultural
education classroom research in these two areas over the past decade.
Despite this challenging definitional ambiguity, multicultural
education's academic roots are solidly grounded in the perennial
struggle—political and popular, peaceful and violent—for civil rights

that sprang naturally from enslavement and exclusion, two conditions that were, and remain, antithetical to the rhetoric that serves to define, guide and morally justify the democratic essence of the United States of America and its inhabitants (Gay, 2004).

The multifaceted goal of multicultural education in the United States is to (a) develop research-informed frameworks of understanding of the various groups that comprise the nation, both historically and currently; (b) influence the socialization processes and outcomes of historically underrepresented groups through enhanced and relevant access to, participation in and benefit from institutional experiences, including educational, economic and civic; and (c) serve as a long-term, broad and accessible gateway to formally educate the American public about itself, in order to move from internal conflict and fragmentation to national consensus and social cohesion—to participate equally and freely in the dynamic social architecture and construction of our democracy. These elements represent a wide-ranging and complex goal, which is justified by the principles in our founding documents and sustained by ongoing research-informed results and their interpretation and transmission, particularly through our schools, universities and teacher-education programs. Why multicultural education is needed and the degree to which it has been successful thus far are questions well worth exploring, as many scholars and professional writers place culture wars at the forefront of divisiveness in the United States.

Equity and Self-Image: One Dimensional vs. Plural Dimensional Democracy

Multicultural Education in the United States exists because equity for specific cultural groups within our national borders has generally and consistently remained an elusive reality, a perceived right and a specific goal rather than an achieved state. The groups that have historically been identified most saliently are African Americans, Asian Americans, Hispanic Americans, Native Americans, and women in the above groups and within the dominant White group (Caiazza, Shaw, & Werschkul, 2004; Washington Times, 2005), together with poor Whites (Porter, 1981). Equity is a term that requires definition, as it is used in many cases to be identical to access or equality, and it is neither. Equity, as used here, consists of three interrelated elements: access, participation, and benefit (see DeVillar, 1986, 1999; DeVillar and Faltis, 1994). The term differs from its near-cognate *equality* in that equality is associated with rules of law. Equity, in contrast, is associated with principles of natural justice which, ultimately, can guide, challenge, or change—in a word, supersede—law-governed equality.

In light of our nation's continued situational context regarding the unresolved legacy of racism and related inequities, and their lingering effects, the following definition of equity by Aristotle in *Nicomachean Ethics* (in DeVillar, 2000) not only maintains its currency in today's multicultural U.S. context, but serves also to frame the perspective, both historical and contemporary, within which multicultural education is described, analyzed and understood:

> Our next subject is equity and the equitable...and their respective relations to justice and the just.... [The] equitable is just, but not the legally just but a correction of legal justice....And this is the nature of the equitable, a correction of law where it is defective. (p. 322)

There is a corollary to the role of equity that must accompany any treatise addressing multicultural education in the U.S., and that is the notion of *participatory democracy*, as collectively and intellectually idealized and officially transmitted through schools, in the United States. Again, Aristotle's words, not only demonstrate their continued relevance, but embody the very essence and value of participatory democracy (in DeVillar, 2000):

> If liberty and equality, as is thought by some are chiefly to be found in democracy, they will be best attained when all persons alike share in the government to the utmost. (p. 322)

Thus far, the American law of the land has vacillated between upholding racism and ethnocentrism—the particularistic-exclusionary paradigm—on the one hand, and mandating decisions aligned with its universalistic-inclusionary rhetoric. Our national rhetoric over the past few decades has been characterized by references—popular and official—to our plural national society, which Calhoun (2002) defines as a society "composed of multiple ethnic, racial, religious, national, tribal, and/or linguistic groups that retain their cultural identities and social networks but participate in shared political and economic systems" (p. 364).

So, in our national context of perpetual ambivalence that continues to favor the White segment of our putative plural society, we continue our twofold national struggle for equity in the Aristotelian sense and comprehensive participatory democracy. For many, our national rhetoric *is* our national practice, and therefore there is no need for subjecting our nation to internal scrutiny. But our national rhetoric *is not* our national practice. Consequently, we, as a nation, must continue to question the extent to which "liberal conceptions of justice... [that] support.... Individual rights and freedoms, equality before the law, and various privileges and protections associated with citizen autonomy are protected by principles of justice" (Christman, 2009), as these principles for the vast majority of our national history have not held true in law or practice for whole groups of our citizenry. Resolving this long-standing dilemma depends, perhaps ironically and certainly obviously, on justice being achieved within our participatory democracy, which amounts to achieving a state where our national practice reflects its foundational rhetoric. Christman (2009 in reference to Habermas, 1994) postulates this achieved state of justice as comprising

> that set of principles that are established in practice and rendered legitimate by the *actual* support of the affected citizens (and their representatives) in a process of collective discourse and deliberation. (Autonomy, Justice and Democracy, para. 3)

In a word, the people, rather than *a favored group of people* as has been our case.

It is evident, then, that within the self-designated context of our U.S. democratic nation, the complex thrust of multicultural education is professionally motivated and characterized by the perennial struggle-bound quest for equity. Our equity quest remains imper-ative—if consistently challenged—in order that the term American can itself reflect the whole of the populous rather than, as has historically been the case, a particular part of it. John Dewey (*Nationalizing*

Education 1916, quoted in Gordon, 1964) understood and underscored this fundamental, although ideal rather than lived, principle of national identity and community in his speech to the National Education Association of the United States:

> Such terms as Irish-American or Hebrew-American or German-American are false terms because they seem to assume something which is already in existence called America, to which the other factor may be externally hitched on. The fact is, the genuine American, the typical American, is himself a hyphenated character. This does not mean that he is part American and that some foreign ingredient is then added. It means that, as I have said, he is international and interracial in his make-up. He is not American plus Pole or German. But the American is himself Pole-German-English-French-Spanish-Italian-Greek-Irish-Scandavian-Bohemian-Jew and so on. The point is to see to it that the hyphen connects instead of separates. And this means at least that our public schools shall teach each factor to respect every other, and shall take pains to enlighten all as to the great past contributions of every strain in our composite make-up. I wish our teaching of American history in the schools would take more account of the great waves of migration by which our land for over three centuries has been continuously built up, and made every pupil conscious of the rich breadth of our national make-up. When every pupil recognizes all the factors which have gone into our being, he will continue to prize and reverence that coming from his own past, but he will think of it as honored in being simply one factor informing a whole, nobler and finer than itself. (pp. 139–140)

Some fifty years later, Milton Gordon (1964), summarizing the general scholarly perspective relative to an *actual* American core culture, wrote:

> If there is anything in American life which can be described as an over-all American culture which serves as a reference point for immigrants and their children, it can best be described, it seems to us, as the middle-class cultural patterns of, largely, White Protestant, Anglo-Saxon origins, leaving aside for the moment the question of minor reciprocal influences on this culture exercised by the cultures of later entry into the United States, and ignoring also, for this purpose, the distinction between the upper-middle class and the lower-middle class cultural worlds. (pp. 72–73)

While this perspective was generally and strongly both embraced by professionals and the community-at-large, a more appropriate word than *actual* would be *fabricated* as the complex cultural character—

our thwarted national character—was usurped by White America and access to it restricted by law, policy, practice, and custom.

In sum, from its ideological roots to its post mid-20th century practice, the United States prized a specific monolithic cultural image and character associated with a particular group. Moreover, through laws and practice, this dominant *soi-disant* core culture controlled and restricted access—to greater or lesser degrees—by other cultural groups in the United States to the institutions that served to mold its own members. This contradictory model of culture—universally inclusive and pluralistic in rhetoric, selectively particularistic and monocultural in fact—within a self-designated democratic context from its inception set the stage and tone for major struggles by members of the excluded groups (and supported to differing degrees by members of the dominant culture group) to match United States practice with its rhetoric.

The American Ideological Dilemma: Liberty, Justice and Inclusiveness for Whom?

The term *ideology* may be defined in various ways and depending on the source one uses or with the discipline one selects. As, for example, the "Doctrines, beliefs, ideals of a person or social group" (Page & Thomas, 1980, p. 169); as a "cohesive set of beliefs, ideas and symbols through which persons interpret their world and their place within it" (Calhoun, 2002, p. 222); or, more elaborately, as a "systematic and all-embracing political doctrine, which claims to give a complete and universally applicable theory of man and society, and to derive therefrom a programme of political action" (Scruton, 1982, p. 213). The unifying power of ideology, as well as its imposing and destructive power, is immense, as it carries within it the illusion of objectivity and righteousness coupled with the passion, strength and certainty of faith. Theodorson and Theodorson (1969) articulate this operational principle in their definition:

> A system of interdependent ideas (beliefs, traditions, principles, and myths) held by a social group or society, which reflects, rationalizes, and defends its particular social, moral, religious, political, and economic institutional interests and commitments. Ideologies serve as logical and philosophical justifications for a group's patterns of behavior, as well as its

attitudes, goals, and general life situation. The ideology of any population involves an interpretation (and usually a repudiation) of alternative ideological frames of reference. The elements of an ideology tend to be accepted as truth or dogma rather than as tentative philosophical or theoretical formulations, despite the fact that ideologies are modified in accordance with sociocultural changes. (p. 195)

Marx and Engels (Scruton, 1982, p. 213) addressed the particularistic-universalistic power element of ideology by characterizing it as a self-serving mechanism of the ruling group (particularistic) that functions to "naturalize the status quo...by persuading oppressed classes to accept the descriptions of reality which render their subordination 'natural' (universalistic). Allport (1958) articulates the lifelong impact of ideological conditioning and at the same time acknowledges that its rhetoric may well outstrip its practice:

> ...one must never forget that *official doctrines* do not always correspond to the actual views or practices of the adherents. Often they express ideals rather than attainments. Yet they are psychologically important, for where they exist they inevitably point the minds of group members in a common direction, and present norms for their behavior which from childhood onward leave their impression. (pp. 92–93)

The salient ideological lines of the United States Declaration of Independence (July 4, 1776) serve, at once, as the foundational-cum-generative credo of American democracy, and, as importantly, as its guardian (National Archives and Records Administration, n.d.).

> We hold these truths to be self-evident, that all men are created equal, that they are endowed by their Creator with certain unalienable Rights, that among these are Life, Liberty and the pursuit of Happiness.—That to secure these rights, Governments are instituted among Men, deriving their just powers from the consent of the governed. (para. 2)

Thus, *liberty* and *justice, equality* and *participation in governing* comprise essential, unalterable elements of the self-professed American character, and are fundamental to the practice and preservation of American democracy (see M. Adler, 1981). Far from being values contained within only one document—albeit one of preeminent status—the values were quickly reiterated within the

Constitution (1787) of the United States in its Preamble (American Civil Liberties Union, n.d.):

> We the people of the United States, in order to form a more perfect union, establish justice, insure domestic tranquility, provide for the common defense, promote the general welfare, and secure the blessings of liberty to ourselves and our posterity, do ordain and establish this Constitution for the United States of America. (p. 1)

The foundational values of American democracy, those of *liberty* and *justice for all*, were again brought to the fore of professed American national identity in the Pledge of Allegiance, written in August 1892 by Francis Bellamy, a Christian socialist; the Pledge was modified in 1923–1924 under the leadership of the American Legion and Daughters of the American Revolution to specifically mention the United States of America, and again in 1954 by a successful campaign spearheaded by the Knights of Columbus (Baer, 1992), to ultimately read:

> I pledge allegiance to the Flag of the United States of America and to the Republic for which it stands, one nation, under God, indivisible, with liberty and justice for all.

In the Pledge, we have ideological juxtapositions—the state and religion, as opposed to remaining separate as decreed—together with the then accepted-yet-invidious contradiction of exclusion by race, religion, ethnicity, gender and other group markers, in the same rhetorical breath that consecrates unity, liberty and justice for all. The border that was to separate state and religion remains permeable, an expression of sustained ideological conflict, exacerbated by those who see our nation as Christian. In like manner, the rationalization of past and present exclusion, regardless of the form it may take, and denial of its effects remain embedded in our current cultural composite, strengthening our national fragmentation and constraining meaningful movement toward national unity.

Ideology is not constrained by physical borders and the promise of America spread freely and rapidly throughout the globe. Beyond its vast geographic borders, during this same 100-year period from the late 1700s to the late 1800s, the word *America* also traveled to lands throughout the globe, with the same universal meaning for prospective immigrants and refugees: *freedom*. The value of this place name, a collectively accepted metaphor for the perceived American spirit of freedom—the land for everyone and anyone, regardless of circumstance—is perhaps best exemplified by the poem of Emma Lazarus (1849–1887), a precocious writer and successful poet born in New York City to wealthy and prominent parents who were Sephardic Jews and pre-Revolutionary War settlers there (Jewish Women's Archives, 2010). The poem, *The New Colossus* (1883), is engraved on the pedestal of the Statue of Liberty, yet another majestic, ubiquitous icon of American freedom:

The New Colossus

Not like the brazen giant of Greek fame,
With conquering limbs astride from land to land;
Here at our sea-washed sunset gates shall stand
A mighty woman with a torch, whose flame
Is the imprisoned lightening, and her name
Mother of Exiles. From her beacon-hand
Glows world-wide welcome; her mild eyes command
The air-bridged harbor that twin cities frame.

"Keep ancient lands, your storied pomp!" cries she
With silent lips. "Give me your tired, your poor,
Your huddled masses yearning to breathe free,
The wretched refuse of your teeming shore.
Send these, the homeless, tempest-tost to me,
I lift my lamp beside the golden door."

The dream, of course, did not match the reality, yet lives of immigrant individuals and groups fared better than had they stayed within their home countries. Segregation, ethnocentrism, religious bigotry, and racism, together with sexism, prevailed in the United States towards immigrants identifiable as belonging to particular groups deemed to be outside the circle of Americanness. An individual's or group's color, nevertheless, made it easier to eventually fall within the circle (White) or to remain outside it (non-White). The problem of color and its attendant issues remain—racism, segregation and societal bias—an integral part of our nation's unresolved cultural dilemma.

Bilingual Education Act and Controversy

In like fashion, and without irony, the Bilingual Education Act of 1968 "clearly represented an ambiguous commitment" to an effective bilingual education approach, and after a half dozen years "the law's instructional objectives were still unclear and its prescribed methodology was still ambiguous" (Salomone, 1986:88–89). In 1974, the Supreme Court ruled in favor of Chinese students in San Francisco regarding their right to receive instruction in a language they could understand (Baker & Prys Jones, 1998). The *Lau v. Nichols* (1974) ruling mandated that school districts take "appropriate action to overcome language barriers," interpreted by legal scholar Salomone (1986, p. 101), as conveying "that schools merely do something." Thus, "the kind of bilingual education needed to achieve equality of educational opportunity for language minority children was not defined" (Baker & Prys Jones, 1998, p. 548).

This continuing, viral-like ambiguity led ultimately to hostile statements and actions by our nation's leaders, beginning with former President Reagan who contested, even repudiated, the use of languages other than English in the U.S. classroom. Reagan's statement in the March 3, 1981 edition of the *New York Times* (quoted in Baker, 1981) displayed a resounding ignorance of bilingual education pedagogy and policy, but did serve to fan the reactionary flames of public opinion toward bilingual education and students, to whom he referred to as "them," isolating Americans, particularly of Hispanic and Asian descent, from their mainstream, monolingual English-speaking American counterparts:

> It is absolutely wrong and against the American concept to have a bilingual education program that is now openly, admittedly, dedicated to preserving their native language and never getting them adequate in English so they can go out into the job market. (p. 194)

The hostility toward bilingual education continued to manifest itself in the official voices of Administration officials, including Reagan's Secretary of Education, William Bennett, and the public media, each choosing to misrepresent the goal and research-based achievements of comprehensive bilingual education programs (Baker, 2006). The fundamental goal of bilingual education is to teach subject matter in the first language of the student as he or she is learning English. In this way, the students learn subject matter content in their native language as they learn English sufficiently to receive all subject matter instruction in English within regular classrooms with their native English-speaking peers.

That the actual goal of bilingual education has generated so much negative reaction, hostility, and that it remains misunderstood today, particularly in light of sound research on the benefits of well-designed and implemented bilingual education programs (e.g., Ramirez, Yuen, Ramey, & Pasta, 1991; Ramirez, Pasta, Yuen, Billings, & Ramey, 1991; Willig, 1988, 1985), illustrates the long-term effectiveness of the conscious and official cultural reproduction of intergenerational naïveté that sustains negative stereotypes and practices toward groups designated as "minority," "disadvantaged," "historically under-performing," and the like within the United States. It is important at this point to repeat that this restrictive socialization phenomenon (DeVillar, 1994) maintains our national populous in "a perpetual state characterized as foolishly credulous," as the *Shorter Oxford English Dictionary* (2007) reminds us. It is, more fundamentally, deleterious to the welfare of the United States as it foments national fragmentation through continued distrust, misunderstanding and prejudice toward particular groups of Americans—designated or perceived as less than American on the basis of race or its socially constructed derivatives mentioned throughout this book—by Americans who are socialized to feel that they are the mythical "mainstream" (read "real") American. An interesting account of surveys involving responses of Tea Party members illustrates the above point (Kroll, 2010):

> [T]his burgeoning grassroots group, surveys show, is staggeringly White, older, and fairly affluent—[it is] a group that tends to view the world through a racial lens: according to a recent study from the University of Washington, 73% of Tea Party supporters concurred with the statement: "If Blacks would only try harder, they could be just as well off as Whites." Only one-third of Americans who reject Tea Party positions agree. In general, those who back the Tea Party are more likely to hold negative opinions of both Blacks and Latinos—a claim that movement regulars in all-White crowds vehemently contest. In fact, when it comes to race, it goes a lot

> deeper than that.... [R]ace is a through-line that connects the unrest of our
> nation's past to today's "patriots." (para. 7)

The recent expulsion of Mark Williams, leader of Florida's Tea Party
Express, by the National Tea Party Federation (*The Week*, July 30,
2010, p. 19) for his racist remarks in a "parody letter" he composed
adds credence to the strong, explicit racist sentiments within the Tea
Party, within its leadership and membership. Williams' composition
(Cohen, 2010) was in the form of a letter from NAACP President Ben
Jealous to President Abraham Lincoln

> begging him not to free the slaves because it would mean 'we Coloreds ...
> having to work for real, think for ourselves, and take consequences along
> with the rewards.' (footnote 2)

Earlier, in April 2010, the founder of the Springboro Tea Party
(southwest Ohio), Brian "Sonny" Thomas, tweeted "Illegals every-
where today! So many spics make me feel like a speck. Where's my
gun?" (McCarty, 2010, para. 1). Again, members and supporters of the
Tea Party distanced themselves from the person and language.
Nevertheless, it is yet another indicator that racism is prevalent and
explicit with its leadership and general membership ranks.

Learning a non-English language exists, of course, as an object of
study as well as in exceptional curricular programs offered, for
example, by international schools in the United States (K12
Academics, 2010) and international baccalaureate programs, which
nationally number more than a thousand (International Baccalaureate
Organization, 2010). But foreign language education is far from being
generalized to the American public school student; moreover, few
students who have taken two or more years of a foreign language in
high school can actually display even beginning proficiency in it.
Bilingual education, likewise, does not generally serve as an accepted
alternative to monolingual education for the 5 million-plus students,
designated now as English Language Learners (ELLs), who could
benefit from it. In what type of schooling circumstances are these
students currently in? Crawford and MacSwan (2008) provide us with
a telling summary:

> The Urban Institute (Cosentino de Cohen et al., 2005) reports that 70 percent of ELLs are now concentrated in majority-minority, under-resourced schools and in classrooms where teachers have considerably less experience and fewer credentials than those serving English-proficient students....As a result, ELLs have among the highest failure and dropout rates of American students. (p. 1)

A substantial lack of funding targeted to the needs of ELLs exacerbates the vicious cycle in which they have been placed.

In *Castañeda v. Pickard* (1981), the ruling by the Fifth Circuit Court of Appeals provided a three-tier analytical model to determine statutory compliance for federal courts to apply in determining "appropriate action of language remediation programs" (Salomone, 1986, p. 103). Twenty-seven years later, on December 15, 2008, Crawford and MacSwan (2008) wrote a letter to then President-Elect Obama "on behalf of [our] nation's 5.1 million English language learners (ELLs) [who] 'represent the fastest-growing student population, [and are] expected to make up one of every four students by 2025.'" In it, they proposed that federal dollars be made available in the form of grants to jump-start professional development, research and programs that address the court's three-tier model as "the unique needs of *these* children have all too often been ignored or treated as an afterthought by policymakers." Crawford and MacSwan (2008) summarize the Court's still-unattended to 1981 ruling and three-tier analytical model:

> A "good faith" effort to serve ELL students was insufficient, the court ruled. Rather, a district's program must meet certain objective standards. First, the pedagogy must be research-based – or at least be based on a theory with some expert support. Second, it must be provided sufficient resources and personnel to give the theory a chance to work. Third, it must be periodically evaluated and, if necessary, restructured to ensure that students are progressing. (p. 7)

We consider ourselves to be a nation that adheres to the *rule of law* as well as one comprised of reasonable people, who, as the Fifth Circuit Court noted in its 1981 ruling, can disagree, including experts, on ways in which to effect educational change. This perception, commonly voiced in professional, community and media circles, can certainly be assessed as self-adulatory, and as a self-serving means to sustain the status quo and avoid change. The Court illustrated this latter point by delimiting the parameters of its ruling, stating that an action based on educational theory needed to be undertaken, but not prescribing the particular educational theory to which an educational institution must adhere (*Castañeda v. Pickard*, 1981):

> The state of the art in the area of language remediation may well be such that respected authorities legitimately differ as to the best type of educational program for limited English speaking students and we do not believe that Congress in enacting § 1703(f) intended to make the resolution of these differences the province of federal courts. The court's responsibility, insofar as educational theory is concerned, is only to ascertain that a school system is pursuing a program informed by an educational theory recognized as sound by some experts in the field or, at least, deemed a legitimate experimental strategy. (para. 59)

In the *Castañeda v. Pickard* case, among the 30 core terms comprising the disagreement between the parents of students whose predominate language was not English and the school district within which they were enrolled were "speaking...segregation...bilingual...hiring...barrier...curriculum...promotion...appropriate action ...administrators...skills...teach...disparate impact...labor market...employment discrimination ...[and] unlawful discrimination." Twenty-seven years after the 1954 *Brown* decision mandating desegregation and 17 years after the 1964 Civil Rights Act, these terms served to characterize the continuing deleterious effects of exclusion, on the one hand, and the differential quality of public schooling that existed for segregated minority groups, on the other.

The extent to which teachers were prepared to effectively teach Hispanic-origin students who were not sufficiently proficient to receive instruction in English was at the forefront of concerns articulated by the 5th Circuit Court, particularly as this was seven years after the Supreme Court's *Lau v. Nichols* (1974). The Circuit Court questioned the reliance by non-Spanish speaking teachers upon Spanish-speaking teacher aides, as aides were not qualified to take the place of certificated teachers; it also questioned the 100 hours of Spanish language instruction to qualify teachers to instruct in a bilingual classroom, as it proved to be an ineffective means to learn Spanish well enough to instruct students whose dominant language was Spanish and whose English language proficiency was inadequate to understand subject matter instruction in English.

To compound the problem of providing unqualified teachers to students in bilingual classrooms, the district's evaluation protocol following the 100-hour course consisted of an examination process in which teachers wrote a paragraph using a Spanish-English dictionary, read orally from a book in Spanish, and answered questions orally by the district's certification committee. Even after such a simple examination process, the court found "There was no formal grading of the examination; the certification committee had no guide to measure the Spanish language vocabulary of the teachers based on their performance on the exam" (*Castañeda v. Pickard*, 1981). Yet, as in the case of *Brown* where the force and velocity of implementing desegregation was diluted by the "with all deliberate speed" statement, the Fifth Circuit Court used similar imprecise wording, including "as soon as possible...conduct a hearing," and "should also assure that [the district] takes whatever steps are necessary to acquire validated Spanish language achievement tests."

And, even in the face of linguistically unqualified teachers being assigned to the bilingual classroom, the Circuit Court's statement did not address the effects on the students' continued lack of exposure to quality, understandable instruction and the devastating effects of such a lack on students' learning and performance outcomes, choosing instead to state their decision in vague, open-to-interpretation language that could as easily reinforce the status quo as lead to some kind of modified hiring or professional development outcomes:

> Although we certainly hope and expect that RISD will attempt to hire teachers who are already qualified to teach in a bilingual classroom as positions become available, we are by no means suggesting that teachers already employed by the district should be replaced or that the district is limited to hiring only teachers who are already qualified to teach in a bilingual program. We are requiring only that RISD undertake further measures to improve the ability of any teacher, whether now or hereafter employed, to teach effectively in a bilingual classroom. (The Bilingual Education and Remedial Education Programs, para. 34)

Since our New World revolutionary birth, we have yet to reach our Harlem, our promised land, "our ... chance [to move] toward the larger and the more democratic ... from medieval America to modern" (Locke, 1925, in Bracey et al., 1970, p. 337). Locke (1925a, b) well understood, as did Allport (see *The Nature of Prejudice*, 1958), a principle of unity that remains valid and in urgent need of our making it operational today: social interaction and cooperation are fundamental to all-inclusive integration, itself a condition for our transformation to national unity. Conversely, segregation inhibits, if not prohibits, achievement of this goal (DeVillar & Faltis, 1991). Locke (1925a, p.630) also understood clearly that marginalization was a result of societal "proscription and prejudice" that forcibly placed African-origin individuals, "dissimilar elements" to one another, "into a common area of contact and interaction." Locke (1925a, p. 630) viewed Harlem as unique from commonplace African American ghettos in its diverse composition of African-origin groups ("the African, the West Indian, the Negro American"; the northerner and southerner; "the peasant, the student, the business man, the professional man, artist, musician, adventurer and worker, preacher and criminal, exploiter and social outcast"). It was, according to Locke (1925a, p. 630), their goal, their challenge, to transform from a "common condition" to a "common consciousness," from experiencing a "problem in common" to experiencing a "life in common." As stated earlier, we, in the United States, as a people, and as multiple groups, have yet to reach our Harlem, our common consciousness, our life in common.

Multicultural Education and the Current Status of Minority Groups

Members of minority groups, regardless of their position and integrity, remain second-class citizens and suspect of anti-American behavior, as recently demonstrated in the Shirley Sherrod fiasco, in which her eloquent comments on our nation's need to transcend race were edited by conservative blogger, Andrew Breitbart, and distributed by Fox News, to portray her as a racist. Ms. Sherrod was promptly misjudged and chastised by NAACP President Ben Jealous and fired from her United States Department of Agriculture post by the Obama administration (O'Keefe, 2010). Within two days of her forced resignation, the full story was known and Ms. Sherrod received an apology from her boss, as well as from Press Secretary Robert Gibbs for the "whole Obama administration," and received an offer of reinstatement in another position within the USDA, which she subsequently declined to accept (CNN, 2010). Yet, the language used by Press Secretary Gibbs to justify the Administration's recanting its previous judgment and decision toward Ms. Sherrod is convoluted and inaccurate. George Orwell in his novel *Nineteen Eighty Four* (1949) introduced the notion of doublethink as the conscious ability to believe in two contradictory ideas simultaneously. The notion of doublethink was later applied by Cummins (1999) to exemplify the coercive relations of power within the bilingual education debate in the United States—that is, essentially supporting bilingual education programs in funding and rhetoric, yet denying the effective type of bilingual education programs needed by the children for whom they were designed. By doing so, academics and media commentators articulated doublethink statements as a means to "denying bilingual students their linguistic as well as educational rights" (Cummins, 1999, p. 16). Gibbs' statement regarding President Obama's rationale for his administration's initially supporting the actions taken against Ms. Sherrod and then rejecting them in favor of supporting her, is a concrete example of doublethink (Jalonick & Evans, 2010):

> The president had been briefed, Gibbs said, and "he talked about the fact that a disservice had been done, an injustice had happened and, because the facts had changed, a review of the decision based on those facts should be taken." (para. 9)

The point must be made that the facts had *not* changed; rather, the actions of the Obama Administration toward Ms. Sherrod were flawed, ill-advised, premature and based on a *purposeful media distortion* by Breitbart *of the facts* presented by Ms. Sherrod, which once distributed, were believed by leaders within the Obama Administration and the NAACP. Facts did not change; they were brought to light. The distinction is important, as decisions made on the basis of distortions are faulty from the beginning and should never be called facts or confused with facts. Yet, according to Mr. Gibbs, speaking on behalf of President Obama, a distortion is equivalent to a fact.

Similarly, it is a distortion of the facts—cultural, racial, societal, economic and otherwise—when the sacrifices and contributions by groups of Americans who are characterized by their absence of Whiteness—that is, as non-White—are excluded from texts and other representational media that socialize generations to what it is to be American and who participated in its making. The facts are that Hispanic Americans shared life and death at the battle of the Alamo, fighting against the Mexican army alongside American heroes whose names we know all too well. Also, the facts are that African Americans fought and died on the fields of our Civil War, and that Jews, African Americans and other minority group members contributed innovative forms to our culture of entertainment, and that of the world's, as well as to our intellectual, creative or scientific advancements. Yet, acknowledgment and integration of these sacrifices and contributions are denied their rightful place in the historical, social and cultural tapestry that textbooks and other forms of representational media weave commercially and educationally for our nation. Thus, the sacrifices and contributions are denied by the very fact of their continued absence.

The recent Texas social science textbook standards and curriculum authorization process, and its result, is a case in point. It is evident that our nation's drive toward greater cultural fragmentation is fueled by contradictions and denials. These two forms of negative expression, in turn, have been identified as manifestations of yet a greater societal ill, summed up by *The Week* (August 6, 2010) as "White and Black Americans still view each other with resentment and fear." But it isn't "Black" Americans who decided what was to be deleted, revised or inserted in the Texas social science textbook standards and curriculum, which is a display of what can happen when resentment and exceedingly poor judgment are combined with the abuse of power. The state of Arizona is blazing a similar backward path away from inclusive and quality education that manifests an insensitivity to developing the hearts and minds of children born to poor parents. Ken Silverstein, writing about conservative politics and actions in Arizona in the July 2010 issue of *Harper's*, states that Republican Representative John Kavanaugh believes that the benefits of all-day kindergarten "dissipate by third grade for all but poverty level" and that the state should offer Medicare only to people at one-third of poverty-level income—which works out to less than $7,500 for a family of four—as opposed to the current practice of offering it to everyone at poverty level and below. "We can't afford to be that generous anymore," [Kavanaugh] said. (p. 42)

One wonders what groups are included in the "we" Mr. Kavanaugh so exclusively alludes to.

Of course, resentment and fear extend beyond black and white, as we have documented throughout this text. Nor are these negative emotions that persistently inform social practice relegated to urban areas, as bell hooks (2009) demonstrates in her recent work about long-standing Black-White tensions in rural Kentucky, and that other writers (Gonzalez, 2003; Saenz & Torres, 2003—both works referenced in Tiekin, 2010) document with respect to Native American and Hispanic presence and contribution in rural and non-metropolitan areas of America (McConnell & Miraftab, 2009). These intergroup cultural, racial and ethnic tensions remain a complex phenomenon that is difficult to perceive, much less address or disentangle. More so, when our national intellectual and popular communicative platforms skirt these tensions, complicit in main-taining their invisibility, as a means to continue the mythology of the American rural landscape, past and present. In the shockingly eloquent judgment of Attorney General Eric Holder, we have yet to transcend these ethnic-racial phobias in our nation's urban, suburban and rural contexts, because we remain "a nation of cowards." Attorney General Holder (U.S. Department of Justice, 2009) addresses our historical and present inability to discuss race, naturally or comfortably, preferring, as we do, to avoid the topic, and living with the societal division that continues to prevail in the absence of any sustained, meaningful and productive interracial discourse:

> One cannot truly understand America without understanding the historical experience of Black people in this nation. Simply put, to get to the heart of this country one must examine its racial soul. Though this nation has proudly thought of itself as an ethnic melting pot, in things racial we have always been and continue to be, in too many ways, essentially a nation of cowards....We, average Americans, simply do not talk enough with each other about race. It is an issue we have never been at ease with and given our

nation's history this is in some ways understandable. And yet, if we are to make progress in this area we must feel comfortable enough with one another, and tolerant enough of each other, to have frank conversations about the racial matters that continue to divide us....This nation has still not come to grips with its racial past nor has it been willing to contemplate, in a truly meaningful way, the diverse future it is fated to have. To our detriment, this is typical of the way in which this nation deals with issues of race. And so I would suggest that we use February of every year ... to foster a period of dialogue among the races. This is admittedly an artificial device to generate discussion that should come more naturally, but our history is such that we must find ways to force ourselves to confront that which we have become expert at avoiding....It is not safe for this nation to assume that the unaddressed social problems in the poorest parts of our country can be isolated and will not ultimately affect the larger society....Perhaps the greatest strength of the United States is the diversity of its people and to truly understand this country one must have knowledge of its constituent parts. But an unstudied, not discussed and ultimately misunderstood diversity can become a divisive force. (paras 1–12)

As a nation, we remain composed of parallel cultures—unequal in power, status, economics and other forms of capital, even trajectory—that interact without integrating. Multicultural education is ultimately a vision of intergroup integration, driven by the engine of equity. It is within the context of the school that formal socialization occurs and that the vision of peoplehood—Americanness—is fostered, practiced and internalized. Schooling also affords the academic and social preparation to enable its graduates to seek and secure opportunities on an equitable basis. Yet our schools have been segregated by law and by fact for over a century, emulating and fueling the larger, inequitable divisions among groups within our nation. Thus, the question remains as to the effectiveness of schools in playing a change-agent, rather than a status quo, role in contemporary society.

Chapter 7

The Continued Multicultural Struggle: Religion, Education and Music

I acknowledge that to molest any person, Jew or Gentile, for either professing doctrine, or practicing worship merely religious or spiritual, it is to persecute him; and such a person, whatever his doctrine or practice be, true or false, suffereth persecution for conscience.

—Roger Williams, 1644

Our form of government has no sense unless it is founded in a deeply felt religious faith—and I don't care what it is.

—President Eisenhower, 1952

Racial discrimination trumped religious bigotry in our nation in terms of legally enforced exclusion, although the two institutions, one secular, the other, spiritual, have been intertwined throughout our history, and remain so. Nevertheless, as important as religion is in American life, it has been used, in different periods of our history, to restrict group access to liberties our founding documents espouse and that our nation cherishes in principle. We begin this chapter by addressing religious intolerance in the United States to properly position it vis-à-vis discrimination, racial and otherwise.

The Role of Religion in America and Americanness

Purposeful exclusion, and the socialization process that accompanies the action, has created an America where all groups are not viewed as American. Exclusion has been based, mainly, but not solely, on wealth, racial and ethnic and gender designations, and for the greater part of our nation's history was legally sanctioned (Jackman, 1994), at the federal level or as a state right. Religion, of course, has been a highly contentious social and ideological issue in the creation and development of American life, biased generally toward Protestantism and away from Catholicism and all other forms of Christianity—such as Eastern Orthodoxy—as well as non-Christian faiths, including Buddhism, Hinduism, Islam, and Judaism, among others. Freese (2008, The History of American Identity) writes of the then-mainstream reaction to the rise of U.S. immigrants who were Catholic:

> But in a country which had always defined itself as Protestant in stark opposition to Catholicism, this openness changed when, in the half-century before the Civil War, immigration led to a massive growth of the Catholic population. In 1790 there had been only 35,000 Catholics, but when by 1860 their number had grown to 3.1 million, religion began to play a major role in the definition of national identity. Anti-Catholicism led to ... bitter fights about educational policy. New public schools were set up as 'Americanizing' institutions meant to counter the detrimental effects of the parochial schools founded by Irish immigrants. Thus, national identity was no longer a primarily ideological notion, but religion, education, and cultural customs and values became important ingredients. (para. 5)

Although racial discrimination trumped religious bigotry, this not to minimize that, historically, Protestantism—acknowledging that it is "an agglomeration of competing denominations and sects" (Wuthnow, 2005, p. 84)—has been the religious unit most identified with Americanness, however contradictory the notion is to our Constitutional principle of religious pluralism embodied in the First Amendment. In his influential work, *Assimilation in American Life*, Gordon (1964) pointed out that White Protestants were heavily homogenous religiously in that their marriage partners were overwhelmingly of the same faith—91 percent; in making this point, Gordon also characterized the privileged status of Protestantism in the United States:

> White Protestants, of course, being the largest ethnic group in America, the culturally dominant group, and the group whose historical role has the greatest degree of popularly accorded legitimation, can afford to be relaxed about their own communalism. (p. 222)

Jews were even more likely to marry a partner of their own faith (93%), while "comparable" (White) Catholics were less prone to marry exclusively within the faith than either Protestants or Jews, but still generally homogenous (78.5%). All three figures were indicators, according to Gordon (1964), of strong ethnic communality, and, by the same token, ethnic group separateness—a segregative phenomenon, Gordon (1964, pp. 222–223) surmised, that was expressed in the local affiliations of national organizations (e.g., Boy Scouts of America, Girl Scouts of the United States of America), leading to increased religious and racial fragmentation.

Until the late 1950s in the United States, Jews and Catholics were suspect, marginalized, ridiculed and the objects of both misinformation and disinformation, as currently, with increasingly graceless and fuliginous hyperbole, are Muslims. Definitely, Muslims, along with Buddhists and Hindus, in the middle of the last century were, as Herberg wrote in 1955 (quoted in Wuthnow, 2005, p. 34) "obscurely un-American." In fact, from our earliest beginnings in what is now the United States, Wuthnow (2005) emphasizes:

> American Christians have thought of themselves as the reigning power and the dominant cultural influence. It was thus possible to ignore the presence of devotees of other religions or to regard them variously as proto-Christians, potential converts, degenerate heathen, or in some other way that did not fully take into account the complexity of their beliefs and practices. (p. 35)

Davis (2010, p. 87) adds a biting reality to the way in which the above religio-centric perspective was carried out: "religion has often been a cudgel, used to discriminate, suppress and even kill the foreign, the 'heretic' and the 'unbeliever'—including the 'heathen' natives already here." Religious intolerance was the order of the day and practiced from our historical beginnings in 1620 toward Catholics and non-Puritans, particularly Quakers, and dissent within the Puritan ranks could well lead to banishment, as it did in the case of Roger Williams, who, as a preacher, preached religious tolerance—considered "Satan's policy" by his religious confreres and colonial administrators. Williams' (Davis, 2008) words, written in 1644, reflected the truth and value of interfaith tolerance:

> I acknowledge that to molest any person, Jew or Gentile, for either professing doctrine, or practicing worship merely religious or spiritual, it is to persecute him; and such a person, whatever his doctrine or practice be, true or false, suffereth persecution for conscience. (p. 94)

This spirit of tolerance was later echoed by Thomas Jefferson, James Madison, John Adams and George Washington in their purposeful and ardent belief in the separation of church and state, which was made explicit in our nation's Constitution, as well as in letters, speeches and laws prior to and after its signing.

This perspective of religious tolerance, however well-grounded in the interpretation of scripture, did not translate into general practice, and, as Daniels (1991) states, by

> the beginning of eighteenth century, if not before, the character of what was to become the United States was pretty well set. It would be English and Protestant. And it would rapidly adopt migration myths that had little relation to what had been seventeenth-century realities. (p. 52)

Myth-making was applied by the Second Continental Congress in 1775 in justifying armed conflict with England in which it was stated that "Americans were all descendents of persons who had left the Old World 'to seek on these shores a residence for civil and religious freedom'"—which in reality accounted "only a minor fraction of Europeans...and not one of the three hundred thousand immigrants from Africa" (Daniels, 1991, p. 52). Religious, racial and ethnic exclusion was structured and incorporated early on to establish the particularistic version of the misnamed and incomplete American narrative. Throughout the 18th century, one's religion affected his political expression. In Massachusetts, only Christians could hold public office, and, if one were Catholic, he would have to renounce "papal authority," and in New York, by state constitution, Catholics were banned from holding public office (Davis, 2010, p. 87). The first half of the 19th century also played upon the fear of Catholicism and papal allegiance, such that "Anti-Catholic venom was part of the typical American school day, along with Bible readings"— accompanied by separate but related incidents such as the burning of a Catholic convent, the torching of houses, destruction of Catholic churches, and the massacre of 20 or more people (Davis, 2010, p. 94).

The Mormon religion (The Church of Jesus Christ of Latter-day Saints) caused problems for mainstream Christians and politicians. Founded by Joseph Smith in 1830, he was tarred and feathered in 1832 for his beliefs and, by 1838, he and his followers were expelled from Missouri by its Governor, Lilburn Boggs, but not before a mob of vigilantes "massacred 17 church members, including children, at the Mormon settlement of Haun's Mill" (Davis, 2010, p. 94). Smith was murdered in 1844, as was his brother Hyrum, by another mob of vigilantes while both were in a Carthage, Illinois jail, and, as Davis (2010, p. 94) points out: "No one was ever convicted of the crime."

Today, the conflictive division among Christian inclusivists (those who believe that, for them, Christianity is best, but that all religions offer an equally good way of knowing God), exclusivists (those who believe that "only Christianity is ultimately true)," and those who are pluralistic in their belief ("spiritual shoppers") manifest differing degrees of tolerance toward religious freedom in the United States (Wuthnow, 2005, p. 190). Conflict and issues of tolerance surrounding the fact of increasing religious diversity within our nation adds to our present fragmentation. The discord regarding the appropriate degree of religious tolerance toward "non-traditional" Christian religious groups inclines toward the vociferous, volatile and vituperative, and conflicts with the letter and spirit of our Constitution, making evident a demonstrated need for a thoughtful, negotiated resolution in keeping with the First Amendment.

Glenn Beck's comment on his CNN Headline News show on November 14, 2006, illustrates the type of negative attitude and rhetoric associated with religious intolerance that persists—even toward our elected officials who practice a faith other than "main-stream" Christian—and the ease with which such divisive and arrogant statements are disseminated nationally. Speaking to Keith Ellison (Democrat, Minnesota), the first American of Muslim faith to be elected to Congress (November 7, 2006), Beck's comment—as well as provoking and reinforcing, on the one hand, religious and ethnic suspicion, anxiety and discord, and, on the other, reflecting a patent bigoted and immodest American arrogance—was also a striking example of the multiple application of synecdoche. In this case, the more inclusive term *Muslim* being equated with the less inclusive, but infinitely more alarming, term *terrorist*, and, in the same breath, the infinitely less inclusive use of *I* (meaning Beck) being equated with the more inclusive phrase "a lot of Americans" (Media Matters for America, 2006):

> And I have to tell you, I have been nervous about this interview with you, because what I feel like saying is, "Sir, prove to me that you are not working with our enemies." And I know you're not. I'm not accusing you of being an enemy, but that's the way I feel, and I think a lot of Americans will feel that way. (paras. 10–11)

Four years later, on Monday, October 18, 2010, Juan Williams, a popular author (*Eyes on the Prize*), contributing journalist to highly regarded magazines (e.g., *The Atlantic, Ebony, Fortune, The New Republic*), and employed by National Public Radio (NPR) as well as Fox News, appeared on *The O'Reilly Factor*. Juan Williams echoed the spirit of intolerance and fear voiced by Fox commentator Glenn Beck in 2006, when he expressed his concerns regarding the appearance of "people in Muslim garb" on planes, for which he was subsequently fired (Folkenflik, 2010):

> [H]ost Bill O'Reilly asked him to comment on the idea that the U.S. is facing a dilemma with Muslims.... Williams responded: 'Look, Bill, I'm not a bigot. You know the kind of books I've written about the civil rights movement in this country. But when I get on the plane, I got to tell you, if I see people who are in Muslim garb and I think, you know, they are identifying themselves first and foremost as Muslims, I get worried. I get nervous.'.... Late Wednesday night, NPR issued a statement praising Williams as a valuable contributor but saying it had given him notice that it is severing his contract. 'His remarks on *The O'Reilly Factor* this past Monday were inconsistent with our editorial standards and practices, and undermined his credibility as a news analyst with NPR,' the statement read. (paras. 2–7)

The same day Juan Williams was fired by NPR, he was offered a three-year, nearly $2 million contract by Fox News Chief Executive Roger Ailes (quoted in Gold, 2010), who described Williams as

> a staunch defender of liberal viewpoints since his tenure began at Fox News in 1997.... He's an honest man whose freedom of speech is protected by Fox News on a daily basis. (para. 3)

These unsubstantiated fears stated by commentators, public figures and others, continue to be widely disseminated and viralized by the media—information distortions disguised as cultural units called *memes* "propagating like a contagious disease," as Hirschorn (2010) characterizes the malicious phenomenon—today as in the past. More than 300 years after John Williams' plea for religious tolerance, and despite our Founders' prescient statement separating Church and State—prominently positioned as our Constitution's First Amendment—in 1960, presidential-hopeful John F. Kennedy was subjected to similar taunts and suspicions based on the fact that he was Catholic, as was Mitt Romney during his 2008 presidential primary campaign for being a Mormon.

Outlandish claims, such as the accusation that President Obama is a Muslim, and whose official acts can be maliciously interpreted by associated un-American cultural factors, are viralized by partisan commentators and politicians, current and previous, who control a spot-lighted space on the media stage. The ex-Speaker of the House (1995–1999), Newt Gingrich, for example, chose September 11, 2010, to engage in spreading the disease of rumor and sophomoric interpretation regarding President Obama rather than curtailing it. Gingrich did so by first selecting the outlet (*The National Review*) that would make the malicious meme net-borne, predicting its spread—in static and modified forms—among the countless techno-ports that would serve both as landing/launching and cloning/reproductive sites. Gingrich's approach, facile and flawed as it was with respect to credible substance, spread successfully in the immediate term, achieving its intended goal as a malicious meme (i.e., to damage). Aping Dinesh D'Souza's slant presented in the September 26, 2010 issue of *Fortune*, and made available on September 9, 2010, Gingrich dutifully served in the role of human (rather than technological) host, transmitting previously produced semantic material by D'Souza, albeit insignificantly altered in syntactic form (Costa, 2010):

> What if [Obama] is so outside our comprehension, that only if you understand Kenyan, anti-colonial behavior, can you begin to piece together [his actions]?.... That is the most accurate, predictive model for his behavior. This is a person who is fundamentally out of touch with how the world

works, who happened to have played a wonderful con, as a result of which he is now president.... I think he worked very hard at being a person who is normal, reasonable, moderate, bipartisan, transparent, accommodating—none of which was true...In the Alinksy[1] tradition, he was being the person he needed to be in order to achieve the position he needed to achieve. ... He was authentically dishonest. (paras. 3–5)

It is evident that religious preference, and its corollary, religious tolerance, do not exist in a vacuum within the United States, especially in politics where, once again ignited by the Cold War's emphasis on the "threat of godless Communism from abroad" (Wuthnow, 2005, p. 30), religion has been actively connected to foreign policy and economic platforms. The late Samuel Huntington published an article in *Foreign Policy* in 2004 entitled "The Hispanic Challenge," which—summoning the vacuous language laden with stereotypic perspectives of many late-19th and early-20th century reporters who wrote on Mexicans—demonstrates religious intolerance toward Catholicism even as he simultaneously touts Anglo-American cultural and Protestant religious primacy (Huntington, 2004):

America was created by 17th- and 18th-century settlers who were over-whelmingly White, British, and Protestant.... They initially defined America in terms of race, ethnicity, culture, and religion....Most Americans see the creed as the crucial element of their national identity [and] the product of the distinct Anglo-Protestant culture of the founding settlers....[which includes] the English language; Christianity; religious commitment; English concepts of the rule of law, including the responsibility of rulers and the rights of individuals; and dissenting Protestant values of individualism, the work ethic, and the belief that humans have the ability and the duty to try to create a heaven on earth, a "city on a hill."...In this new era, the single most immediate and most serious challenge to America's traditional identity comes from the immense and continuing immigration from Latin America, especially from Mexico, and the fertility rates of these immigrants compared to Black and White American natives....This reality poses a fundamental question: Will the United States remain a country with a single national language and a core Anglo-Protestant culture? (pp. 31–32)

Huntington (2004), apparently not satisfied with the flagrant trans-gressions he has already committed regarding any semblance of research-informed, objective scholarly writing, continues his *Heart-of-Darkness* type mental journey deeper into a morose netherworld where danger lurks in the form of groups whose behavior threatens his life and those like him. Huntington sees his world through a distorted lens that focuses on cultural conflict but does not see that our nation has itself induced and perpetrated it through a twisted doctrine of racial and religious superiority. Once at his destination, Huntington's confusion as to where he has arrived intellectually is apparent, as what he thinks of as the zenith is, in fact, the nadir of his journey—the production and justification of an apocalyptic vision of White nationalism (Huntington, 2004):

> A plausible reaction to the demographic changes underway in the United States could be the rise of an anti-Hispanic, anti-Black, and anti-immigrant movement composed largely of White, working- and middle-class males, protesting their job losses to immigrants and foreign countries, the perversion of their culture, and the displacement of their language. Such a movement can be labeled "White nativism.."...These new White nationalists do not advocate White racial supremacy but believe in racial self-preservation and affirm that culture is a product of race. They contend that the shifting U.S. demographics foretell the replacement of White culture by Black or Brown cultures that are intellectually and morally inferior....White nationalism is "the next logical stage for identity politics in America," argues Swain, making the United States "increasingly at risk of large-scale racial conflict unprecedented in our nation's history." The most powerful stimulus to such White nativism will be the cultural and linguistic threats Whites see from the expanding power of Hispanics in U.S. society. (p. 41)

A more recent manifestation of this rhetorical, even jingoistic, tripartite tool (i.e., religious intolerance toward Catholicism combined with Anglo-American cultural and Protestant religious primacy) to dismantle a country's, group's or individual's credibility was addressed by *The New York Times* reporter Matt Bai in a September 15, 2010 article in which he articulated that the recent combined critiques of President Obama's putative "cultural affinity" by Dinesh D'Souza, Newt Gingrich, and Mississippi Governor Harley Barbour were targeted to clearly imply

> that [Obama] is neither suitably Christian nor American in his values, [which] adds a sinister subtext to the argument against his economic agenda. It suggests that Mr. Obama is oddly indifferent to the effects of his policies on ordinary Americans because, at the end of the day, he doesn't share their experience. Mr. Obama's alleged sympathy for so-called Muslim extremists

who would desecrate the World Trade Center site, his socialist African ancestry and his early years in Indonesia—all of this creates a shadowy archetype that every conservative enclave (fiscal, foreign policy and religious) can find a reason to fear. (paras. 11–12)

The nexus formed by Anglo-Saxon exceptionalism and religion also continues in our nation through the religious, largely Protestant, media. One salient example—as it claims to have a subscription base of "1 million readers in 120 countries" and has published for decades—is *The Philadelphia Trumpet*, a magazine published 10 times a year. *Trumpet* carries embedded in its pages—and electronically through its daily media website *theTrumpet.com*—the message of "prophetic significance...[seeking] to show how current events are fulfilling the biblically prophesied description of the prevailing state of affairs just before the Second Coming of Jesus Christ" (theTrumpet.com, n.d.). Its editor in chief, Gerald Flurry, as well as the magazine's writers, interpret all natural and human phenomena through its exclusive resource: the King James Version of the Holy Bible. *Trumpet* does more than prophesize—it raises issues of threats to Anglo-Saxon (in this case, meaning "America and Britain") preeminence by the European Union, an entity that is "*imperialist* [original emphasis] in motive and intent" and, according to *Trumpet*, began to reconstruct itself once again into the Holy Roman Empire in the Balkan wars of the 1990s, "the first territorial war of the seventh and final resurrection of an ancient entity: the Holy Roman Empire" (Fraser, 2010). The fear, of course, encompasses the threat of Catholicism as well as non-Anglo Saxon cultures.

Trumpet also uses its magazine as a bully pulpit, excoriating those whose politics or lifestyles conflict with those of its Oklahoma-based Philadelphia Church of God. Witness the words of the magazine's editor in chief (Flurry, 2010):

There are many people, especially on the left, who fuel...deadly division by playing the race card. White, left-wing radicals are allied *with the majority of the non-White population* [emphasis added]. Extreme radicals have gotten control, What they really want is control of America! And they will do just about anything to get it.... A deadly, racially charged time bomb is about to explode. (p. 1)

There is no room for alternate life styles or gender preferences (Hilliker, 2010a):

> some delusional academics seem to think there are no inborn psychological differences between boys and girls—only what society teaches them. Absolute poppycock. Without prodding or guidance, from very early on my daughters would pick up a doll and begin cradling it and cooing to it. My son pulls the head off to see what's inside…. For the sake of order and organization, God created men to fulfill one role within the family and within society, and created women to fill a different and beautifully complementary role…. We parents must equip our sons to resist feminization…. Boys have a natural tendency to want to conquer—to storm the backyard and erect a barricade. We want to encourage that, not squelch it. (p. 3)

In a companion article by Hilliker (2010b), the title shares the sect's absolutist belief toward homosexual unions and family life: "There Is No Such Thing as Two Fathers," and its text squarely holds President Obama accountable for any progress or legal success to the contrary:

> President Obama used this past Father's Day to show his support for homosexuals raising children…. In June [2010], completely outside the purview of elected legislators, the Obama administration's Labor Department unilaterally announced that the Family and Medical Leave Act (FMLA) now covers 'all families, including LGBT [Lesbian, Gay, Bisexual, Transgender] families'…. All this language is framed to sound like it promotes family in general—that it is just win-win all around. In truth, it represents the ceaseless efforts of self-professed intellectuals to popularize deviant sexuality…. It is impossible to encourage *both* deviant sexuality and traditional family; they are diametrically opposite. And traditional family must be vigorously promoted and defended if it is to thrive…. Today's society is forcefully pursuing a contrary, anti-Bible agenda that is dismantling families and leading to our ruin. (p. 35)

And, finally, *Trumpet* spreads racial fear through sensationalist headings and articles disguised as journalism: "The President, the Black Panthers, and the Coming Racial Explosion: Truth is trampled in the street and judgment is turned around backward" reads an article by Morley (2010), who writes:

> It was clear that many non-White people feel the justice system is racially biased against them—that Black people cannot get justice—that the law does not protect them…. This is a view that President Obama became

intimately familiar with from his time as a community organizer in Chicago, and from his close association with racially charged preacher Jeremiah Wright. And he seems to be trying to fix it.... Unfortunately, President Obama's fix will only make matters worse.... If America is not careful, it may soon have White-empowerment groups becoming mainstream too. (pp. 8–9)

This widespread faux-journalism spreads and reinforces division, particularly along lines of culture, race, and religion (together with other phobias, such as homophobia) within our nation and across its borders, and complements the widespread faux-scholarship school of thought and writing style of Huntington and D'Souza and the even more widespread distortion-as-entertainment-as-political soapbox-as-news propagated by Fox media and its contract players that include Beck, among others of similar ilk. Incessant, inflammatory rhetoric on these multiple fronts, fueled by distortions and jeremiads, divides while accusing, and simultaneously calls adherents to again take control and regain perceived lost or diminished privileges. Such rhetoric has its rewards, Pyrrhic though they may prove to be—as in the case of Beck, whose annual income, through his enormous audience base, which includes television and radio audiences of 9 million and 3 million, respectively, and a readership audience of 3 million, is estimated to approach $32 million (Buckley, 2010).

We are increasingly distant, both chronologically and in our intolerance, from successfully practicing our principle of religious freedom and tolerance, itself a cornerstone in the construction of our democratic American identity and system of governance—and from the civility that should accompany, even anticipate, it. Former President Eisenhower addressed the necessity of religious freedom and tolerance for our American system, which Einhorn (2010) posits was a lived principle that imbued our national cultural character during that same period:

the values that constituted the American 'civil religion,' defined as a kind of nationalistic ethical creed with a vaguely Christian accent and epitomized by the 1952 words of President Eisenhower: "Our form of government has no sense unless it is founded in a deeply felt religious faith—and I don't care what it is." (p. 32)

Clearly, as a nation, as we struggle continually with our economic future, individually and nationally, we remain entangled in the pernicious knot of our own making: the contradictory attempt to justify and sustain the subordination of groups by race, culture, and religion within the context of American democracy. Such a struggle is, inevitably, a losing one, as the universal principles promoted, guaranteed and protected by our Constitution and its Amendments are stronger than any one group's attempt, however dominant, to deny, limit or otherwise curtail them. The notion of Aristotelian equity continues to thrive as it is a natural condition and, where absent, a natural response to injustice. By definition, our continuing national inability to resolve through practice these three conditions of unity (race, culture and religion) in accordance with the mandates of our Constitution reinforces and exacerbates our metacultural frag-mentation and squanders our human, social and political capital.

Moreover, in the current global development context, the continuing high degree of national fragmentation affects drastically our ability to attain and sustain the ever-increasing levels of mass academic achievement, professional productivity, and innovation across disciplinary and sector spheres. This inability erodes and compromises our economic standing as a leading global competitor and our political credibility as a world leader, which propels us toward a downward trajectory of deterioration, as other nations and regions prosper, while accelerating dramatically their level of productivity and global competitiveness. This, of course, is the case of China, a nation that ubiquitously extends its geopolitical influence globally and vies with mounting success to achieve and exert a predominant role in world leadership. Our internal conflict and fragmentation bode ill for our nation's ability to engage in global competition or partnership, as interests demand, with China or other countries in rapid economic, and geopolitical, acceleration, such as India or Brazil.

The problem of national unity, of metacultural unity, under our current conditions of cultural fragmentation—to include serious differential schooling facilities, experiences and outcomes; religious intolerance and nativism; and economic degeneration of the poor and middle class as the net economic assets of the wealthy continue to increase disproportionately—is clear. How to respond effectively to the problem to redeem the hopeful trajectory of our American character—particularly in its original Zangwillian cultural fusion sense—given our tendency to distance ourselves, one group from another, in a climate not conducive to civil discourse, objective negotiation or the seeking of common goals, is far from clear.

Texas Textbook Controversy and Implications

It is ironic and lamentable that, after centuries of explicit racial and ethnic segregation and violence toward these groups, each of which was commonplace practice in the United States until 1965, our official cultural response has been to hide this history from our students in favor of transmitting our nation's rhetoric of freedom and equality, rather than present our persistent struggle to negotiate these two foundational elements of our aspired-to national character. The recent Texas textbook controversy, where more than a hundred amendments to the proposed social science textbooks were recommended by the 15 state school board members, serves as a relevant and timely example. Ten of the 15 members are Republican, seven of whom reportedly vote as a conservative bloc, while the remaining five are Democrats. The conservative and Christian perspective of the board permeates the vocabulary and subject matter selection and approach. The premise initiated and acted upon by Senator Joseph McCarthy (Republican) that our federal government had become infiltrated by 200 card-carrying communists, for example, is presented as viable, when, in fact, as Arthur Miller writes (2006):

> his accusations were proven to be untrue, and he was censured by the Senate for unbecoming conduct[; nevertheless,] his zealous campaigning ushered in one of the most repressive times in 20th-century American politics. (para. 1)

Moreover, the Texas social science textbook curriculum "plays down the role of Thomas Jefferson among the founding fathers [and] questions the separation of church and state" (Birnbaum, 2010, para. 2), as well as places less attention on the civil rights era and the role of Hispanic Americans in Texas and U.S. history. Further, as Birnbaum reports:

Discussions ranged from whether President Reagan should get more attention (yes), whether hip-hop should be included as part of lessons on American culture (no), and whether President of the Confederacy Jefferson Davis' inaugural address should be studied alongside Abraham Lincoln's (yes). (para. 6)

The Texas textbook controversy has gained nationwide attention particularly as Texas is the "single largest textbook purchaser in the country" and there is apprehension that as Texas goes, so goes the nation, particularly given the expense of developing textbooks. Textbook publishers counter that they are in a position to quickly accommodate to changes as information can be readily integrated and substituted. Thus, publishers "will start with a core national narrative and edit to suit the sensitivities and curriculum standards of various states and districts" (Thevenot, 2010, para. 5). It is still too early to gauge the local and national effects of this proposed conservative, Christian-focused set of textbooks on the millions of school-age students who may be subjected to use it throughout much of their K–12 schooling experience. However, purposely reinforcing a bigoted status quo will not serve as a positive force to move us toward understanding and resolving inter-group differences, metacultural cohesion, substantive educational reform and development alternatives, heightened innovation and productivity in relevant areas of scientific, technological and economic advancement, global competitiveness and cooperation, or sustained national prosperity.

Revisionist phenomena of the type illustrated above, if not yet a trend, historically coincide with, parallel and continue our nation's attitude toward exalting that which is considered White and criticizing, diminishing, or leaving out the presence and contributions of groups considered non-White within the American experience, as discussed earlier (see Chapter 2). On May 21, 2010, the Texas State Board of Education approved the conservative-revisionist high school textbook standards by a 9 to 5 vote, ushering in a decade-long period of instruction that will be characterized and influenced by a deeply partisan formal textbook adoption, ultimately affecting the schooling, and even the minds, attitudes and behaviors, of 4.8 million students in Texas. The Associated Press (Ripley, 2010) assessed the decision thus:

The partisan board has amended or watered down the teaching of the civil rights movement, slavery, America's relationship with the U.N. and hundreds of other items. ... They dictate how political events and figures will be taught to some 4.8 million schoolchildren in Texas and beyond for the next decade. (para. 3)

The board also approved the study and value of notions that are intellectually and ethically suspect such as American exceptionalism, as well as antagonistic toward and anathema to our democratic model. The statement by Senator Albert Beveridge (Schoultz, 1998), recorded in the *Congressional Record* on January 9, 1900, summarizes the notion of American exceptionalism:

God has not been preparing the English-speaking and Teutonic peoples for a thousand years for nothing but vain and idle self-contemplation and self-admiration. No! He has made us the master organizers of the world to establish system where chaos reigns. He has given us the spirit of progress to overwhelm the forces of reaction throughout the earth. He has made us adept in government that we may administer government among savage and senile people. Were it not for such a force as this the world would relapse into barbarism and night. And of all our race He has marked the American people as His chosen nation to finally lead in the regeneration of the world. This is the divine mission of America, and it holds for us all the profit, all the glory, all the happiness possible to man. We are the trustees of the world's progress, guardians of the righteous peace. (p. 90)

A head-in-the-sand perspective deleted any mention of Hip-Hop and thus students' ability to associate with and explore creatively and analytically the complex cultural dynamics relating to this enormously lucrative and identity-influencing phenomenon that transcends class, race and ethnicity and has had a global and national impact. There is a general sense of social connectedness, including a shared resistance to perceived foibles of a nation's mainstream culture, embedded within Hip-Hop's complex genre. This sense expresses itself in popular, non-standard language—using not only a vocabulary considered profane by standard language and the normative social canons of mainstream societies, but a whole, rule-governed vernacular grammar of its own. Connectedness manifests itself through the means of respectful imitation and local originality that attracts and attaches itself to audiences, universally through media and, more locally, through live performance. Its complement is the individual spirit that is nurtured, developed and expressed explicitly through writing and performance, even within a Hip-Hop group context. The absence of Hip-Hop in the state's curriculum is even more ironic when its role as a major contributor to the music industry, consumer patterns and entrepreneurial spirit of the free enterprise system, which extends to China and other parts of the globe, is considered (see, for example, the ethnographic work on Hip-Hop culture in Beijing by Steele, 2006 and the spate of video-rich websites available on this topic).

Jazz and Hip-Hop: Marginalized Origins, Core Contributions

The description of jazz, a phenomenon that sprang from our nation's earlier context of racism, segregation and group inequities during the early decades of the 20th century, by J. A. Rogers in the March 1925 issue of *Survey Graphic*, contains elements that remain germane in understanding, on the one hand, Hip-Hop's origins, popularity and ability to cross national, cultural and class borders and, on the other, the persistent segregated settings and inequitable conditions in the United States that foment the creation of these similar cultural phenomena:

> Jazz is a marvel of paradox: too fundamentally human, at least as modern humanity goes, to be typically racial, too international to be characteristically national, too much abroad in the world to have a special home. And yet jazz in spite of it all is one part American and three parts American Negro, and was originally the nobody's child of the levee and the city slum....But somebody had to have it first: that was the Negro. What after all is this taking new thing, that, condemned in certain quarters, enthusiastically welcomed in others, has nonchalantly gone on until it ranks with the movie and the dollar as the foremost exponent of modern Americanism? Jazz isn't music merely, it is a spirit that can express itself in almost anything. The true spirit of jazz is a joyous revolt from convention, custom, authority, boredom, even sorrow—from everything that would confine the soul of man and hinder its riding free on the air.... It is the revolt of the emotions against repression. (p. 665)

The contextual well spring from which both popular cultural forms sprang was decidedly American—specifically, the America of the marginalized—although its creations were immediately identifiable and accepted, as well as imitated and adapted, by marginalized (and mainstream) performers, producers and audiences globally. Politics and economics aside, for the moment, Hip-Hop as been defined as (Dyson, 2004)

> still fundamentally an *art form* that traffics in hyperbole, parody, kitsch, dramatic license, double entendres, signification, and other literary and artistic conventions to get its points across. (p. xii)

Dyson's (2004) reference to the cross-border influence of Hip-Hop in the early 21st century is virtually indistinguishable in effect and tone from that of jazz scripted by Rogers in 1925:

> When I was in Brazil recently and went to the "Black Six," a hip-hop club in Rio, I might as well have been in Harlem or Philadelphia. (Dyson, 2004, p. xiv)

> It follows that jazz is more at home in Harlem than in Paris, though from the look and sound of certain quarters of Paris one would hardly think so. (Rogers, 1925, p. 665)

DJ Kool Herc (2005), the originator of Hip-Hop music in 1973, stresses the social connectedness as key to the universal appeal of Hip-Hop:

> To me, hip-hop says, 'Come as you are.' We are a family. It ain't about security. It ain't about $200 sneakers. It is not about me being better than you or you being better than me. It's about you and me, connecting one to one. That's why it has universal appeal. It has given young people a way to understand their world, whether they are from the suburbs or the city or wherever. (p. xi)

Hip-Hop, of course, is as complex and varied a phenomenon as any other sector within our nation, whether political, economic, religious, recreational, medical, educational or cultural. Its successes and contributions have been enormous and beneficial; its imperfections or legal transgressions involve individuals, like in any sector, and thus do not define the whole; transgressions need to be assessed objectively, understood, and, where legally warranted, reprimanded or castigated. The *New Yorker* (Wilkinson, 2010) profile of Gil Scott-

Heron, called by many the "godfather of rap," speaks to the uneasy balance between creativity, economic hardship, marginality and dependency, and attests to the high visibility and wide audience interest in Hip-Hop as a relevant American phenomenon. The artist-philanthropist balance struck by Raymond Usher IV stands in noteworthy contrast to the above type of Hip-Hop artist profile. Usher, a 31-year-old rhythm and blues/hip-hop artist who has sold 45 million albums globally, amassed five Grammy Awards and a plethora of related awards, including "multiple NAACP Image Awards," established the New Look Foundation in 1999 when he was 21 years old "to reach talented youth from diverse socio-economic back-grounds and provide them with a chance to learn firsthand about the business side of the sports and entertainment industries" (New Look Foundation, 2010). Achievements of the New Look Foundation, as its President, Shawn H. Wilson elaborates upon below, relate to developing leaders with a passion for educational attainment and engagement in service, community and professional activities, both locally and globally (New Look Foundation, 2010):

> We are proud to report that 98% of New Look alumni graduate from high school and 100% of those graduates attend college. While those results are enough to recognize our youth as leaders, they are also currently serving as Congressional aides, sitting on non-profit Boards of Directors, starring in major motion pictures, interning at major media outlets, attending prestigious universities with academic and athletic scholarships, starting their own non-profits and businesses, and so much more. The New Look Foundation has worked with over 7,500 youth and delivered over 118,000 hours of training! We have been able launch an international campaign to engage millions of youth in service, travel to Asia and Africa to introduce the New Look model to communities around the world, forge new partnerships with organizations ranging from the UN Foundation to the Clinton Foundation to the Corporation for National and Community Service, and rapidly mobilize youth to support relief efforts for one of the world's most devastating natural disasters in Haiti. (paras. 2–3)

In a recent album that has sold 5 million worldwide *Here I Stand* (2008), Usher, the artist, struggles creatively to explore, understand and articulate musically the conflicts within him as a man, successful entertainer, African American, and human being as he continues to develop and interact with life. His goal is to convey musically the opportunities that present themselves in his life to stray from or adhere to the values of which he has become conscious and desires to follow in a way that resonate with the general public, or as the article in the *New Yorker* (Frere-Jones, 2008) interprets Usher's intent, perhaps somewhat unflatteringly:

> His songs balance on a moral and formal fulcrum: salacious stories and club beats over here, vows to reform and slow, throaty singing over there. It's the Saturday-night, Sunday-morning dichotomy....Usher's songs strive for as wide a demographic as possible, and his personal story—as recounted endlessly in entertainment magazines—hews to whatever product he is currently hawking. (paras. 2–3)

Hip-Hop, then, is the American-spawned global phenomenon— with all the free enterprise virtues and imperfections, pioneer spirit, creative forces, perseverance-in-the-face-of-adversity ethos and race-, ethnicity- and class-busting energy that collectively characterize the American success story—that the Texas Board of Education recently denied as having value as a cultural area of study within the state's social science curriculum. The persistent issue of mainstream denial regarding the presence of long-term, mainstream racism (in the extended sense of the term used in this volume) and of the contributions of minority groups to the establishment and success of the United States must be recognized and addressed by our government and corporate leaders, media and universities, including by faculty within our teacher education programs.

Chapter 8

Educating for Failure: From De *Jure* to *De Facto*

While the nation struggles to strengthen the economy, the educational capacity of our country continues to decline.

—J. M. Lee, Jr. & A. Rawls, 2010
College Board Advocacy and Policy Center

Put differently, the persistence of these educational achievement gaps imposes on the United States the economic equivalent of a permanent national recession.

—McKinsey & Company, 2009

Cycle of Educational Underperformance

Since mid-20th century, schooling has been the general gateway to sustained employment, income, and middle class status in the United States (Salomone, 1986, pp. 1–2). It remains so. Despite the economically disastrous recession which we in the United States currently experience, the evidence in comparative economic well-being continues to reinforce the quote attributed to Derek Bok, two-time president of Harvard University: "If you think education is expensive, try ignorance." The clarion call relates to the *societal* imperative for a formally-educated populace in our democratic nation—a goal that was transformed in 1954–1964 in terms of *what groups* would be included within the societal imperative, and one that, nationally, we continue to fail to reach, or to even demonstrate substantive progress. Race—in all its continuing non-scientific, popular misconceptions, which can include one's color, (mis)perceived ethnicity, religion, etc.—and its corollary, poverty, continue to serve as barriers to our national community's ability to *generally* develop the long-term symbiotic social and academic skills within our students required for successful school completion and career development. This negative phenomenon is especially visible among students from designated minority groups, such as African American and Hispanic American, as well as in other less populous, but no less important, groups.

There was a particular period, 1964–1976, in our turbulent struggle for equity in public schooling where African American and Hispanic American students "had an equal chance of attending college as a White high school graduate" (Gándara & Orfield, 2010, p. 21). However, the educational policy and support slope that we, as a nation, had successfully negotiated, once scaled, proved significantly slippery and ephemeral. As Gándara & Orfield (2010, p. 21) point out "the era of affirmative action was on life support [compounded simultaneously by the fact that] fewer colleges were built, admissions standards were raised and tuition constantly went up faster than family incomes as state support declined." Recent statistical analyses regarding public education in the United States, reported in *The Condition of Education, 2010* (Aud et al., 2010), demonstrate that differential performance in elementary and secondary school educational achievement relates to the type of school—high poverty or low poverty—students attend. Students who attend high poverty schools exhibit lower achievement in the critical subject matter areas of math and reading than their counterparts who attend low poverty schools. Currently, 16,122 schools, 17 percent of U.S. public schools (approximately 94,835), are designated as high-poverty—that is, schools in which at least 75 percent of students are eligible to receive free or reduced lunch. This figure includes public elementary and secondary schools. As can be surmised by information shared in earlier chapters regarding segregation and net wealth, a greater percentage of African American, Hispanic American, and Indian/Alaska Native students attend high poverty schools than do White or Asian American/Pacific Islander students (and, within these two groups, a greater percentage of Asian American/Pacific Islander students attend high-poverty schools than do their White counterparts).

The amount of high poverty schools, moreover, is increasing across elementary and secondary school categories. In the 1999–2000 school year, 15 percent of our nation's *public elementary* schools were designated as high poverty; that percentage had increased to 20 percent by the 2007–2008 school year, the latest figure available. Similarly, for the same school year periods, high poverty *public secondary* schools increased from 5 percent to 9 percent. Thus, while growth in high poverty schools continues in both public elementary and secondary school settings, the growth *rate* is considerably higher for public secondary schools (80% increase) than for public elementary schools (33%). One of every five students in our nation's public elementary schools attends a high-poverty school; one in every 16, a public secondary school (Aud et al., 2010). Unless and until we, as a nation, implement relevant, substantive changes that actually work, both long-term and across the board, our nation's combined schooling-societal problem will remain the same in form, but exacerbated in degree and in negative returns. More high poverty schools, combined with continuing lower performance in critical subject matter areas for students enrolled in these schools, will continue to translate into predictably higher rates of under-performance, with concomitant lower rates of completion of the K–12 schooling cycle, lower rates of postsecondary school enrollment, lower rates of postsecondary degree completion, and lower rates of majoring, for those who would earn a postsecondary degree, in an area of specialization such as science, math, engineering, computer science/technology, pre-medicine or other area where math and science would have a substantive role in their degree program and future professional career.

Underperformance and Incarceration

Of course, this cycle of educational underperformance also translates into higher rates of incarceration and the misplaced, although required to varying degrees, investment, for which there is little-to-no human, social or cultural capital return, in prisons and their associated complex infrastructure. Our nation has "the highest homicide rate and the highest incarceration in the developed world," which translates into 1.7 million prisoners, 700,000 offenders in jails,

4.3 million ex-prisoners on probation, and 700,000 parolees (Kleiman, 2010). African American and Hispanic Americans are overrepresented in incarceration rates as figures from June 30, 2004, demonstrate: for every 100,000 individuals in the nation, 393 Whites were incarcerated in contrast to 957 Hispanics and 2,531 African Americans (Wagner, 2005, cited in Prison Policy Initiative, n.d.). Mauer (2009) places the incarceration numbers in a more telling perspective, both for children and for our nation:

> There are many indicators of the profound impact of disproportionate rates of incarceration in communities of color. Perhaps the most stark among these are the data generated by the Department of Justice that project that if current trends continue, one of every three Black males born today will go to prison in his lifetime, as will one of every six Latino males (rates of incarceration for women overall are lower than for men, but similar racial/ethnic disparities pertain). Regardless of what one views as the causes of this situation, it should be deeply disturbing to all Americans that these figures represent the future for a generation of children growing up today. (p. 1)

The national phenomenon of children whose parents are or have been incarcerated continues to grow, along with racial disparities in disproportionate sentencing and incarceration, and increased high-risk consequences for the children, as research by Wildeman (2009) demonstrates:

> (1) 1 in 40 White children born in 1978 and 1 in 25 White children born in 1990 had a parent imprisoned; (2) 1 in 7 Black children born in 1978 and 1 in 4 Black children born in 1990 had a parent imprisoned; (3) inequality in the risk of parental imprisonment between White children of college-educated parents and all other children is growing; and (4) by age 14, 50.5% of Black children born in 1990 to high school dropouts had a father imprisoned. These estimates, robustness checks, and extensions to longitudinal data indicate that parental imprisonment has emerged as a novel—and distinctively American—childhood risk that is concentrated among Black children and children of low-education parents. (para. 1)

The degree of educational attainment of the parent plays a vital role in this bleak and spreading scenario regarding parental incarceration, childhood disadvantage, and increased risk of antisocial and self-destructive behavior of the parents' children, as a survey article in *The New York Times* (Eckholm, 2009) recently reported:

> Recent studies indicate that having an incarcerated parent doubles the chance that a child will be at least temporarily homeless and measurably increases the likelihood of physically aggressive behavior, social isolation, depression and problems in school—all portending dimmer prospects in adulthood. (para. 4)

Research by Wildeman and others (Wildeman, 2009/2010) provides substantive evidence for the above statement, as "Prior research suggests that having a parent go to prison compromises child wellbeing and that these effects linger, leaving children of incarcerated parents at elevated risk of social exclusion later in life"— the exception being in those cases where the parent was abusive.

Unmarried Mothers and the Effect on Children

Associated with persistent, transgenerational underperformance in education is the rising phenomenon of the high percentage of unmarried women giving birth in our nation, which now accounts for 41 percent of all births and is more than double (18.4%) that of 1980 (Ventura, 2009). Births by unwed mothers accounted for 35.7 percent of all national births in 2004 and 5.3 percent in 1960 (Child Trends Data Bank, n.d.), representing a consistent and steep increase. Recent statistics (2008) cited in a news article by Associated Press reporter Jesse Washington (2010) illustrate the pervasiveness of the unmarried mother phenomenon and indicate the individual and social consequences associated with it:

> Children of unmarried mothers of any race are more likely to perform poorly in school, go to prison, use drugs, be poor as adults, and have their own children out of wedlock. The Black community's 72 percent rate eclipses that of most other groups: 17 percent of Asians, 29 percent of Whites, 53 percent of Hispanics and 66 percent of Native Americans were born to unwed mothers in 2008, the most recent year for which government figures are available. The rate for the overall U.S. population was 41 percent. This issue entered the public consciousness in 1965, when a now famous government report by future senator Daniel Patrick Moynihan described a "tangle of pathology" among Blacks that fed a 24 percent Black "illegitimacy" rate. The White rate then was 4 percent. (paras. 7–9)

Although Washington (2010) also comments that "42 percent of all Black women and 70 percent of professional Black women are unmarried," statistics tend to generally work against women who have children born out of wedlock, as well as their children, economically and otherwise (R. Johnson & M. Favreault, 2004, cited in Child Trends Data Bank, n.d.).

The increase in the percentage of births by African American unwed mothers has tripled since 1965, but for White unwed mothers it has risen by seven and a quarter (7.25) times, or more than double the percentage in increase in births by African American unwed mothers. The statistics for Hispanic and Native American unwed mothers are equally disconcerting, particularly given the context of challenging health, economic, social and educational circumstances within which the children will be raised—including birth fathers who are absent or incarcerated and multiple males who were birth fathers to siblings within the same household—and what the future may hold in store for many, if not most, of them. A recent analysis published by the National Center for Health Statistics (Ventura, 2009) describes the disadvantage at which children of unwed mothers are likely to begin life at the point of birth:

> Nonmarital births are at higher risk of having adverse birth outcomes such as low birthweight, preterm birth, and infant mortality than are children born to married women. Children born to single mothers typically have more limited social and financial resources. (p. 1)

In terms of age, in 2004, nearly all births (97.4%) to girls younger than 15 were by unwed mothers; more than 8 out of 10 births (82.4%) of teenagers who gave birth did so as unwed mothers; more than half (54.8%) of women 20–24 years of age who gave birth were unwed at the time of birth; and nearly one out of five (18.2%) of women over 40 years of age who gave birth were unmarried (Child Trends Data Bank, n.d.). Data available for 2006 indicate that the birth rates of unmarried mothers have been relatively stable within the youngest age categories (15–17 years old) since 1980, about 20 births per 1000, except for a spike in 1995; births rates for women between the ages of 20 and 39 have risen sharply, doubling (41 to 80 per 1000) in the 20–24 years old category and more than doubling in the 25–29 (34 to 75 per 1000), 30–34 (21 to 55 per 1000), and 35–39 (10 to 27 per 1000) years old categories (Ventura, 2009), and all are above the rates of 15 to 17 year olds. Births rates for unwed mothers in the 18–19 years old category spiked from 39 per 1000 in 1980 to 67 per 1000 in 1995 and have remained relatively high since then, at 59 per 1000 in 2002 and 62 per 1000 in 2006 (Ventura, 2009). In 2007, the 1,714,643 children born out of wedlock represented "an historic peak" in our nation (Ventura, 2009), a dubious achievement in light of the disadvantages mentioned above and, as the disadvantages are not foreseen to diminish on their own, a substantive policy, economic, training and research and development outlay for our nation. The duration of cohabitation relative to the probability of it leading to marriage was reported by Bramlett and Mosher (2002):

> [F]or all women, the probability of a first premarital cohabitation becoming a marriage is 58 percent after 3 years of cohabitation and 70 percent after 5 years of cohabitation.... The probability that the first cohabitation becomes a marriage within 5 years is 75 percent for White women, 61 percent for Hispanic women, and only 48 percent for Black women. (p. 12)

Income influences the probability of cohabitation leading to marriage, although significantly less so for low-income ($25,000 or less) Whites and high-income ($50,000 or more) Whites (73% vs. 77%) than for low-income African Americans and high-income African Americans (39% vs. 71%); religious affiliation and educational attainment, as well as prior experience within an intact family (i.e., father and mother present) also exert influences on cohabitation leading to marriage (Bramlett & Mosher, 2002). Thus, race, ethnicity, income, education, religious affiliation, and having been part of an intact family influence the probability that a child will be raised within a household having a mother and a father. The probability of first cohabitation disruption is relatively high at the all-women level, 39 percent within the first three years and 49 percent within the first five years; African American women "are more likely to experience a cohabitation disruption than either White or Hispanic women" (Bramlett & Mosher, 2002, p. 14). Corroborative findings from recent research articles in the *Future of Children* (2010) journal, jointly published by Princeton University's Woodrow Wilson School of Public and International Affairs and the

Brookings Institution, were summarized by Kay Hymowitz (2010) in the *Los Angeles Times*, providing insight into the type of everyday experiences that children, primarily from minority families, within these unmarried-couples' environments are subjected to:

> [W]ithin five years, a tiny 15% of the unmarried couples had taken wedding vows, while a whopping 60% had split up. At the five-year mark, only 36% of the children lived with their fathers, and half of the other 64% hadn't seen their dads in the last month. One-half to two-thirds of the absent fathers provided little or no financial support. A parental breakup is hard enough on kids, but the prevalence of what experts call "multipartner fertility" is salt in their wounds. By the time the children were 5, 20% of their mothers had a child by a different man; 27% of the kids were living with their mother's new live-in partner. These relationships tended to reduce father involvement: Dads are less likely to come around when a new man is in the house. In the long run, it's not even clear that the new boyfriends are good for the women involved, because mothers with children by more than one man "reported significantly less available [financial] support than those with children by one man." (paras. 3–4)

The United States is not alone in the rising trend of births on the part of unmarried women, as the percentages of births to unwed women in Europe and other countries are also widespread. Comparing data from the United States to those of particular European or other countries must be done with extreme caution as the contexts, conditions, and consequences may differ substantially— for example, variables that require consideration include the comparative rationale, degree and duration of cohabitation, the degree of a traditionally intact family structure, the parents' educational attainment, and the stability and source of income, regardless of the marital status of the mother. Nevertheless, studies do compare these data, which, at the aggregate level, demonstrate a common rising trend. Reporters Stein and St. George (2009), for example, citing figures from the 2009 NCHS study, stated that the phenomenon of births to unmarried mothers in the United States is "starting to look more like that in many European countries [as] the proportion of babies born to unmarried women is about 66 percent in Iceland, 55 percent in Sweden, 50 percent in France and 44 percent in the United Kingdom." The NCHS study (Ventura, 2009, p. 5) included fourteen countries, six of which had higher percentages of births to unwed mothers than did the United States—the four mentioned above and Norway (54%) and Denmark (46%). The Netherlands (40%) tied with the United States, while Ireland (38%), Germany (30%), Spain (28%) and Italy (21%) had lower percentages, as did the non-European countries listed among the fourteen, Canada (30%) and Japan (2%). Comparative growth rates among the countries between 1980 and 2007 relative to births to unwed mothers varied: Netherlands, 900%; Spain, 600%; Ireland, 560%; Italy, 425%; France, 355%; United Kingdom, 267%; Norway, 260%; Germany, 150%; Canada, 131%; United States, 122%; Japan, 100%; Iceland, 65%; Denmark, 39%; and Sweden, 37.5%. Again, while sheer percentages indicate clearly that all countries have experienced substantial increases in the birth rates of unmarried mothers, they neither characterize nor reveal the extent to which the respective cultural phenomena influencing the birth rates are comparable in context, conditions or consequences.

In the specific case of the United States, as we have seen, the disadvantages are salient and threatening to a child's well-being, however measured, and thus to their future as productive individuals and contributors to our society in all its forms, but particularly socially, politically and economically. The numbers of low-income and at-risk children with these and related characteristics are entering our schools in significant numbers and, in many cases, comprise a majority of school enrollments. This demographic phenomenon, coupled with the probability of below-standard academic performance and disruption of the schooling completion cycle, is a poor platform for the development and dissemination of cultural, social, and economic capital (Bourdieu, 1986), much less its creative or synergistic expression as a driver of innovation. Traditionally, our schools and communities have not fared well in transforming low-income children, particularly from differentiated groups, into high- or even average-performing students who complete the minimal schooling cycle that is high school.

Currently, the numbers of poor and underprepared children continue to explode, and our school teachers, administrators and infrastructure, both human and physical, remain themselves underprepared and underfinanced to competently serve their charges' urgent, non-traditional and high-maintenance needs in ways that lead to competitive learning outcomes and enhanced school-completion rates. Thus, there appears but exiguous hope for successfully reversing this phenomenon of substantive and persistent loss of capital, in its cultural, social and economic forms. Yet, we must identify, implement, monitor, assess and refine new ways and continue to improve existing ways of nurturing and nourishing this generation, and each new generation, regardless of the challenges presented, but particularly if a substantive percentage of the generation is at risk. We have no recourse but to do so, if our nation is to regain its own upward trajectory of development, productivity, influence, and, especially, well-being—a course from which our nation has deviated for more than three decades, particularly at the expense of its middle and lower classes.

Economic Impact of Achievement Gap

There is a financial loss to our nation's 2008 Gross Domestic Product (GDP) associated with the "underutilization of human potential"—that is, the achievement gap, measured by race, ethnicity, income or geography, national or international. Depending on which variable is being measured, the estimates range from a 2008 GDP higher by $310 billion to $525 billion (2 to 4 percent) if the gap between our nation's African American and Hispanic student performance and White student performance had been closed; $400 billion to $670 billion higher (3 to 5 percent) if the gap between low-income and higher-income students had been closed; $425 billion to $700 billion higher (3 to 5 percent) if the gap between low-performing states and all other states had been closed; and $1.3 trillion to $2.3 trillion higher if the gap had been closed between our nation's educational achievement levels and those of countries who outperform us, such as Korea and Finland (McKinsey & Company, 2009). Our nation's financial loss is augmented by the education debt it has created and that is composed of the "historical, economic, sociopolitical, and moral decisions and policies that characterize our society" (Ladson-Billings, 2006, p. 5). Referring to the economic aspect of the education debt, Ladson-Billings provides insights into current funding disparities in segregated schools, reminding us that they have "occurred over centuries" (Ladson-Billings, 2010):

> The economics of the education debt are sobering. The funding disparities that currently exist between schools serving White students and those serving students of color are not recent phenomena. Separate schooling always allows for differential funding. In present-day dollars, the funding disparities between urban schools and their suburban counterparts present a telling story about the value we place on the education of different groups of students. The Chicago public schools spend about $8,482 annually per pupil, while nearby Highland Park spends $17,291 per pupil. The Chicago public schools have an 87% Black and Latina/o population, while Highland Park has a 90% White population. Per pupil expenditures in Philadelphia are $9,299 per pupil for the city's 79% Black and Latina/o population, while across City Line Avenue in Lower Merion, the per pupil expenditure is $17,261 for a 91% White population. The New York City public schools spend $11,627 per pupil for a student population that is 72% Black and Latina/o, while suburban Manhasset spends $22,311 for a student population that is 91% White (figures from Kozol, 2005). (p. 6)

The persistent and multifaceted achievement gap we have sustained across generations in the United States casts a growing and threatening shadow on our nation's current preeminence in economic productivity—approximately $15 trillion per annum—as well as its ability to produce, much less rely on, sufficient domestic human capital for technological innovation and a growth-oriented service sector. McKinsey & Company (2010) places the threat in clear competitive perspective:

> Put differently, the persistence of these educational achievement gaps imposes on the United States the economic equivalent of a permanent national recession. The recurring annual economic cost of the international achievement gap is substantially larger than the deep recession the United States is currently experiencing. The annual output cost of the racial, income, and regional or systems achievement gap is larger than the US recession of 1981–82 [a deep recession that lasted 16 months and was, at the time, the longest U.S. recession since World War II (CNBC.com, 2007)]. (p. 6)

Increasing Poverty Level

The fact that poverty, as a national *growth* phenomenon, continues its 35-year (1975–2009) trend upward, while its current *rate* of 14.3

percent, or 43.6 million Americans, is the highest since 1994 (Poverty Rising in the U.S., 2010), relays a strong message that the barriers to closing the achievement gaps and increased national productivity not only continue but that they are in danger of widening. The five states with the highest percentage of poverty were, in rank order, Mississippi, Arizona, New Mexico, Arkansas, and Georgia (see DeVillar & Jiang, 2007). And, as members of our nation's Hispanic-origin population have the highest growth rate in the nation and account for 22 percent of our current (2008, latest figure available) public school enrollment, or more than 10 million students (Aud et al., 2010), one can predict that more poor students will continue to populate our high-poverty schools.

Year-over-year poverty levels for all racial/ethnic groups rose, as did the poverty level of children. Specifically, poverty levels with respect to Hispanics was 23.2 percent in 2008 and increased to 25.3 percent in 2009; for African Americans, the levels were 24.7 percent and 25.8 percent, respectively; for Asian Americans, 11.8 percent to 12.5 percent; and for non-Hispanic Whites, 8.6 and 9.4 percent, respectively; the percentage of children living in poverty in our nation rose from 19 percent to 20.7 percent (Income, Poverty and Health Insurance Coverage in the United States, 2010). The poverty rate of native-born Americans increased from 12.6 percent to 13.7 percent, while that of foreign-born Americans (resident and naturalized) rose from 17.8 percent to 19 percent. Non-Hispanic White Americans comprised 42.5 percent of all Americans in poverty. Many Americans, moreover, have been touched by poverty in the first decade of the 21st century. During the 4-year period of 2004–2007, for example, DeNavas-Walt, Proctor, and Smith (2010) report in their U.S. Census study on income, poverty and health insurance coverage that "[a]pproximately 31.6 percent of the population had at least one spell of poverty lasting 2 or more months."

The median income of female heads of family with no husband present was worse in 2009 ($32,597) than in 2008 ($32,947), and significantly trailed that of married couple family households, whose median income in 2009 was $71,830, and that of male heads of family with no wife present, whose median income in 2009 was $48,084. Female heads of households with no husband present earned 45 percent of what married couple households earned, and 68 percent of what male heads of households with no wife present earned. Regarding racial and ethnic differences, the median income for non-Hispanic White householders in 2009, at $54,461, was 67 percent greater than that of African American households ($32,584), 43 percent greater than that of Hispanic American households ($38,039), and 17 percent less than that of Asian American households ($65,469) (DeNavas-Walt et al., 2010). Comparative per capita median income figures among the racial and ethnic groups reflected a similar profile, as individuals who were designated as White earned $30,941 (100%), as Asian, $30,653 (99%), as African American, $18,135 (57%), and as Hispanic American, $15,063 (49%). Women's earnings (36,278) for 2009 were 77 percent of Men's ($47,127). Overall, DeNavas and her colleagues (2010, pp. 10–11) state that the national figures of income disparity suggest that income inequality has been rising for decades: "Over the 1967-to-2009 period, all equivalence-adjusted inequality measures increased more than the money income inequality measures."

Resegregation, the Culture of Schooling and Performance Outcomes

As can be surmised, traditionally and to the present, the economic status of a household, particularly its intergenerational persistence, together with the race or ethnicity of the residents (note that these two terms are not mutually exclusive), have strongly influenced where a family lives, the density of similar households in the neighborhood, and, thus, the location of the public school that a student, or group of students, will attend. The profile of a school is not uniform and, once again, both traditionally and currently, is associated with the community in which it is located. Thus, the school-site building, facilities, administration, teachers, staff, resources and curricula will vary according to the particular type of student body served. The types of variation that influence the quality, consistency and durability associated with the above elements, and therefore the school as a viable educational context, include: (1) the quality, size and overall operational quality of the school site; (2) the professional preparedness and readiness (goodness of fit, both academically and culturally, with the school-community context, as it were); (3) the average duration of its instructional staff; (4) the quality of the curriculum and resources available to the students and teachers; (5) the type, degree and relevance of expectations that teachers and administrators have for the students; and (6) the know-how teachers, staff and administrators have to effectively help the students (a) feel secure and welcome, (b) achieve grade-level requirements and beyond, and (c) competently and competitively prepare themselves for postsecondary institutional access and success.

Differentiation in household income and quality of school infrastructure, curricula, resources, personnel and leadership, while important in depicting critical intergroup differences within our national context regarding schooling contexts and experiences, does not explain our educational decline when competing internationally, for even when this set of complementary factors depicts our advantaged schools, our students' scores are not competitive in the global arena. As a nation, we are struggling with two interrelated and complex academic performance dilemmas in our public schools: steady declines, both domestically and globally, that transcend students' advantaged status. As stated earlier in this text, our nation is consistently declining in international status vis-à-vis other nations, whether industrialized, post-industrial or developing, who outperform us in math, science, and cognitively demanding reading.

Stanford University economist Eric Hanushek states in *The Atlantic*, in reference to his study on comparative performance across countries on advanced level in math proficiency, that the United States "does not do a good job of educating kids at the top" and that "even our most-advantaged students are not all that competitive" (A. Ripley, 2010, pp. 96–97). Our "relatively privileged" students do not perform as well as their counterparts in other countries, such as Poland, for example, or Iceland, France, Estonia or Sweden (A. Ripley, 2010, p. 97). In fact, the spot that our nation earned, based on the six percent (6%) of our nation's 15-year-old students who performed at the advanced level in math proficiency on the PISA international test, was 31st, well behind the top five countries, specifically, Taiwan's twenty-eight percent (28%), Hong Kong's twenty-four percent (23.9%), Korea's twenty-three percent (23.2%), Finland's twenty percent (20.4%), and Switzerland's nineteen percent (19.1). We were well behind Liechtenstein (16.1%), New Zealand (15.9%), Macao-China (14.1%), Slovenia (11.4%), and Estonia (10.1%), not to mention twenty other countries (Ripley, 2010). Within this same ranking, 31 (62%) of our states fell below our nation's international ranking of 31st place. The state with the highest percentage of PISA-tested students was Massachusetts, whose 11.4 percent, equaled that of Slovenia's, and was 88 percent that of the next highest country, Austria, and 41 percent that of the top ranking country, Taiwan, where 28 percent of the PISA-tested students performed at the advanced level in math proficiency.

While our top universities are still globally respected and in constant demand by the best students throughout the world, other nations have successfully initiated accelerated competitive strategies to build their own world-class research universities and educate their own students and those from other countries. Stanford University President John Hennessy, writing in the November/December 2010 issue of *Stanford*, highlighted the contrast in American's perceptions of the United States as a "scientific powerhouse." In 1999, nearly half of those polled "rated scientific advances among the country's most important achievements; by [2009], only 27 percent thought so" (Hennessy, 2010, p. 6). Thus, as our national educational performance declines in math, science and reading, and our academic competitiveness is consistently overshadowed by the higher educational performance of scores of countries in Asia and Europe, we ourselves—the American public—are expressing a loss of confidence in our nation as a leader in scientific advances. There is, of course, reason for concern: In 2009, for the first time, "non-Americans were granted more U.S. patents than resident inventors [50.7% and] for only the second time in the last 25 years, patent applications fell overall in the year ended Sept. 30 [2009]" (Arndt, 2010, p. 29).

President Obama's speech to Congress on February 24, 2009, contained a cautionary aphorism within a larger picture of our material excess and educational complacency. The particular segment of his speech was itself a rallying cry for timely, positive and widespread educational change—of course, for reform to work, it must be supported by timely, positive and widespread allocation of resources:

> Our children will compete for jobs in a global economy that too many of our schools do not prepare them for....[W]e have lived through an era where too often, short-term gains were prized over long-term prosperity.... A surplus became an excuse to transfer wealth to the wealthy instead of an opportunity to invest in our future.... Now is the time to act boldly and wisely —to not only revive this economy, but to build a new foundation for lasting prosperity.... Right now, three-quarters of the fastest-growing occupations require more than a high school diploma. And yet, just over half of our citizens have that level of education. We have one of the highest high school dropout rates of any industrialized nation. And half of the students who begin college never finish. This is a prescription for economic decline, because we know the countries that out-teach us today will out-compete us tomorrow. (paras. 8–64)

It is well understood that, nationwide, our school-sites within states and across states are urgently in need of reform. Caitlin Flanagan, writing in *The Atlantic* (2010), shared her highly personal critique of the dysfunctional state of education in California:

> I have spent my whole life, it seems, in and around schools.... I taught in Louisiana and Los Angeles for more than a decade; I have volunteered in all sorts of schools, am now a mother of elementary-school students. I have never seen an entire school system as fundamentally broken and rudderless as the California public schools, a system in which one out of five high-school students drops out before graduation, and in which scarcely 60 percent of the African American and Hispanic students leave school with a diploma. These young people are cast adrift in a $50 billion system in which failure is almost a foregone conclusion. (p. 111)

Even with a stellar university system of global recognition and contribution as is the University of California, California's problem extends to its postsecondary institutions, prompting the need for a new vision for student success, particularly regarding Hispanic and African American students, by the year 2020 (Lay, 2010):

> [California] has fallen in rankings and now lags behind many other states in the production of college graduates. In 2006, California ranked 23rd among states in its share of 25- to 34-year olds holding at least a bachelor's degree, down from eighth position in 1960. California colleges and

universities, both public and private, award relatively few baccalaureates, given the size of the state's youth population: California ranked 43rd among states in the ratio of bachelor's degrees awarded in 2006 to high school diplomas awarded five years earlier. (p. 6)

The declining numbers of postsecondary education graduates relative to the increase in college-age students is, of course, a national problem, the severity of which has been quantified in various recent reports. Lay (2010) quotes both from 2010 reports by Carnevale, Smith and Strole and the Lumina Foundation for Education, respectively, to illustrate the required pace if our nation is to attain parity in this critical area of national need:

> The Georgetown University Center on Education and the Workforce shows that by 2018, we will need 22 million new college degrees—but will fall short of that number by at least 3 million postsecondary degrees, Associate's or better. In addition, we will need at least 4.7 million new workers with postsecondary certificates. At a time when every job is precious, this shortfall will mean lost economic opportunity for millions of American workers. [Carnevale, Smith and Strole, 2010] (p. 5)

If our nation is to achieve its goal of leadership in the proportion of college graduates—to include associate degree holders—it will require radically improved recruitment and retention rates, as Lay (2010) reports:

> The Lumina Foundation for Education projects that reclaiming the global lead in college attainment will require increasing college attainment rates among adults from 37.9 percent to 60 percent. Lumina finds, "[i]f the rate of increase over the last eight years continues, the U.S. will reach a higher education attainment level of only 46.6 percent by 2025, and the shortfall in college graduates will be just under 25 million." (p. 5)

College-bound students in these envisioned heightened percentages is only a part of the story, as we must be able to retain and graduate them once they are enrolled; we must also control the enormous acceleration of tuition increases that have made postsecondary attendance a major debt-accumulation experience for students, as Stanford president John Hennessy (2010) observes:

In recent years, college tuition has risen faster than the Consumer Price Index, while increases in family income above inflation have stalled. Middle-income families are having a progressively more difficult time affording college, and students attending institutions without robust financial aid programs must decide if an undergraduate degree in worth significant debt. (p. 6)

To complement this postsecondary scenario of change, we also must, as a nation, effectively and concomitantly improve the quality of the P–12 experience and our high school graduation rates across all groups. Toward this end, we propose that P–12 reforms include the transformation of school site cultures to serve as communities of transformation for all students and our nation. To accomplish this goal, school-site communities must be student-centered and parent/guardian-friendly, within which teacher-informed programs operate and teachers form a relevant component in all aspects of leadership, at all levels of decision-making, relative to policy, design, practice, and assessment. School sites, moreover, must be communities accessible on a daily basis to students and parents/guardians, in which schedules begin well before the first class period and end well after the last class in the regular curriculum day. Our nation's school-site communities must be resource-rich, offering nutrition, respite, and recreation—before, during and after the official school day—and serve as welcoming, rigorous contexts where all learners can thrive through their participation in extensive socioacademic learning and skill development activities throughout the regular and extended day, week and year.

We need to achieve this transformation to substantively enhance our elementary and secondary school students' socioacademic outcomes through the professional development, expertise and leadership of our nation's teachers, and the optimum allocation of school-site resources. To not attend to this need is to opt for an aphotic future characterized by the maintenance and exacerbation of our existing network of differentiated infrastructure, treatment and outcomes within resegregated and mainstream schools. Such schools are increasingly producing students who are unprepared to competently or effectively meet competitive challenges or contribute, through innovation or new knowledge, to our nation's complex panoply of needs, much less maintain our geopolitical leadership status and influence, as the following section demonstrates.

Demographic Distribution and Disparate Academic Performance

The common trend evident in comparative household income and educational attainment rates across racial and ethnic groups is also visible when average reading scores of White Americans on the National Assessment of Educational Progress (NAEP) are compared with those of Asian/Pacific Islander, Hispanic and African Americans, in fourth and eighth grades, for the years 1998 and 2007. As the White American fourth grade and eighth grade average reading scores (225 and 270, respectively), in 1998, were the highest, each is used as the initial referent from which all other groups' reading scores are compared. Asian/Pacific Islander American students generated average reading score gains greater than any other group at both grade levels and years, a phenomenon that led them to parity in average reading scores with the White American group by 2007 at both grade levels.

In the case of African American and Hispanic American students, the gap narrowed by 2 percent and 3 percent, respectively, from 1998 to 2007 in the fourth grade, but remained virtually identical at the eighth grade levels. African American students' average reading scores from 1998 to 2007 at the eighth grade remained 10 percent lower than the White American average reading score; the average reading score gap for Hispanic American students during this same period exhibited a change of 1 percent, from a 10 percent gap to 9 percent. Thus, average reading scores at the eighth grade level for three of the four groups remained relatively flat over the ten-year period, which meant that the average reading score gap between White American students and their Hispanic American and African American counterparts was either nominally narrowed (Hispanic American students, 1% difference in 10 years) or not narrowed (no difference after 10 years in the case of African American students).

The average reading score of Asian/Pacific Islander Americans, in contrast, changed sufficiently to place them at parity with the White American group at both grade levels over the 10-year period. In similar manner, NAEP data show that the average reading scores among 13- and 17-year olds remained flat between 1984 and 2004 and gaps in achievement relative to African American and Hispanic American students remained stable when compared to their White American counterparts, as did the gap in mean math scores among students in these same groups (Kirsch, Braun, Yamamoto, & Sum, 2007).

These data results are especially disconcerting for two reasons: (1) educational research and associated reforms—including more than a half-century of supposed desegregation plans—have been in place to address and rectify this persistent disparity, and (2) population projections indicate that students from Hispanic, Asian, African American, and Multiracial categories now comprise, and will continue to comprise, the overwhelming increase in enrollment figures, as the non-Hispanic White population continues to decline relative to the replacement level of its particular category (NHW). The disparity is transformational in terms of race and ethnicity, particularly as the non-Hispanic White population, from 2030 to 2050, "would contribute nothing to the Nation's population growth," and, conversely, "after 2020 the Hispanic population is projected to add more people to the United States every year than would all other race/ethnic groups combined" (Day, 1996). Disparities in schooling extend beyond reading and mathematics, and include type and nature of curricular offerings, and the structure of the schools themselves, including the professional preparation and experience of the teachers (Darling-Hammond, 2006, 2010).

Disparities, of course, exist not solely in performance results, but also in the way groups of students are assessed for instruction and where they will go to school. Thus, in our nation, too many minority and poor students are kept, in part, from quality and integrated schooling due to the persistent practice of two phenomena: tracking and resegregation. Tracking (Oakes, 2005)—also conflated with ability grouping, although distinctions might be made in particular cases—reduces educational opportunities for students placed in low-tracks, who, as it were, are disproportionately represented by their socio-economic condition (poor) and racial/ethnic category (e.g., African American, Hispanic American). Students assigned to the lower tracks generally remain within the assigned track throughout their schooling experience (Burris & Welner, 2005). The continuing pattern of intense resegregation within America's neighborhoods (Orfield, 2001; Orfield & Lee, 2006) keeps students from distinct racial and ethnic groups from interacting with one another throughout their schooling experiences, which reinforces social distance and the unfounded beliefs, negative attitudes, wary behaviors, and flawed stereotypes regarding groups that segregation reproduces. Also, there is the salient, unresolved issue of quality, to which we now turn.

Teacher Quality, Student Diversity and Academic Outcomes

The differential level of teacher quality between schools that serve low-income students and those that serve middle class and above students sustains inequitable schooling and contributes to stark differential educational experiences and performance results between underrepresented minority group students and students from groups that are middle class and above. Carey (2007) provides criteria that were applied to determine a teacher quality index (TQI),[1] which lends insight into the effects of teacher quality on student advanced math performance and college entry and retention in Illinois. Results indicate that the level of teacher quality is important to student academic success and subsequent college choice, subject matter preparation and retention, since

> students who take advanced math courses in schools that employ the fewest well-qualified teachers are far less likely to be adequately prepared for college, or to succeed in college, than students who take the same courses— or even less advanced courses—at schools with the most well-qualified teachers. (para. 3)

As alarming, but certainly consistent with the model of persistent inequity within which our nation's schools and the general society operate, and that parallels findings by Oakes (2005), is that students who do not enroll in advanced courses "do poorly across the board," and that the poorer the school's students, the higher the percentage of "least qualified teachers" (Carey, 2007), such that

> 56 percent of schools that were in the top 10 percent in terms of poverty—the poorest schools in Illinois—were in the bottom 10 percent in terms of TQI.

> By contrast, less than 1 percent of the schools with the fewest poor children
> were in the lowest TQI category. Low-income students, who face some of the
> greatest barriers to education, are much less likely to be taught by teachers
> with the best qualifications. (Ready or Not, para. 8)

At the national level, in 1998, African American, Hispanic American, and American Indian/Alaska Native high school graduates remained less likely than their White American or Asian American counterparts to have taken higher level mathematics courses. With respect to the lower end of advanced math courses, Algebra II, African American students, in 1998, were roughly at the level (56%) where White American students were in 1990 (53%), while Hispanic Americans remained even lower (48%) in 1998 than White American students in 1990 (53%), although the percentage point gains were greater within the respective African American (15 percentage point) and Hispanic American (13 percentage points) student groups than in the White American group (9 percentage points) (National Science Foundation, 2003).

A sobering statistic relates to the fact that achievement gaps exist for these groups across socio-economic status classes, and sometimes even larger in the middle and upper income classes than in the poor (Steele, 2004). Referring once again to Carey (2007), the dropout rate for those students who were "least" or "not" prepared for college, based on the amount of high school advanced math courses completed and scores obtained in 2002, was internally and comparatively high:

> Three years later, 41 percent of students who entered as "Not" or "Least"
> ready had dropped out of the system, four times the attrition rate of those
> who were "More" or "Most" ready. (Ready or Not, para. 12)

Thus, socio-economic class and non-White status remain barriers to quality and integrated schooling. Addressing, much less resolving, the problem is made more difficult—even though it has persisted as practice and has been studied as a problem since the 1920s (Glass, 2002)—as the vast majority (74% as reported in one recent survey) of "Americans believe that the achievement gap between White students and African American and Hispanic students is primarily due to factors unrelated to the quality of schooling that children receive" (Burris & Welner, 2005, p. 594).

While there is general consensus among educational researchers that there is a difference between wealthy and low-income/poverty schools, and that *the quality of teachers* is a factor in student academic performance, controversy continues with respect to what type of teacher (that is, traditionally certified, alternatively certified, or non-certified) is most effective in the low income/poverty schools. A recent study published by Mathematica Policy Research, Inc (Decker, Mayer, & Glazerman, 2004) compared the three categories of teachers in a research sample that included 17 schools, 100 classrooms, and nearly 2,000 students within five national regions (Chicago, Houston, Los Angeles, New Orleans, and the Mississippi Delta), and found that the students who were taught by alternatively certified teachers (in this case, from the "Teach for America" program) had higher performance results in math than did students in classrooms with certified or non-certified teachers, and equal results in reading performance. Nevertheless, the gains, while significant within the sample, still placed the grades 1 through 5 students at the 17th percentile in math achievement.

Academic achievement, moreover, may differ according to a student's racial and ethnic group designation. For example, according to a report (Jacobson, Olsen, Rice, Sweetland, & Ralph, 2001), African American students, regardless of gender, scored lower on math and reading tests in every grade from first through twelfth than did their White American student counterparts, over a period from the late 1970s to the early 1990s, regardless of similar academic achievement between students from each racial group in earlier grades. This finding led the researchers to the implication that

> Black-White disparities in educational achievement can widen as students progress through elementary or secondary school. (p. xv)

Psychologist-scholar Claude Steele, writing in *The Atlantic* in 1992, elegantly expressed the longevity and effects of this achievement gap-expanding phenomenon:

This pattern has been documented so broadly across so many regions of the country, and by so many investigations (literally hundreds), that it is virtually a social law in this society—as well as a racial tragedy. (para. 13)

This differential continues to persist. In 2000, for example, National Assessment of Educational Progress (NAEP) academic achievement research results demonstrated that at the 4th, 8th and 12th grades, statistically significant disparities continued between White (and Asian) students and their lower-scoring African American and Hispanic American student counterparts, and no gains occurred to narrow the achievement gap between 1990 and 1999 (National Science Foundation, 2003). A corollary statistic of regrettable dimensions is that, according to the NAEP 2004 *Trends in Academic Progress* report published by the National Center for Educational Statistics (Perie, Moran, & Lutkus, 2005), Hispanic American and African American 17-year-olds demonstrate math and reading achievement that compares with that of 13-year-old White American students. Perhaps of greater importance is the fact that when comparing average scores from 1971 to 2004, the highest average scores by African American students reported in 2004 do not equal the lowest average score by White American students in 1971, in either math or reading. A similar, but not absolutely comparable, pattern is evident when comparing Hispanic American and White American students, from 1973 (first year that survey results were available for Hispanic American students) average scores to 2004 average scores in both subject matter areas; in only one case was Hispanic American students' highest average score in 2004 higher than that of White American students in 1973: in the 9-year-old student category in math, the average score of Hispanic American students in 2004 was 230 and that of their White American student counterparts was 227 in 1973.

The salient question one must address is how this current state of schooling affairs—this *status quo* of historical exclusivity in the face of multiple reform movements and critical legislation—has come to pass. From a legal perspective, consideration must be given to the fact that since 1954 there has been continuous confrontation between states rights and the Federal Government regarding the interpretation, and thus, application, of fundamental notions that could transform U.S.

society (and culture) from its legally sanctioned exclusionary behaveiors to one consistent with the principles espoused in its official, supposedly legally binding, rhetoric. The question is especially poignant as more than a half-century has transpired since the landmark *Brown v. Board of Education* Supreme Court decision (1954) overruled the *Plessy v. Ferguson* 163 U.S. 537 (1896)[2] separate-but-equal policy, and mandated that schools be desegregated. In *Brown*, segregated schools—data were regularly compiled only for the 17 southern states that had the segregation law on their books—were deemed "inherently unequal" and, consequently, were ordered to desegregate. The geopolitical designation *South* was defined as the 11 states of the Confederacy: Alabama, Arkansas, Florida, Georgia, Louisiana, Mississippi, North Carolina, South Carolina, Tennessee, Texas and Virginia; Border states were Delaware, Kentucky, Maryland, Missouri, Oklahoma and West Virginia. These 17 states all had legal state-imposed segregation prior to the 1954 *Brown* U.S. Supreme Court decision. Regrettably, in *Brown II* (1955), the Supreme Court mandated that desegregation transpire "at all deliberate speed," which effectively meant that no specific time line was mandated. *Brown I* was said to have "moral clarity without explicit doctrinal foundation;" *Brown II* was said to have neither and diminished "the moral imperative of the first decision" (Hutchinson, 1992, pp. 94–95). Nevertheless, a 58-year legal era of apartheid (1896–1954) was, with respect to equal access to educational and public services, theoretically over. What ensued, however, was a 10-year struggle between the States Rights advocates (as educational policy resides within each state), the Federal Government, and civil rights advocates.

In 1957, the Arkansas National Guard in Little Rock was federalized and combat-ready paratroopers sent in by then President Eisenhower to "reestablish order and allow a federal court desegregation decree to be carried out" (Salomone, 1986, p. 45). In 1958, the Supreme Court's decision in *Cooper v. Aaron* successfully challenged the ability of the state government to stall or otherwise thwart desegregation due to anticipated racial unrest, as had been the argument of then Governor Orval Faubus. During this period, in spite of the federally funded anti-poverty programs and the Civil Rights Act of 1964 that prohibited discrimination on the basis of race, color and national origin in federally assisted programs (Salomone, 1986, p. 4), the United States experienced a move in educational policy and practice from one of segregation-by-law (*de jure*) to one of segregation-in-fact (*de facto*)—98 percent of Southern Blacks still attended segregated schools in 1964 (Orfield, 2001)—and a concomitant lowering in the quality of public schooling (Salomone, 1986, p. 10). Desegregation was so opposed by southern states that "at least 137 new laws and state constitutional amendments had been enacted to delay or prevent the process" and by 1964, they had reached 200 (Salomone 1986, pp. 45–46). In 1979, twenty-five years after *Brown*, the U.S. Supreme Court found in *Columbus Board of Education v. Penick* (1979) had yet to

> disestablish its dual system and [thereby] failed to discharge its duty [to desegregate] and that in the intervening years since 1954 there had been a series of Board actions and practices that..."intentionally aggravated, rather than alleviated," racial separation in the schools. (para. 1)

In 2006, more than sixty years after *Brown*, some 400 of the nation's 15,000 school districts remained under court orders to desegregate (ABC News, 2006). Ironically, in 2007, the Supreme Court decided upon two cases regarding school desegregation in school districts in Seattle, Washington and Louisville, Kentucky. The Supreme Court ruled—although divided starkly along ideological lines, 5 to 4—that "both school districts' practices violated the equal protection clause of the 14th Amendment to the Constitution" (Glass, 2008), thus invalidating voluntary school desegregation plans, even when using race as a means to assign "some students to schools in an effort to end racial isolation and prevent re-segregation" (Totenberg & Kaufman, 2007).

Gary Orfield is past director of the Civil Rights Project at Harvard University and since 2007, when the project was transferred to UCLA, its co-director, as well as professor of Education, Law, Political Science and Urban Planning there. Orfield has studied the phenomenon of civil rights and school segregation in the United States for more than 30 years. Since its inception in 1996, the Civil Rights Project has commissioned more than 400 reports and issued 12 books. Orfield's 2001 and 2007 studies illustrate in detail our nation's move toward resegregation, which began in the 1990s largely due to three Supreme Court decisions between 1991 and 1995 and authorized a return to segregated neighborhood schools and limited the reach and duration of desegregation orders. The three Supreme Court cases were *Board of Education of Oklahoma v. Dowell,* 498 U.S. 237 (1991), *Freeman v. Pitts,* 503 U.S. 467 (1992), and *Missouri v. Jenkins,* 115 S. Ct. 2038 (1995).

Additionally, Orfield reported that Hispanics "have been more segregated than Blacks now for a number of years, not only by race and ethnicity but also by poverty (Orfield, 2001, p. 2). Orfield and Lee's (2006) study reported that, although the South maintained its status "by a small margin" as the least segregated region in our nation for Black students, the percentage of Black students in majority non-White schools had increased from 61 percent in 1991 to 71 percent in the 2003–04 academic year; in the same time period, Black student enrollment in majority non-White schools in the Border states increased from 59 percent to 69 percent, constituting a definite trend toward resegregation. Orfield and Lee (2006) conclude that:

> These changes and the continuing strong relationship between segregation and many forms of educational inequality, compound the already existing disadvantage of historically excluded groups. (p. 4)

Elementary and secondary schooling practice continues to favor the tracking model despite the general finding that it is detrimental academically to lower-income and non-White students (Glass, 2002; Wheelock, 1992; Oakes, 1985, 2005) and "does not result in the equal and equitable distribution of effective schooling among all students" (Wheelock, 1992). Tracking is not equitable for academic, social or psychological reasons, nor does the practice reflect, as Oakes (2005) states, America's fundamental rhetoric on equality:

> [A] very American notion [is] called equality and ... this ideal seems unwittingly subverted by tracking in schools [; that is] those children who seem to have the least of everything in the rest of their lives most often get less at school as well. (p. 4)

Today, U.S. schooling enrollment patterns continue to reflect this exclusionary ethnic-enclave pattern, defined by race, ethnicity and class, as well as geography. As we have seen, the official perception that we have of ourselves as a nation has been based on that of a particular group—designated traditionally and mainly as White, Anglo Saxon, Protestant (WASP). Elite private schools that cater to children from the upper socio-economic class remain modeled along these lines, as Cookson and Persell (1985) claim in *Preparing for Power: America's Elite Boarding Schools*:

> [T]he idea of sending a child away to school has distinctly European—especially British—overtones, and it is on the East Coast where the British influence is most strongly felt. One of the hallmarks of the American upper class is its Anglophobia, and a good many prep schools were founded on the British model. (p. 4)

Thus, throughout the course of our history, and particularly due to legal and economic (class) factors based on racial or ethnic exclusion, both legal and social, we have kept ourselves, as a nation, from a universally meaningful positive and productive democratic experience. Due to these perceived differences, which have been driven by a dominant White American societal reluctance, if not refusal, to integrate, we have yet to see, much less to value or apply, our sense of national cohesion. This previously legal, and now social, exclusionary phenomenon has created, on the one hand, a persistent chasm and vacuum between racial and ethnic groups, particularly regarding schooling—the nation's most important formal, long term socialization institution—and, on the other hand, persistent negative stereotypes and conflict.

Alain Locke (the prominent African American, who was a Harvard-, Oxford-, Berlin-educated philosopher, professor at Howard University, and principal figure in the Harlem Renaissance and New Negro Movement), writing in 1925, understood the negative consequences of segregation and the positive consequences of integration (cited in DeVillar & Faltis, 1991):

> The fiction is that the life of the races is separate, and increasingly so. The fact is that they have touched too closely at the unfavorable and too lightly at the favorable levels....There is a growing realization that in social

effort the co-operative basis must supplant the long-distance philanthropy, and that the only safeguard for mass relations in the future must be provided in the carefully maintained contacts of...both race groups. (p. 32)

This sentiment was not new among the African American intelligentsia. In 1896, Booker T. Washington wrote that Tuskegee University was founded in 1881 precisely to provide industrial education to African American students as a means to establish effective race relations:

> Nothing else so soon brings about right relations between the two races in the South as the industrial progress of the negro [sic]. Friction between the races will pass away in proportion as the Black man, by reason of his skill, intelligence, and character, can produce something that the White man wants or respects in the commercial world. ... We find that as every year we put into a Southern community colored men ... who produce something that makes the White man partly dependent upon the negro, instead of all the dependence being on the other side,—a change takes place in the relations of the races. (para. 16)

The view of education for African American men as an economic industrial trade enterprise was considered too narrow by other members of African American intelligentsia, particularly the eminent scholar-activist, W.E.B. DuBois, who in a 1902 issue of the *Atlantic Monthly* wrote that postsecondary education for African Americans must meet universal ("Harvard, Yale, Oberlin and seventy other leading colleges") rather than particularistic standards of higher learning:

> We shall hardly induce Black men to believe that if their bellies be full it matters little about their brains....The function of the Negro college then is clear: it must maintain the standards of popular education, it must seek the social regeneration of the Negro, and it must help in the solution of problems of race contact and cooperation. And finally, beyond all this, it must develop men. (para. 29)

Steele (1992) suggests that African American students have dissociated with schooling achievement in order to maintain their positive self-esteem, and therefore, "schooling must focus more on reducing the vulnerabilities that block identification with achievement," particularly by attending to the following four conditions:

1. The student must feel valued by the teacher for his or her potential and as a person.
2. The challenge and the promise of personal fulfillment, not remediation (under whatever guise), should guide the education of these students.
3. Racial integration is a generally useful element in this design, if not a necessity.
4. The particulars of Black life and culture—art, literature, political and social perspective, music—must be presented in the mainstream curriculum of American schooling, not consigned to special days, weeks, or even months of the year, or to special-topic courses and programs aimed essentially at Blacks. (Elements of Wiseness, para. 2)

The University of Texas Arlington (2006) report cited earlier summarizes comparable statistics on academic disparities and contributes the following four recommendations regarding criteria that post-secondary education institutions should follow in their collaborative efforts with preK–12 school systems to enhance achievement and retention of African American, Hispanic and other historically underperforming student groups:

1. Help build the data systems necessary to understand teacher effectiveness and how it is distributed;
2. Help [educators] understand the practices and characteristics of teachers who produce strong learning gains for students;
3. Produce more teachers with the commitment and skills to teach all students to high levels, and don't put [an institution's] stamp of approval on those without the necessary characteristics; and
4. Join in the effort to make sure [those] students in high poverty and high minority schools get the teachers they need to succeed.

Teacher Preparation Programs and Future Teachers

Thus, currently our nation's schooling is generally characterized by exhibiting and reinforcing the continued maintenance and spread of societal schooling practices that are antithetical to favorable schooling experiences and outcomes for African American, Hispanic American, American Indian/Alaska Native, and Asian/Pacific Islander American groups, among others. Major schooling factors that researchers identify that contribute to this status quo behavior include, as we have mentioned, resegregation, inconsistent teacher quality, and tracking.

There are other frameworks that delve specifically into categories within these three major elements.

M. Cochran-Smith (2003; Cochran-Smith, Davis, & Fries, 2004) applies her 8-category framework to assess multicultural teacher education programs and research literature regarding those programs. The categories are diversity, ideology, knowledge, teacher learning, practice, outcomes, recruitment and selection, and overall coherence. Cochran-Smith (2002) also devised a complementary 4-point framework to assess external factors, which may be interrelated with the previous 8-category framework, and whose elements include institutional capacity, relationships with local communities, governmental and non-governmental regulations, larger societal context (described in Cochran-Smith et al., 2004). However, as Cochran-Smith and her colleagues point out (Cochran-Smith et al., 2004, p. 965), there is little evidence that teacher education programs are becoming more multicultural or responsive to students' needs, partly due to the "conservative multiculturalism" that stresses high-stakes testing over alternate forms of student assessment, confuses universally required mass testing with equity, and assimilation with preparation for democratic engagement. Other contributing factors the researchers point to include (a) the strong role of the federal government in research, which is exerted through funding requirements; (b) research within multicultural education that is heavily weighted toward action research designed and conducted by educators, to include university faculty and preK–12 teachers, which is problematic in terms of traditional criteria for objectivity, measurement, and generalizability; and (c) a lack of research that relates teacher education, to teacher practice, to student outcomes.

Our nation's declining and increasingly uncompetitive educational performance, both nationally and globally, is a major problem that we need to respond to. We need to do so in such a way that our students throughout the educational pipeline demonstrate that they are learning. Moreover, that they are learning in a manner that will sustain and continually enhance not only their individual and socio-familial lives, but also the wellbeing of our nation. We understand in an ideal sense that each generation must contribute relevantly to our nation's growth and development trajectory, economically as well as geopolitically. We now need to understand the urgency with which we must make tangible the ideal through concrete actions that will lead us, as a nation, to our goals in keeping with our ideals.

A parallel and interdependent major problem is our mounting resegregated schooling contexts—which are themselves a strong and unblinking signal, on the one hand, of the lack of value that we, as a nation, have placed in them as viable and relevant institutions of education and, on the other, the disregard with which we hold the diverse and low-income populous that they are societally obligated to serve. This is ironic, as we need to be a cohesive and educated community if we are to develop, express and refine the elements required for sustained innovation and productivity in all of our societal sectors, but particularly science and technology.

In combination, the two factors of declining educational performance and resegregated schooling contexts have served to curtail meaningful, transformative progress toward achieving our foremost national goals in the critical areas of national concern and priority. Specifically, we must attend to (1) realizing substantive domestic educational reforms; (2) markedly improving our international educational standing; (3) thoroughly preparing students to contribute consistently, relevantly and creatively to innovation and patent generation in the sciences and technology; (4) motivating and preparing students to contribute to our nation's economy in ways that sustain and enhance our domestic and global productivity in increasingly diverse, efficient and effective ways; and (5) closing persistent educational, income and communication gaps among racial, ethnic and gender groups that currently fragment our nation. These problem areas, together with the barriers they impose and the pressures they exert on us nationally, are too costly in terms of the loss in human, social, cultural and economic capital, and lead in a recurring loop-like manner to inevitable consequences that diminish us domestically and globally. If we are to affect the type of purposeful and positive high-performance change needed to prevail as a major nation that leads and inspires, then we must be surefooted, rather than ambivalent, in moving toward our national goal of metacultural cohesion. To cohere as a nation, we must, in turn, resolve to integrate, to communicate and to cooperate.

Chapter 9

Envisioning Metacultural Cohesion: Championing Integration, Communication, Cooperation, Critical Inquiry and Culture

> Groups are cohesive when group-level conditions are producing positive membership attitudes and behaviors and when group members' interpersonal interactions are operating to maintain these group-level conditions. Thus, cohesive groups are self-maintaining with respect to the production of strong membership attractions and attachments.
>
> —Noah E. Friedkin

Power Distance, Inequality and Resistance: The Paradox of Competing Paradigms

The two-part question regarding our nation's culture—our metaculture—focuses first on its relationship to the subordinate cultures that are embedded within, yet peripheral to, the dominant culture and, second, on how we are advancing or diminishing our metaculture by this dominant-subordinate relationship. All cultures are composed of groups and, as such, the unit of analysis of any culture is at the group level. At the same time, individuals comprise groups, and may influence the nature and trajectory of the group, and therefore the culture. In the case of the United States, our metaculture is grounded in our founding documents—seen as immutable—and the amendments and laws that support it, and which are subject to revision, as illustrated in earlier chapters of this book. Thus, as a nation, we ideally uphold and are guided by the values embedded in our founding documents and our behaviors ideally uphold and are guided by the amendments and laws we have passed and that apply universally.

Within this scenario, cohesion, then, represents the degree to which our national rhetoric (that is, the body of beliefs, values, and principles that characterizes our fundamental sense of nationhood) corresponds to our national practice (our behaviors) toward all members of our nation. This same body of beliefs, values, and principles should guide our practice in global interactions as well. In an ideal world, there would be a one-to-one correspondence between our metacultural rhetoric and our practice, and cohesion would be absolute. This standard as an ideal is common enough, as is the distance from the standard in reality. Thus, the question to address is the degree of correspondence between our nation's rhetoric and its practice.

In our nation's specific case, from its earliest days, we exhibited a severely narrow particularism that favored one group—namely, White male property owners—over all others. Hence, our actual practice began remarkably distant from our rhetoric, and in direct opposition to its universality. In actuality, then, our practice was to exert superiority by a particular group over other groups within our nation—thereby creating the "other." This practice served, in turn, as a means to assert distance, dominance and control over many groups in general by one group in particular; at the same time, the practice established hierarchies that enabled all to explicitly distinguish, for example, the dominant from the subordinate, the strong from the weak, the privileged from the masses, the masters from the slaves, the owners from the workers, the rich from all other income classes, and the leaders from the followers, as well as men from women, and Whites from all other groups designated as non-White.

Obviously, the particularistic practice with which we began our metacultural expression did not correspond to our metacultural rhetoric or to the diverse groups' sense, who were not equally privileged, of how to live it. Different groups, moreover, were less distant, less dominated and less controlled. The notion of *power distance* (Hofstede, 2001) addresses the degree to which those who are not as privileged within a nation (or unit within it, such as school, family, office, etc.) "handle" inferiority, specifically:

> The extent to which the less powerful members of institutions and organizations within a country expect and accept that power is distributed unequally. (p. 98)

In our country's particular case, the other groups that constitute our nation did not generally expect or accept that power be distributed unequally, and our nation's history has been characterized by the negotiated tension between the two streams of thought—the one, exclusive; the other, inclusive. Both terms, of course, even when operationally defined, are not inherently stable and depend not only on the times in which they are used, but on the groups who use them. Racism was our nation's legally sanctioned right to privilege and dominance over others based on one's perceived Whiteness or lack thereof. As the term "White" or its equivalent grew broader, thus enabling ethnic-White groups previously excluded to enter into the fold of privilege, racism did not follow suit, as it had set and maintained the legal bar of separation and differentiation by race sufficiently high, it was thought, that no non-White group was expected to reach the exclusive and rarified heights of the White group and form part of that community. But non-White groups, and their White comrades-in-arms, did not agree with that expectation and designated non-White groups, as well as women, who were disenfranchised from voting, struggled incessantly to be treated equally and equitably.

It is not an exaggeration to state that our metacultural rhetoric, which has not changed in terms of our founding documents, was finally extended to all groups within the traditionally excluded bloc with the passage of the Civil Rights Act in 1964 and by the Voting Rights Act of 1965. The latter Act belatedly enforced the right to vote by African Americans as mandated by the Fifteenth Amendment (1870) and its amendments of 1970, 1975, and 1982, which were enacted to extend protection against voter disenfranchisement to Hispanic Americans, Asian Americans, and Native Americans. Poll taxes in state elections, however, were allowed until 1966, when the Supreme Court decided in *Harper v. Virginia State Board of Elections* that such taxes were unconstitutional as they discriminated unfairly against the poor (Thernstrom, 1992). The inclusive move by our nation's highest court, nevertheless, did not extend to it being disposed to interpret our Constitution to embrace group rights to proportionate representation. Rather, according to Thernstrom (1992), the Court deemed it expedient to remain firmly in the legal space of individual rights for two interrelated reasons:

> [W]hen the state categorizes individuals for political purposes along lines of race and sanctions group membership as a qualification for office, it inhibits political integration; the commitment to the group is heightened at the expense of the sense of common citizenship. (p. 902)

The notion of individual rights positioned dichotomously and mutually exclusively against group rights is, in actuality, a highly selective value and practice within our nation—simply, it is a false dichotomy. This historical characteristic—the very paradox that characterizes our Gordian knot dilemma—has both sufficient academic and entertainment value to be in vogue as the subject still strikes at the core of our national identity, our Americanness, and the degree of group privilege that was granted White Americans, while at the same time severely subordinating groups designated as non-White. John Lahr (2010, p. 88), writing in *The New Yorker*, reviews the play *A Free Man of Color*, and states that it "takes place in the racial mosh pit of pre-Purchase New Orleans, position[ing] its fun and fury strategically at the moment when manifest destiny and moral travesty collide." Joseph Ellis' (2007a) work, *American Creation*, illustrates the nature of the stage upon which our founding fathers constructed the "triumphal and tragic elements" that constitute our ongoing dilemma: In terms of space (land expansion) and pace (evolutionary approach to social and political change), the founding perspective proved to be favorable, excepting, of course, the enormous miscalculation of the predicted attrition of slavery; race, however, "proved impervious to any imaginative response whatsoever" as

> it was psychologically impossible for the founders to imagine the peaceful coexistence of Whites and free African Americans in the same nation-state.... Without any historical precedents to guide them, the founders could imagine a secular state and a large-scale republic, but they could not imagine a biracial society. As a result, whenever race entered the founding conversation, tragedy prevailed. (pp. 18–19)

The language of the Louisiana Purchase Treaty (1803) included guarantees relative to the French inhabitants (under Spain's dominion) whose territory was to be ceded to the United States (National Archives, 1996):

> The inhabitants of the ceded territory shall be incorporated in the Union of the United States and admitted as soon as possible according to the principles of the federal Constitution to the enjoyment of all these rights, advantages and immunities of citizens of the United States, and in the mean time they shall be maintained and protected in the free enjoyment of their liberty, property and the Religion which they profess. (Art. III)

However, as the racially and culturally diverse inhabitants in many cases "did not match the picture of American settlers that [President Thomas] Jefferson saw in his mind's eye.... [He] opted to grant those rights only to the 'White inhabitants'" (Ellis, 2007, quoted in Lahr, 2010, p. 88). What Jefferson saw in his mind's eye was articulated in his draft of a proposed amendment to the Constitution in July, 1803 (*Downes v. Bidwell*, 1903 in Justia.com, n.d.):

> Louisiana, as ceded by France to the United States is made a part of the United States. Its White inhabitants shall be citizens, and stand, as to their rights and obligations on the same footing with other citizens of the United States in analogous situations. (Statement by Mr. Justice Brown, p. 182 U.S. 253)

What Jefferson also saw in his mind's eye was the power, morally questionable in today's world, that privilege accorded one to define one's distance from his public beliefs relative to his private practice. By having the privilege to do so, Jefferson engaged in doublethink and duplicitous practice: publicly eschewing freeing slaves and touting the social harm of miscegenation, while maintaining an intimate relationship with Sally Hemings, a slave he owned and by whom he probably fathered children, as Ellis (U.S. History, 2000) described in an online, live webcast conversation with middle and high school students from across the nation:

> I say Jefferson plays tricks inside himself. He's the kind of man who plays hide-'n'-seek inside of himself and instead of seeing him as kind of an outright hypocrite, I see him as a man of great duplicity, internally. With the

Sally Hemings thing, I think you've got to start thinking in terms of hypocrisy. Because this really does mean that he was living a lie for the following big, big reasons. One of the reasons Jefferson gave as the reason he could not assume a leadership issue on the problem of slavery is he didn't think it was possible for Blacks and Whites to live together in the same society and he feared if they were, it would produce what is called "miscegenation," the coming together of races, which he disapproved of. There he is, living a considerable portion of his adult life, in a relationship with a Black woman—she's actually a mulatto woman—and in that sense violating the very thing that he claims stands in his way of freeing the slaves. So he also never acknowledges his paternity. That is to say, some planters had children with slaves and they took them on as their own children. Jefferson never did that. Jefferson refused to acknowledge that they were his children. He didn't allow them to escape or include them in his will. (U.S. History, 2000, J. Ellis transcript, para. 80)

But Jefferson was not alone in exercising this voluntary White privilege in self-deception; it was an exclusive group phenomenon, as demonstrated by the custom in early nineteenth-century Louisiana (Louisiana State University Libraries, n.d.):

Proslavery writers in the eighteenth century argued that race mixing would result in a weaker White race even while they ignored "plaçage" [placing a young, free Black woman by her parents under the protection and care of a White male of means, generally to serve as his mistress and bear his children], concubinage, and miscegenation. Southern Whites tended to express horror at race mixing, even while they engaged in it. As if in defense of their behavior, proslavery "advocates suggested that the availability of slave women, who were powerless to resist the unwanted sexual advances of White men, helped guard White women from the lust of White men." (Wall, p. 72) Also in Louisiana laws were enacted to protect White women from slave and free men of color by requiring that a slave convicted of raping White woman be put to death. There were no laws against White or Black men raping Black women. (Slaves and Free People of Color, para. 2)

In 1810, the census conducted in the Territory of Orleans, virtually what comprises the present state of Louisiana "minus the parishes east of the Mississippi River," reported that there were more than 76,000 residents, divided almost equally by race—half of whom were African American and half of whom were White (Louisiana State Museum, n.d.). Louisiana, having more than the 60,000 residents required for statehood, was admitted into the Union on April 30,

1812, and, as mandated by its state constitution, voting was restricted to White males who paid taxes, which eliminated two-thirds of the White male population, as well as all White women and non-Whites (Louisiana State Museum, n.d.).

The Louisiana Purchase was of extraordinary importance to our nation's development: It covered an area of 828,000 square miles, served as a critical step in our envisioned Westward expansion, effectively doubled the size of our nation, placed the port of New Orleans and Mississippi under our control, and ultimately was the space from which thirteen states, in whole or in part, would be established (Arkansas, Colorado, Iowa, Kansas, Louisiana, Minnesota, Missouri, Montana, Nebraska, North Dakota, Oklahoma, South Dakota and Wyoming). It was perceived as the first foreign country that was added to our nation, and also demanded a national policy toward the Native Americans who resided within its boundaries. As the White group's identity was absolutely privileged over that of the groups comprising the collective term American Indian, Ellis (2007a, p. 9) claimed that "the seeds of Indian extinction east of the Mississippi were indisputably sown in the late eighteenth century," as "demography trumped honor and diplomacy" (Ellis, 2007b).

Jefferson's formal thought regarding the rights of Indians, to use that era's term, reflected that of the dominant, property-owning, White encroaching group and was displayed early on in his career. In 1774, at the age of 33, Jefferson wrote in *A Summary View of the Rights of British America* that American lands were "undoubtedly of the allodial nature" (quoted in Jennings, 2000, p. 79). The use of this technical term meant, to Jefferson, that no land in America was held by a feudal landlord, as claimed by the king of England, or by Indians, as these same lands were held by, and to be allotted by, a society with civil institutions, which the Indians presumably did not have. Thus, Jefferson "neatly suppressed with one phrase any rights to be claimed by king *or* aborigines" (Jennings, 2000, p. 79). Again, Jefferson was not alone in this thought, much less its practice. Frontier Revolutionaries, as Jennings (2000) illustrates, were of like mind, which they expressed in action:

> Frontier Revolutionaries...practiced total war against Indians. Their aim
> was not merely to win but to extirpate the Indians, to which end they used

methods that had originated under Oliver Cromwell in Ireland and had been continued by the duke of Cumberland in Scotland's Highlands. Kill, burn, destroy. Take no prisoners. Leave no property intact, for "the only good Indian is a dead Indian." And the only acceptable land is land "free to be taken".... [T]he great tide of Europe's landless peoples swept all before it. And the imperialists who prided themselves on their virtue behaved toward weaker indigenous peoples as brutally callously as expanding Europeans had during the Middle Ages. (pp. 247, 252)

As a general principle, the above statement is accurate, and particularly evident in the presidency of Andrew Jackson. However, this is not to say that there were no exceptions to it, as there were several towns and elected officials who went on record to support honoring treaties and protest Indian removal. The larger twofold point, however, is that (a) the Indian Removal Act of 1830 passed and was, "in reality, only the first shameful step on the 'Trail of Tears,' the forcible eviction of the Native Americans living east of the Mississippi [that] began in 1838" (S. Cummins, 2009), and (b) the trajectory was direct between the thought of Jefferson, as expressed in his proposed Constitutional Amendment of 1803, quoted below (Brown, 1920), and the legal privileging in 1830 of the White group over that of the Native American:

> The legislature of the Union shall have authority to exchange the right of occupancy in portions where the U.S. have full right for lands possessed by Indians within the U.S. on the East side of the Mississippi, to exchange lands on the East side of the river for those on the West side thereof and above the latitude of 31 degrees; to maintain in any part of the province such military posts as may be requisite for peace or safety; to exercise police over all persons therein, not being Indian inhabitants; to work salt springs, or mines of coal, metals and other minerals within the possession of the U.S. or in any others with the consent of the possessors; to regulate trade and intercourse between the Indian inhabitants and all other persons; to explore and ascertain the geography of the province, its productions and other interesting circumstances; to open roads and navigation therein where necessary for beneficial communication and to establish agencies and factories therein for the cultivation of commerce, peace and good understanding with the Indians residing there. (p. 38)

At this same point in time, Jefferson also recommended to Congress that our nation entice the Native American groups to convert their culture from hunting to one of agricultural, raising livestock, and domestic manufacture to accommodate the rapid population incursion of White Americans (Fengler, 2006):

> In order peaceably to counteract this policy of theirs and to provide an extension of territory which the rapid increase of our numbers will call for, two measures are deemed expedient. First[:] To encourage them to abandon hunting, to apply to the raising [of] [live]stock, to agriculture, and domestic manufacture, and thereby prove to themselves that less land and labor will maintain them in this better than in their former mode of living. The extensive forests necessary in the hunting life will then become useless, and they will see advantage in exchanging them for the means of improving their farms and of increasing their domestic comforts. (para. 3)

The late eighteenth century, according to Ellis (2007b), proved to be a uniquely fertile period in political, economic, cultural and human opportunities that coalesced to produce "the big bang...in the American political universe." As noted previously, however, despite our Enlightenment-rich rhetoric, and even our understanding among leaders that slavery was at best "a necessary evil," "the consciousness of the populous in the late eighteenth century was so racist [that it could be described as] an endemic cancer that has been part of American society from the beginning" (Ellis, 2007b). The words of Senator James Jackson, from Georgia, delivered on February 28, 1803, in the debate as to whether slavery should be allowed in Louisiana, reflect the degree to which slavery was embedded in the American consciousness of the South and the lengths they would go— and ultimately did go—to preserve it (Brown, 1920):

> Jackson, arguing from experience as a Georgia rice-planter, held that slavery was necessary. To exclude slaves would depreciate the value of lands in Louisiana fifty per cent....Full of serious portent for the future, tinged with what might be well called the "higher law" was his statement: "You cannot prevent slavery—neither laws moral or human can do it. Men will be governed by their interest, not the law." (p. 111)

As much to the point is the question of belonging, as African Americans were never considered to be a viable part of our nation's society, even by the White Americans who advocated for their freedom; the general consensus was that they should be shipped to the Caribbean or Africa were it granted—although this was economically prohibitive. The notion of integration, from an American societal perspective, gathered critical mass and surfaced in the mid-twentieth century (Ellis, 2007b). The rights of Native Americans were no less violated, as their presence and way of life were considered incidental to the stampede for land by the White American populous, the states and the federal government.

The respective power distance paradigms in play, then, have been substantively different. The privileged White American group paradigm has relied on the three elements of exclusion, particular, non-transferable advantage, and abuse by law or custom to maintain distance from equality and preserve the White American way of life. In contrast, the general paradigm of our nation's non-privileged groups has been based on inclusion, universal advantage, and equity under the law (de jure) and in fact (de facto). The tension caused by the oppositional values and trajectories between the two paradigms has informed the definition and character of Americanness from our inception to the present day, and will continue to do until our nation's practice more fully and equitably corresponds to its rhetoric.

The White American paradigm, of course, has been dominant from our colonial beginnings and has been supported by law and practice to varying degrees until the last quarter of the twentieth century. Racism, in the words of Ellis (2007b), "was present then; it is certainly present now [but] it is on the defensive." The countervailing phenomenon to the practice of particularism has been the solid, persistent strength of belief by the non-privileged groups in the immutability of our national rhetoric and that struggle is not only inevitable, not only just, but that it is demanded if we are to adhere to our founding rhetoric. At present, the equity-driven struggle for inclusive education continues to base itself on the strength and promise of our founding rhetoric.

The Goal of Education and the Socioacademic Achievement Framework

The goal of all our nation's schools should be clear, regardless of socio-economic, racial/ethnic profile or other dimensions, including geography or gender: To provide a successful socioacademic experience for each student that results in the acquisition, appreciation, development and refinement of four fundamental areas of skill:

1. Cognitive, affective, and intellectual skills—including original and critical t thinking and creativity—and ethical behavior;
2. Socio-cultural skills that value and embrace collaboration to promote societal development, and well-being within the context of our plural populous. To avoid the possibility of confusion, we must note that the terms cohesion and unity do not correspond to the term uniformity;
3. Academic skills that meet or surpass the competency requirements in the set of subject matter areas associated with the K–16 schooling cycle and that foster the desire and will for life-long learning; and
4. Civic skills that, on the one hand, reflect a knowledge of, and passion for, our nation's core values as manifested in our Constitution, Declaration of Independence, related founding documents, and laws, and that, on the other, strengthen our nation's unity through their consistent and equitable practice within our always-evolving democratic context.

By meeting this fourfold goal, our nation's students will be prepared—individually, socially, politically and culturally—to undertake their careers, as well as to initiate their lifelong engagement as productive members in the negotiated development and trajectory of our democratic society, and to relevantly participate in and contribute to current and future global dynamics that affect us collectively as a human society.

To support this educational goal, DeVillar and Faltis (DeVillar, 1994; DeVillar & Faltis, 1991, 1994; DeVillar, Faltis, & Cummins, 1994) proposed the socioacademic achievement framework, whose key elements of integration, communication and cooperation reflect principles of successful intergroup collaboration and achievement found, respectively, within Allport's (1954) contact theory; Vygotsky's (1962, 1978) work regarding socio-cultural interaction in context, with particular emphasis on the zone of proximal development; and cooperative learning, particularly the research-based models and activities of Johnson and Johnson (2009a, 2009b, 2000, 1994). The socioacademic achievement model established a platform sustained by educational equity and presented a counter-narrative to the dominant cultural narrative, which legitimated the traditional instructional model. The standard model of instruction consisted of segregation (within schools and classrooms through various forms of tracking or ability-grouping); routine-driven, one-way teacher talk that seeks known information in predictable response patterns at the expense of two-way, authentic communication espoused, for example, by Goffman (1981); and competition among students that stresses individualism and independent work at the expense of social interaction, collaboration, and positive interdependence.

Thus, the socioacademic framework promotes discourse founded upon a counter-narrative that reflects "Mark Freeman's use of the term counter-narrative [as] those 'culturally-rooted aspects of one's history that have not yet become part of one's story [but are necessary in that they] surge into reflection, infusing one's history with new meaning, complexity and depth'" (quoted in Andrews, 2004, p. 5). The part of our national history that has yet to become a substantive and everyday part of our national story, and practice, relates to equity-based inclusion—that is, inclusion that ensures access to quality teaching, resources, and learning contexts, within which all students can participate meaningfully and derive relevant and substantive benefit from their educational experience.

The Role of Context

We use the term context to conform to the definition of one of its synonyms, *milieu*, to embrace operationally the diverse social and cultural elements within our national setting and the more abstract element that informed our context—the spirit of Americanness, so to speak—that has allowed and enabled our long-term, dynamic and troubled discourse of negotiation relative to the conflict produced by these two co-existing, yet ultimately mutually exclusive, paradigms of American nationhood. This milieu is not only unique but overwhelmingly powerful. It is the spirit that guides and informs our consciousness, and that has led to negotiated actions that express our belief and adherence to our nation's egalitarian rhetoric. We have made relatively slow progress in our own minds, as "justice delayed is justice denied." Yet, there can be no denial that progress has been made and in the direction of our rhetoric. Our gains in inclusiveness have been a result of our willingness to struggle and resolve, a value which not even the Civil War could alter. The Civil Rights era was another case of massive struggle and resolution, particularly in the legal arena, but extending to important areas of practice as well.

But there is much yet to discuss, to negotiate, before we achieve our envisioned state of unity. Moreover, our trajectory toward unity can be threatened internally, if we allow our nation to be defined, determined and debilitated by an unsustainable and unchallenged interpretation of free market capitalism at the expense of refining and controlling the reins of our representative democracy. Our persistent levels of sustained national poverty conjoined unhealthily with the reproduction of naïveté ("sanctioned ignorance" in the words of Spivak, 1988, in Ailon, 2008, p. 901) likewise reinforce and maintain a negative status quo that can only add to an accelerated national and public deterioration relative to fomenting cohesion through integration, communication, and cooperation. On the other hand, there is little doubt that if our discourse were motivated and sustained by a common perspective regarding the need to identify and address the problems at hand, rather than the traditional adversarial positions that have led to war or intense, violent struggle, we would make important gains in terms of peaceful discourse. But our gains would be greater, as they would also occur in the nature and quality of time invested, in the quality and pace of discourse, in the range of avenues for negotiation, and in the quality and pace of achieving our desired results.

Schools remain, in principle, the single greatest formal socialization context within which to continue our national development toward realizing the vision of cohesion embodied in our founding documents. Schools also serve as contexts for refining our social and academic practices based on our Constitutional amendments and laws, both case and statutory. But to effectively model our vision, we now must go well beyond our existing regular school-day contexts and the environments they offer if we are to have any chance of our younger generations valuing, internalizing and putting it into practice.

Our nation's patterns of intensified segregation continue to work against unity by reinforcing distance among American groups in important areas, including social, economic, linguistic and educational. The differential schooling contexts, from buildings to teachers to curricula, combined with family and neighborhood contexts, influence significantly differential schooling experiences and academic outcomes, and lead, consequently, to differential life and career opportunities. It is clear that we cannot afford to ignore the factors that contribute to depressed schooling conditions and outcomes by an increased proportion of our school-aged population. As we have attempted to make clear in this text, the threat and cost to our national political and economic system, as well as to our global geopolitical standing and influence, are too great, and perhaps too near.

Schooling within the Context of the Socioacademic Achievement Framework

The socioacademic achievement framework was developed to respond to a particular and complex need related to American schooling: too many students were dropping out, failing or underperforming, particularly from low-income sectors or racial and ethnic minority groups, or both. Moreover, schooling contexts were not propitious environments for learning-related meaningful interaction or cooperation among students, or for students to interact with other students who were from different racial or ethnic groups or socio-economic backgrounds. If computers were used to mimic the current pedagogical model, then one could predict that they would in fact reinforce the status quo—too many student dropping out, too many failing their courses, and too many underperforming academically—rather than contributing to academic reform. Cummins (1991), in his foreword to *Computers and Cultural Diversity* (DeVillar & Faltis, 1991), summarized the general problem associated with instructional settings in our elementary and secondary schools:

> As the authors point out, typical American classroom still segregates learners from each other and promotes individualistic competitive learning in a context where teachers define their roles as transmitters of knowledge and skills to students who, in turn, are given little option but to define their

roles in terms of internalizing what is transmitted. Within this context, the role of the computer is as an adjunct transmitter of knowledge and skills. (p. vii)

Later in the Foreword, Cummins (1991) states the type of computer-based communication in which students must engage in order for the experience to be meaningful from a socioacademic framework perspective:

> [I]n order to make of the power of the computer as a communicative and discovery tool, students must have some non-trivial reasons for communicating with others and motivation to search out and interpret particular forms of information. In most contemporary classrooms in North America the curriculum has been sanitized such that students are given few opportunities to pursue projects to which they are intrinsically committed. (p. viii)

Cummins, moreover, presaged the operating distinction that later would be made between computer uses that foment a passive consumer nature (i.e., Web 1.0) and those that enable active social participation (i.e., Web 2.0):

> The implicit image of the individual who is supposed to emerge from twelve years of this form of education is considerably closer to a self-centered compliant consumer than to a critical and creative thinker who knows how to cooperate with others in seeking solutions to common problems...DeVillar and Faltis present an alternative to the continued failure of American education. The student who would emerge from the type of educational experience they espouse is one in which collaborative critical inquiry and creative problem solving are highlighted. (Cummins, 1991, pp. viii–ix)

Thus, as noted earlier, the original socioacademic framework promoted a specific type of reform within our schools based on three interrelated principles, independent of whether computers were present or absent, namely:

1. Integration (heterogeneous groupings; following principles of contact theory elaborated upon by Allport, 1954);
2. Communication (both student-teacher and student-student; following forms of talk principles by Goffman, 1981) that presents and negotiates

the learning of subject matter material consistent with Vygotsky's (1934/1962, 1978) zone of proximal development; and

3. Cooperation (differentiated from small group or collaborative learning, but incorporating both through research-based principles and activities associated with cooperative learning, as particularly articulated by Johnson & Johnson, 1975, 1985, 1986, but also other researchers such as Slavin, 1983).

Additionally, two key elements formed part of the achievement whole: equity and cohesion. Equity was defined as a function of access, participation and benefit (DeVillar, 1986, 2000; Faltis & DeVillar, 1987), which meant that access was a necessary but not sufficient component to define equity or realize its intended effects; for equity to be realized, students need to participate meaningfully in the social and learning process and to derive relevant benefit from it. Equity, in our nation's case, will have been realized when any child entering school exits with the same probability of successfully completing the schooling cycle as any other child. That is, current barriers related to *group classifications*, such as race or ethnicity designation or income status, among others, would not serve as predictors for being classified as at-risk or for being at-risk.

The phenomenon of any child falling within the normal distribution curve would eliminate categorization by group membership (African American, Asian American, Hispanic American, etc.)—the skewed curve associated with group school underperformance, failure, and dropouts, will have been, so to speak, de-skewed in favor of symmetry. Furthermore, in light of school experiences framed within the context of integration, communication and cooperation as defined above, students would become more cohesive as Americans, rather than as fragmented according to their *perceived* race or ethnicity or other social marker. Cohesion among previously fragmented groups enables metacultural development, where each individual is free, willing and able to participate relevantly in the democratic process, engaging through negotiation in our nation's multifaceted and complex trajectory of self-determination. The criteria would be met associated with individual-group dynamics relative to cohesion and the type of goals that result from it:

group cohesiveness refers to the degree to which the members of a group desire to remain in the group. Thus, the members of a highly cohesive group, in contrast to one with a low level of cohesiveness, are more concerned with their membership and are therefore more strongly motivated to contribute to the group's welfare, to advance its objectives, and to participate in its activities. (Friedkin, 2004, p. 412)

To the degree that we remain fragmented by design, as is inevitable when the root of racism and related designations that favor one group over another survive, we cannot satisfy the meaning of self-determination: "The aspiration of some group...to form its own sovereign state and to govern itself....Only if a single social entity can be identified...can there be any recognizable process of self-determination" (Scruton, 1982, p. 422). The founding fathers provided our rhetoric, which captured, defined and trans-generationally generates our spirit—a collective spirit, uniquely American, but universal in its egalitarian appeal. We have, however, not lived our rhetoric in the egalitarian manner which corresponds to its spirit. To this degree, we therefore cannot engage in self-determination in the envisioned democratic sense and thus we are not the democratic nation we purport to be. Our persistent internal struggle, with every gain, moves us closer toward the possibility of engaging in productive and authentic self-determination; but we remain far from identifying ourselves, much less operating, as the single social entity mandated by our founding vision.

Refinement of the Socioacademic Achievement Framework

The socioacademic achievement framework has been revisited by its originators (DeVillar, 1994; DeVillar & Faltis, 1994) and refined by researchers (Cummins, 1994; Freedman & Liu, 1996). The original framework, according to Cummins (1994, p. 365), needed to take into account three additional factors to strengthen its theoretical and operational viability as an alternate mode to achieve socioacademic success on the part of students, particularly those from groups traditionally at-risk of underperforming, failing or dropping out: (a) the relevance of societal power relations to the educational development of culturally diverse students, (b) the crucial role that negotiation of identity between educators and students plays in student success, and (c) the importance of curriculum content and the promotion of critical inquiry.

Referring to communication, the second element in the socioacademic framework, Cummins (1994) demonstrates how the framework would benefit from including the element of societal power relations, even within classrooms informed by social learning principles such as those espoused by Vygotsky (1978). DeVillar and Faltis (1991, p. 11) had, as a means to support the condition for authentic communication in the classroom, incorporated four elements associated with Vygotsky's (1962, 1978) social learning theory:

1. The presence of an adult or a more capable peer;
2. the occurrence of social interaction between the learner and the adult or more capable peer;
3. that interaction be carried out in a language comprehensible to both learners and adults or more capable peers; and
4. that the adult or more capable peer operate within what Vygotsky called the learner's "zone of proximal development."

Cummins (1994, p. 365), however, recommended that the framework's *implicit* reference to unequal power relations be made *explicit*, as interactions at the classroom level (microinteractions) reflected and were influenced by the macrointeractions "between subordinated communities and societal institutions establish and controlled by the dominant group." Cummins posited that teachers, to the degree that they accepted the societal status quo and defined their socialization agent roles in keeping with the societal status quo, would be "likely to reflect and reinforce the coercive relations of power that exist in the broader society."

Thus, even within Vygotsky-driven social learning contexts designed to promote two-way communication leading to the knowledge generation and development of thinking abilities, "student and teacher identities are also actively negotiated in the interpersonal space that the ZPD forms" (p. 366). Cummins' major point relates to the patterns that develop within these contexts of interaction, as they can lead to either *coercive or collaborative relations of power*, and "real change in the education of culturally diverse students is likely to occur only when competitive and coercive social structures shift towards cooperative ones" (p. 366). Last, Cummins recommended that the socioacademic framework be refined by incorporating the operating assumption that the curriculum to which students are exposed "is not neutral with respect to power relations between societal groups [thereby necessitating] development of the critical thinking abilities required to deconstruct systematic disinformation used to bolster coercive relations of power" (pp. 386–387). Cummins' insightful critique and recommendations contributed substantively to the refinement and robustness of the socioacademic framework.

Freedman and Liu (1996) applied the socioacademic framework in a study within which a group of twenty-one Asian American students, mainly Hmong (18), at a technology-magnet middle-school in a midwestern state corresponded electronically with culturally dissimilar students and geographies—White Americans in a rural setting; Native Americans on a reservation—at two middle-school sites in two states. Non-Asian American students within the same classes as the Asian American students were also included in the study, making possible inter-cultural site-specific comparisons. The Asian American students interacted within three subject-matter contexts, each having one teacher: art, creative writing, and social studies. A thematic case study approach was used in which qualitative and quantitative methods were applied to gather and analyze information relative to three thematic areas: computer knowledge, learning processes, and communication patterns.

The researchers modeled the students' learning of the curriculum content along the classroom-to-classroom, computer-based collaborative approach used within the Orillas project (Sayers, 1994). In keeping with the Orillas model, two grouping strategies were employed. One being a computer-based pen-pal structure, which enabled students to correspond individually and in small groups with their White American and Native American peers at the two other schools in two other states. The other strategy, a group-to-group structure, facilitated cross-site/cross-state development of collaboratively planned assignments to ensure the engagement of all students in common instructional activities, and allowed for the three-way exchange of completed projects by students.

Methods used to gather information included participant observation (90 hours); pre-study and post-study structured interviews (10 open-ended questions); survey questionnaires (students' computer experience and attitudes toward other ethnic groups); and student journals (thoughts regarding sharing their culture and learning about other cultures, and about the project, communication between people from different cultures, life inside and outside of school, and hopes for the future). Freedman and Liu used a topic-based content analysis technique to analyze the 10-week compilation of network correspondence; pre-determined topics included family, school, community, and social issues, including the importance of family in the students' lives, interactions with students of different ethnic backgrounds, and the like. Pre-determined topics were complemented by free-choice discussion in which students chose to discuss, in some cases, topics specific to their own cultures. The researchers categorized the coded topics thematically—computer knowledge, learning processes, and communication patterns—and then sub-categorized within each theme to identify trends. Post-study interview questions related to the students' experiences during the study, including "their communication with their peer corre-spondents, and knowledge they gained about computers and culture (mainstream American, Hmong, Native American, etc.)" (Freedman & Liu, 1996, p. 49).

Although the students attended a technology magnet school, findings indicated that the majority of the Asian American students had been introduced later to computers (at age 10 years or older) than their non-Asian American counterparts (7 to 9 years of age) at the same school, and fewer had computers at home (30%) than their non-Asian American peers (40%). Asian American students were found to experience "greater difficulty" using computers than their non-Asian counterparts and tended to work on a technical (mechanical manipulation), rather than creative (learning new software, understanding computer processes), level. Asian American boys tended to dominate computer use and talk, as Asian American girls disengaged "without comment," a finding the researchers attributed to the students acceptance of "male domination" within Hmong traditional culture (p. 51), mentioning also that the students lower socio-economic class may also have influenced their behavior.

Freedman and Liu also found that particular male students were identified as leaders to whom Asian American female students, as well as other male Asian American students, deferred; the male leaders controlled computer use to a greater degree than others, were the spokespersons for the group when teachers or researchers asked questions or made comments to the group, and worked at the computer without receiving suggestions from others as to what should be typed. Regarding this latter point, when students who were not identified as leaders were generating e-mails at the computer, other students, including leaders, would make recommendations as to what should be typed. Leadership identification was a function of individual and family factors. These included the length of time spent in the United States and mastery of English, as well as whether a male student's father was a leader in the local Asian community, and "Hmong's traditions of leadership as determined by family, wealth, knowledge, and interpersonal skills" (p. 51).

Asian American students also reported a greater knowledge of computers than their behavior exhibited, which the researchers attributed to the students' beliefs relating to what constitutes computer knowledge (typing, for example) and "a certain cultural disposition toward self-representation. The students were concerned about saving face, and did not want to seem as if they lacked computer knowledge" (p. 51). The Asian American students rarely asked for help, declined it when offered by a teacher, and looked to their peers in those cases where assistance was determined to be really needed. In these latter instances, the peer whose assistance was sought would typically do the work rather than serving as a tutor or otherwise helping the student to learn how to do it. This was not the case for the non-Asian American students, who, in comparable interactions, requested assistance and were engaged in tutor-type, explanation-rich interactions with their peers.

In e-mail interactions with White American or Native American peers, Asian American students, including male leader students, typically did not ask questions of their counterparts, preferring to make comments in response to peer-generated questions; thus, Asian

American students generally were prompted by their teachers to pose questions in their e-mails. The researchers attribute this finding to discourse-related cultural values:

> Asian American students, particularly of the girls, tended to inhibit verbal investigation. Unlike many of the non-Asian students, the Asian American students felt that asking questions, particularly personal questions, was inappropriate; and yet, they were interested in reading and discussing their correspondents' answers to questions. Some of these students learned to ask questions over time as they developed an understanding of the importance of questioning for stimulating responses from e-mail correspondents. However, none of the Asian American students were really comfortable with this part of the project. (p. 52)

Culture also appeared to play a role in terms of how quickly Asian American students would initiate working on a computer-based task assigned by the teacher, when compared to their non-Asian American counterparts. When tasks contained elements that were more familiar to the students, they engaged more rapidly in the assignment. The researchers interpreted this finding to be associated with the Asian American students' "cultural background and life experiences."

Asian American students, unlike their non-Asian American peers, refrained from using trial-and-error or experimental methods required to complete several assignments, stating, when asked, that "they did not think it would help them get an idea" (p. 53). Again, rather than request assistance, many of the Hmong students preferred to engaged in repetitive tasks to feign engagement in the assigned task, which the researchers associated with the cultural notion of saving face. When compared to their non-Asian American peers, Asian American students preferred not to be observed as they worked at the computer or to engage in discussion with a teacher or researcher about their work. Their non-Asian American peers generally did not mind being observed or engaging in conversation with a teacher or the researchers. In keeping with this finding, Hmong students tended to classify themselves as "shy" and speak Hmong when grouped together at the computer.

As cultural events, such as Hmong New Year, occurred during the study, and Hmong students wanted to share their knowledge of it with their electronic correspondents, the students found that they had to learn more about their native culture as they did not know the rationale or meaning associated with certain activities. The seemingly innocuous process of gathering information regarding the Hmong New Year from within the community was tempered by the male dominance cultural tradition, as knowledge and its sharing, particularly regarding rites and rituals, were generally a male domain. Thus, both male and female students were concerned as to the ability of female students to engage in the task, although they expressed a desire to do so. The researchers summarize their finding:

> As a result, a careful process of negotiation with and between the students (and some parents) was undertaken. By the end of the project, the Hmong students had developed a common knowledge and level of comfort; however, the boys retained dominance in leadership, in part as a result of the amount of their cultural knowledge. (p. 54)

There were statistically significant differences in the responses of urban Asian American and urban non-Asian American students regarding friendship patterns (urban Asian American students reported fewer friends with different ethnic backgrounds), cross-cultural cooperation (Asian American students were less likely to cooperate with classmates from various ethnic backgrounds), and preference for inter-group relations (Asian Americans preferred to have *less* contact with people from *inside* their group).

Their findings indicated that students of different ethnic backgrounds may vary with respect to attitudes about and knowledge of computers, cross-cultural communication patterns, and learning processes—in this case, when working in a computer-intensive learning context. Freedman and Liu (1996) conclude that the

> most practical result of the study is that the Hmong students did not use computers in ways similar to their classmates, suggesting that attention be given to cultural differences in learning with computers....Computer networking could be used to help students have contact with people they might otherwise never encounter and provide a level of comfort in communication that students may not even feel with their own classmates. However, as DeVillar and Faltis (1991) argue, networking students should not be considered a replacement for the promotion of positive face-to-face interactions. (pp. 57–58)

These findings led Freedman and Liu to recommend that "an understanding of the cultures of the students" should be added to the socioacademic framework.

The Expanded Socioacademic Framework and Technology for Social Participation

We, the authors, consider the expanded socioacademic framework—to include the two refinements (critical inquiry and culture) offered by Cummins (1994) and Freedman and Liu (1996), respectively—a relevant means to realize long-term social and academic gains within and across student groups. This perspective, we feel, remains valid even, or perhaps more so, in today's intensely electronically centered, computer-mediated social networking context within which students —and to a lesser-but-expanding degree, the general public—operate on what may be termed, without exaggeration, a 24/7 basis. The value of face-to-face contact in social relations, including learning, was based on the operating assumption that, given the constraints of time, resources, and cost, *not* meeting face-to-face would exacerbate barriers to negotiation, understanding, collaboration, cooperation, mastery and similar learning or community-building goals. There were, of course, other associated factors, such as the inability to see a person's non-verbal and paralinguistic behaviors that help us to define and interpret the interaction and, therefore, to make adjustments to it. Setting has been considered important both as a natural (social) and political (power, control) element informing the communicative experience. Simply stated, communicative goal achievement was associated with physical presence.

The constraints of time, resources and cost have been generally resolved, as electronic communication devices are ubiquitous, and getting lighter in weight, smaller in size, and more powerful in transmission/reception strength and application capacity. Image transmission/reception, in still and motion forms, has also been refined to the point that electronic face-to-face (e.g., Skype) is accessible at reasonable costs and virtually without regard for time or space constraints in the developed countries, as well as the developed parts of developing countries, of the world. (There remains the major problem in both developed and developing countries of extending services to underserved, low-income communities.) Thus, our notion of the value of face-to-face contact as a *sine qua non* relative to communication and its valued derivatives such as learning, community building, and the like, must be questioned, particularly as the socio-cultural transformation may have already occurred in practice, leaving theory, research, institutional canons, conventional wisdom, and even opinion, to catch up. Our notion of what constitutes a setting has been similarly transformed in practice, as have been, perhaps, the constraints or advantages associated with it. "Have device, Will communicate" may be the only communicative principle required to achieve the complex and multifaceted goals, whether individual or group, associated with communication.

The essential vehicle and expectation of communication, in its social interaction sense, is conversation. Moreover, within the conversation paradigm, negotiation of meaning is a primary, although not necessarily conscious, process that ideally leads to mutual agreement and understanding; negotiation can also result in transformation through creating meaning that is both socially constructed and socially shared. Thus, the manner in which conversation is modified, produced and shared socially within the context of electronic, image-driven, unconstrained-by-space-and-time, application-rich, handheld devices, or other electronic tool of varying sizes, becomes a relevant question to ponder and pursue. The point of commonality between technology and human communication is conversation, albeit transformed in character and potential power. Conversation within this technological context is reiteratively negotiated and produced, independent of time or space, to socially produce new meaning, refine existing meaning, or reinforce established meaning. Marshall (2010) describes the combinatory phenomenon and its value in the following manner:

> When looking for the common denominators in both the Web 2.0 world and more traditional research contexts, I see participation in conversation as the root activity. This is not simply conversation as a metaphor, but conversation represented by Gordon Pask's conversation theory (Pask, 1975a, 1975b, 1976). This is a well established theory developed in the context of cybernetics. The appeal of these systems, in my opinion, is that they are removing the time and space boundaries which have historically limited human conversations. Now we are able to converse with almost

anyone anywhere and benefit from the preserved conversations of millions of people we will never meet. (p. 3)

A recent review of research, issues and opportunities (Chi, Munson, Fischer, Vieweg, & Parr, 2010) surrounding the relatively new concept of technology-mediated social participation (TMSP) also describes TMSP's societal transformative intent through technology-driven social participation:

> Research on social media has emerged from a set of activities aimed at understanding and developing technologies that enhance the intelligence of users, individually and in social collectives (Bush, 1945), through socially mediated information production and use, particularly in many new popular social websites and networks....Social media create technological, economic, and organizational disruptions that provide foundations to rethink and redefine learning, working, and collaboration and create new support environments for creativity and design, specifically social creativity and collaborative design....By providing infrastructures, seeds, and mechanisms for user-generated content, the fundamental transformation that we seek to understand complements and transcends Web 1.0 environments, which are dominated by broadcast media developed by professional designers for passive users, with the participatory Web 2.0. (2. Introduction, para. 3)

Thus, it is clear that face-to-face interactions, bound by physical presence, as a fundamental criterion for effective communication has been challenged by socially mediated technology participation, and that Web 2.0 is the current platform for enabling users to socially and actively participate, thereby empowering the social group in terms of size (unlimited), space (anywhere/everywhere), time (24/7/365) and meaning (consensus building through negotiation/refinement/ reinforcement of meaning) to address, engage and resolve issues and opportunities, "becoming co-creators of new ideas, knowledge, and products in personally meaningful activities" (Chi et al., 2010).

Within our current societal setting, then, communication is possible through physical and virtual interactions. Technology, at present, enables the two general communication types present in physical social interaction: one-way (passive) and two-way (participatory). The act of downloading text, sound or images, still or motion, to read (e.g., electronic books), listen to (e.g., audio import, storage and playback), or view (e.g., video streaming, DVDs), is considered passive.

Participatory communication is currently characterized by two subtypes: *surface communication* (social media) and *core communication* (social participatory).

The social media network phenomenon has been associated with surface communication, a general form of personally created, ego-fulfilling, instant, continually updated, communicative snippets of relative value in time and substance that are electronically shared with friends, family and others linked to the sender. This socially shared electronic phenomenon takes various specific interrelated forms—public diary, appointment book, scrapbook, messaging device, among others—and is enormously popular and free to subscribers. The leading social media network organization, Facebook, in July 2010 reported that 500 million people across the globe were actively using it (Zuckerberg, 2010). At present, the social contribution of surface media is, arguably, limited in purpose and scope: to inform others within the individual's network of one's activities that may or may not involve or be of interest to recipients.

The purpose of TMSP, a core communication phenomenon, is to bring people together in cooperative groups to address a common issue or set of issues that will contribute to the general good (Chi et al., 2010). As such, TMSP satisfies the two critical criteria associated with our expanded socioacademic (ESA) framework: TMSP's process incorporates all elements of the ESA framework—integration, communication, cooperation, criticalness and culture—and its twofold intent is to (a) foster a general and genuine sense of cohesion, and (b) effect change that contributes to the general good. The general good relates both to the individual and the social, as change within the ESA framework will contribute to the individual's ability to achieve and sustain his or her overall well-being, as well as to contribute meaningfully to that of his or her family, nation and community. Community in the sense we use it embraces the physical and virtual aspects embedded in the term. That is, its operational definition includes the group of people defined by the relatively narrow limits of local borders, as well as those included in the expanded (borderless) sense—namely, the group of people one can reach, interact with, influence, and contribute to regardless of space or time.

The goals associated with change would be consistently approached by the change-agents (anyone participating and contributing to a particular area within a TMSP arena in the positive sense defined here) through social interactions conducted within discourse settings structured by principles of cooperative learning and two-way communication. This scenario and the criteria associated with it allow for open access, negotiation and meaning-making. Discourse, moreover, would be consistently informed and refined by principles of critical thinking and communicative expression that value negotiation as a means to establish points of commonality that lead to action-related contributions. At the national level, for example, the goal of engaging in discourse of this nature relates to ultimately transcending the fear and animosity relative to group differences that our nation has engendered, prolonged and left unchallenged, socially (*de facto*) if not now legally (*de jure*). At the same time, such discourse would foster, instill and allow for the re-emergence of behaviors that reflect, sustain, refine and expand the egalitarian and related set of democratic, unifying principles that comprise our founding rhetoric and define our nation, as a body, and each one of us, as individuals. We would be, so to speak, of like mind with respect to honoring, embodying and acting upon our founding national rhetoric.

Chapter 10

The Reform Imperative and Metacultural Unity

I would like to shout this from the rooftops every time I hear another argument for "talented and gifted" programs, for tougher "standards" and stricter discipline, for streaming or tracking, for merit awards and opportunity schools and honors programs—in short, for any of the hundred and one affronts to equal provision of education. An education that privileges one child over another is giving the privileged child a corrupted education, even as it gives him or her a social or economic advantage.

—Connell, 1993

I am convinced that the current rhetoric of education reform...and how it is to be...delivered...speaks only false promises and portends failure.

—Eugene Glass, 2008

In previous chapters, we shed light on the dualism that has defined and now seriously undermines our development and future, as a people, nation and global leader. The dualism is characterized by the inter-group tensions generated by deeply rooted exclusionary practices based on a dominant-subordinate paradigm that fragments us in constant conflict with the perhaps even more deeply rooted elegant and universal rhetoric that allows each and every one of us to claim equality and unity as our birthright. These tensions continually have surfaced and played themselves out on the broad, variegated socio-political and geographic landscapes of our nation throughout our history. Earlier in Chapter 9, we characterized our national stage as a milieu to distinguish it as a particularly American setting that has enabled us to embrace, at times entangle, operationally both the diverse-*cum*-divisive social and cultural elements and the more abstract elements of equality, freedom and unity without succumbing to a second Civil War or consistent mass violence. Rather, as we mentioned earlier, our milieu has allowed and enabled our long-term, dynamic and troubled discourse of negotiation relative to resolving the conflict produced by these two co-existing, yet ultimately mutually exclusive, paradigms of American nationhood.

The tensions were natural, as was the long-term conflict that ensued, given our explicitly racist, exclusionary status as a nation that, at the same time, purported to be the world's greatest democracy. However, to a great degree and from a legal perspective, the major tensions that had threatened the internal peace and stability of our nation were resolved by 1965. Yet, as we near the half-century mark that highlighted our progress in human rights and democracy, we remain, emotionally, whether as members of the mainstream populous, elected representatives or professional leaders, adamant in clinging desperately to our myopic perspective and archaic belief that a group's physical and putatively cultural differences determine its relative placement on some vague natural hierarchical scale of group performance and privilege. There are many operative terms in the latter statement, but *group*, *natural* and *putatively* are especially key to understanding the distorted logic that characterizes the long-held, but ultimately doomed perspective and belief.

There now appears to exist a distributed understanding that this continued tension is not serving our country well, particularly with respect to generating on a sustained basis a profitable expansion and distribution of income within our internal economy or the dynamic development of human capital. Whether the "wake-up call" was triggered by international events in which we competed, as Secretary of Education Arne Duncan admitted in December 2010 upon receiving the news of our nation's mediocre PISA scores in math, science and reading (Anderson, 2010) or by our domestic inability to reform K–16 educational institutions in the equitable and high-performing vision to which we aspire, the die seems to have been cast. Thus, there will be substantial, energetic—perhaps even frenzied—and highly visible *movement* in the fields of economics and education within our nation for the foreseeable future. Whether the movement is characterized by incremental progress—much less substantive reform or even transformation—is yet to be seen. Definitely, it will be a challenge for us, as a nation or as individual states, to engage in relevant, sustained reform- or transformation-oriented alternatives. The main reason being that the short-term, simple, quick-fix alternative that may sound plausible, particularly when well-funded, has been favored over long-term, research-informed and research-monitored alternatives that are more complex. Anxiousness is no substitute for preparedness.

We conclude, therefore, by presenting recent research-based recommendations as to how our schools can provide the leadership, teachers, curriculum and context to move us toward sustained and generalized quality schooling experiences and competitive achievement outcomes. The desired transformation, of course, will not occur overnight, so the degree to which these, or alternate, recommendations are implemented must be monitored, and assessments regularly and objectively administered, to determine the degree of progress made toward the envisioned goal or set of goals. The type, quality and amount of resources we commit to, and the time we invest in, addressing and meeting our goals will serve to substantively and ultimately erode the fragmentation that threatens our national wellbeing and capital development in all its diverse forms. Our commitment also will place us on an accelerated trajectory toward metacultural cohesion—a cohesion that derives its spirit and impetus from, and reflects the values, principles and practices inherent in, our founding documents, specifically, the Declaration of Independence and the Constitution of the United States.

Research-Informed Recommendations

In actual fact, we have not made substantive progress as a nation insofar as adhering to a framework that would foster socioacademic achievement or promote cohesion. Our national schooling crisis has not improved relative to the three areas of integration, communication or cooperation in the twenty years since the original socioacademic achievement framework was published (DeVillar & Faltis, 1991), much less the two additional areas of critical inquiry and culture that characterize the expanded framework described in Chapter 9. There are, nevertheless, examples of instructional settings that correspond to the ESA framework's elements, but they are the exception that our nation needs to transform into the rule. Darling-Hammond (2010) provides an excellent research-based example of effective practices by a teacher that build cohesion through the incorporation of the essential elements of integration, communication, cooperation, criticalness and culture, as proposed in the ESA framework.

> Maria's teaching illustrates what scholars have found regarding effective teachers of students of color: that such teachers, whatever their own racial/ ethnic background, develop classrooms that create a sense of community and team, featuring cooperative learning strategies and inclusive participation. They use an active, direct approach to teaching: demonstrating, modeling, discussing, organizing engaging tasks, giving feedback, reviewing and emphasizing higher-order skills....[T]hey are able to form and maintain connections with their students, inviting children to share who they are and what they know in a variety of ways. As they develop curriculum, they also draw on cultural referents—texts, examples and models of people and practices—that connect to students' experiences and identities, honor their families and communities, and provide message of inclusion to all students. (p. 213)

The educational issue that we face as a nation relates to successfully educating our nation's children. This problem is compounded for three immediately evident reasons. First, as a nation, we have not been successful historically in serving the academic needs of the majority of students from low-income backgrounds, particularly if they were from racially, ethnically or linguistically distinct groups; thus, we have not only not solved the problem, but it has been exacerbated by the next two factors. Second, as the costs of education rise, budgets are cut, and resources become scarcer, children are coming to school poorer, as poverty is on the increase. Third, our nation's population growth is experiencing a high birth rate among the Hispanic American community, which represents approximately sixteen percent of our population, while the birth rate of African Americans is relatively stable, and that of White Americans maintains itself at approximately a zero birth rate. Asian Americans have the second highest birth rate in the nation. Minority group members now account for 35 percent of our nation's population. Hispanic Americans number 48.4 million; African Americans, 37.7 million; Asian Americans, 13.7 million; Mixed Race Americans, 5.3 million. White

Americans account for 35 percent of our nation's population, number 199.9 million and continue to decrease in proportion to the rest of the population (U.S. Hispanic Population, 2010).

The fact that more poor and minority children will be enrolled in our schools and that our success rate relative to guiding them through the educational cycle remains exceedingly low, leads us to present research-based recommendations from publications by independent scholars or professionals within agencies that address to varying degrees one or more of the five elements associated with the ESA framework. Goal statements and recommendations tend to be stated in a language that is general, which makes measurement difficult. The followings goals and recommendations, then, must be supported by objectives, which generally, and by convention, represent the measurable elements within a proposed program or project. Objectives were not part of the reports or other publications that we reviewed, as they were general in nature. However, the point of sharing the goals and recommendations is to illustrate the shared urgency, mandate for enlightened and comprehensive action, and incipient sense of unity found within the writings of researchers and educational professionals alike regarding educational reform. It is common knowledge among researchers and educational professionals that our nation's schools are severely in need of rapid, substantive and successful reform and that we must transform our declining degree of national school-completion rates, including higher education degree rates, and our competitiveness in the global arena if our nation is to improve its economic base and maintain its global leadership position and credibility.

Darling-Hammond (2010) offers research-informed recommendations in three interrelated areas—the classroom, schools and school districts, and national policy—that contribute to our understanding of what needs to be done to create successful schools, practices and policies throughout our nation. Regarding developing teacher quality in the classroom, we need to develop an infrastructure that will ensure competent and quality teaching as a rule. The placement of "teaching schools" in urban areas to create an environment that would both support school transformation and serve as training for teachers would be a step in the right direction.

Teacher residency models, whereby students learn to teach in the classroom of an expert teacher for a year while taking meaningful and well-constructed coursework from partner universities have produced highly competent and long-term teachers for urban schools. Mentoring by master teachers of new teachers at the beginning of their careers is another essential element that will support successful teacher development. Last, evaluating the efficacy of instruction through the use of performance-based assessment and National Council for Accreditation of Teacher Education (NCATE) standards, as well as providing meaningful and high-quality professional development to enable practicing teachers to continue their growth are important steps to ensure teacher quality and improved student learning and outcomes (Darling-Hammond, 2010).

In the area of schools and school districts, Darling-Hammond (2010) contributes the following research-informed recommendations. High levels of achievement are associated with "smaller, more personalized units in which teachers plan and work together around shared groups of students and common curriculum" (p. 239). Successful schools also are characterized by the presence of collaborative learning structures, maintaining students together across various grade levels, and having the students taught by a common core of teachers who are authorized sufficient time to plan instruction together. Additional characteristics of school and school district success include "involving staff in school-wide problem solving, involving parents in their children's education, and fostering cooperative learning" (p. 239).

Turning to national policy, Darling-Hammond (2010) begins with a quote that sets the stage to see how well we have done relative to the educational achievement goals:

> In 1989, then-President George H.W. Bush and the nation's governors established a set of six national goals to be accomplished by the year 2000. Among these were the goals to ensure that all students enter a school healthy and ready to learn, that the high school graduation rate would increase to at least 90%, that all students would be competent in the academic disciplines—including science, foreign languages, civics, arts, history, and geography, as well as math and English—and be prepared for responsible citizenship, and the United State would be "first in the world in mathematics, and science achievement" by the year 2000. (p. 278)

Darling-Hammond reminds us that these goals were never met, and, even worse, that "we are further away from achieving most of them than we were two decades ago" (p. 278). President Obama has now restated the goal and extended the timeline: "[B]y 2020, America will once again have the highest proportion of college graduates in the world" (Duncan, 2010, p. 69).

Darling-Hammond recommends a new paradigm for national and state education policy guided by "twin commitments to *support meaningful learning* on the part of students, teachers, and schools and to *equalize access to educational opportunity*, making it possible for all students to profit from more productive schools" (p. 279). She deems the following five areas as essential in implementing the new paradigm:

1. Establish nationally meaningful learning goals consistent with the knowledge and skills required for success in the 21st century to guide the development of high-quality standards, curriculum and assessments of student learning in each state.
2. Create intelligent, reciprocal accountability systems that ensure quality teaching and sufficient learning opportunities through government funding and ways to continuously evaluate and improve the quality of curriculum, instruction and school capacity.
3. Ensure equitable and adequate resources provided by federal and state governments so that all students have an adequate opportunity to meet the required learning standards.
4. Develop strong professional standards and supports for all educators that include high-quality teacher preparation, mentoring for new teachers, and continued professional learning and development for their entire career with special incentives and assistance for those who dedicate themselves to working with high-need students.
5. Develop schools organized for student and teacher learning to enable professionals to work collaboratively to build curricula that concentrate on essential subject matter and proficiencies, strengthened by highly informed practices and robust performance assessments that enable students to demonstrate the real world application of learning.

There is a complementary call for K–16 pipeline-sensitive, post-secondary reform. A report titled *The College Completion Agenda: 2010 Progress Report by the College Board* (Lee & Rawls, 2010) presented the following overarching goal identified by the Commission on Access, Admission, and Success in Higher Education, and the ten recommendations to attain it. The Commission was motivated to develop the goal and related recommendations by the declining educational competitive status of our nation when compared to other countries. Specifically, the Commissioner "noted the alarming decline of educational attainment ranking among 25- to 34-year-olds, with the United States ranking 12th out of 36 nations" (p. 9). The multifaceted, pipeline-specific goal statement declared what our nation was to achieve by the year 2025:

> Increase the proportion of 25- to 34-year-olds who hold an associate degree or higher to 55 percent by the year 2025 in order to make America the leader in educational attainment in the world.

This goal is set to be achieved five years after President Obama's goal of 2020, which underscores that nationally linked goals are more likely to be reached, everything else being equal, when we are all on the same page, particularly in terms of schedule. We quote the ten recommendations associated with the goal:

1. Provide a program of voluntary preschool education, universally available to children from low-income families, such that all children at or below 200 percent of the official poverty line have a chance to enter school ready to learn.
2. Improve middle and high school college counseling by meeting professional staffing standards for counselors and involving colleges and universities in college planning.
3. Implement the best research-based dropout prevention programs, which include early identification of those students who are at risk of dropping out and subsequently providing them a safety net.
4. Align the K–12 education system with international standards and college admission expectations so that all students are prepared for future opportunities in education, work and life.
5. Improve teacher quality and focus on recruitment and retention; an education system can only be as good as its teachers.
6. Clarify and simplify the admission process; a transparent and less complex process will encourage more first-generation students to apply.

7. Provide more need-based grant aid while simplifying and making financial aid processes more transparent; to minimize student debt and at least keep pace with inflation, make financial aid processes more transparent and predictable, and provide institutions with incentives to enroll and graduate more low-income and first-generation students.
8. Keep college affordable by controlling college costs, using available aid and resources wisely, and insisting that state governments meet their obligations for funding higher education.
9. Dramatically increase college completion rates by reducing the number of dropouts, easing transfer processes and using data-based approaches to improve completion rates at both two- and four-year institutions.
10. Provide postsecondary opportunities as an essential element of adult education programs by supplementing existing basic skills training with a new "honors GED" and through better coordination of existing adult education, veterans benefits, outreach programs and student aid. (Lee & Rawls, 2010, p. 2)

Another approach to reform is to learn from successful educational systems from around the world. Mourshed and Fenton (2010) recently identified elements from schools they claim are "the world's best," to support successful educational reform in our nation. First, however, they share evidence that serves to justify the need for reform:

> By age three, kids with professional parents are already a full year ahead of their poorer peers. They know twice as many words and score 40 points higher on IQ tests. By age 10, the gap is three years. By then, some poor children have not mastered basic reading and math skills, and many never will: this is the age at which failure starts to become irreversible. (para. 1)

Furthermore, according to the authors, our nation's school should emulate Finnish schools with respect to every child completing basic education; in the United States that would translate to graduating with a regular diploma from high school. Mourshed and Whelan state that KIPP charter schools accomplish this and that eighty percent of their high school graduates "make it to college." The achievement is all the more gratifying as the students enrolled are "from the poorest families." Gaps can be narrowed, as Singapore demonstrated by narrowing the gap among ethnic minorities from 17 percent to 5 percent over a 20-year period. Our nation, in contrast, has lived with heightened gaps for more than half a century. High-quality preschool attendance, more hours and even days spent in school, effective and sustained professional development for teachers, and timely and extensive extra support for students who need it.

These achievements by other countries should alert us to understand that our nation can effect dramatic changes, and that we must not surrender to hopelessness regarding either our educational system or its teachers, and most certainly not our students or their families. In a recent interview in *Ebony* (Barnett & Chappell, 2010, p. 70), President Obama shared his impression relative to the consequences of a sustained achievement gap and the need for reform: "This achievement gap is going to be an albatross around the neck of our economy if we don't solve it." The President also stated that our communities need to sufficiently fund their school districts, and that the federal government should provide "stabilization funds" during periods of recession, such as the present one. He stressed the importance of parents, regardless of income status or length of time in the United States, universally "emphasizing high levels of achievement." The President implies that reform is driven within homes by a commitment to educational high achievement and school completion on the part of parents, whether in dual-parent or single-parent households, as reform at the household level, according to President Obama, "doesn't require money" (p. 71). We understand the need for hope and emotional support, but family, neighborhood and after-school programs are of critical value to complement and reinforce such emotional support with concrete programs and channels related to educational reform. Another area of concern regarding the President's reform agenda is that it is competitively based, meaning that states have to compete for funding, knowing that sufficient funds will not be available for distribution to every state in the amounts requested or even at all. The obvious question to pose is what reforms can take place when there are no funds to effect them? President Obama once again articulates his belief that money isn't required in this instance as well:

> Not all of [the 46 states] got funding in that first year, but because they all were competing for it, they all ended up changing their laws and strengthening reform efforts. So what we've already seen is a much more aggressive reform agenda at the local level with a relatively small amount of

money. How fast we start seeing results...is going to depend on how aggressive that particular school district is. (p. 71)

Commitment and aggressive competition without tangible, nationwide distribution of economic support, appear to be the salient recommendations by the President relative to engaging in and achieving educational reform over the next "decade or 15 years" (p. 72). (President Obama has also informally extended his 2020 timeline by five years to 2025.)

Moreover, school-age children should engage in service, to learn to "give back," which President Obama thinks should start in the home, by doing chores, for example. More structured service experiences are recommended for elementary school students as well, as it presents a "great opportunity to network and get exposure to a wider group of people who can end up being helpful to you" (p. 71). The President is mindful that income status plays a role in the type and degree of service in which a student can engage. Privileged students, for example, can more readily engage in not-for-profit service experiences, while other students must work—and he includes himself in this group, as he stated that "I had to work at Baskin-Robbins...just to make money. So it's not always an even playing field. But I think the general principle applies" (p. 71). There are sufficient gaps in the logic of the President's statements in this interview to question the degree to which the above general principle applies to the priority of service that "gives back" when so many poor and low-income students have so many educationally related needs that remain unattended to by our nation. Thus, although we present these particular recommendations of the President, they neither reflect the elements within the ESA framework elaborated upon in Chapter 10, nor will they contribute to effective educational reform.

Conclusion

It is obvious that educational reform is a major undertaking, but particularly at the national level, where we have engaged in it for decades with minimal results, at best. There seems to be little evidence that we are sufficiently cohesive or even in general agreement at present to engage in reform that is comprehensive and transformative, regardless of the fact that the reform imperative is demanding our informed, immediate and sustained action. As we have illustrated in this work, race, ethnicity and culture have exerted significant influence in how our nation has evolved as a society and cultural entity. The fact that our nation's egalitarian rhetoric was granted to White Americans and denied other groups has led to our current social, economic, and political differences and fragmentation.

As a nation, since the mid-1950s, we have struggled openly and covertly against integration, and our people are as segregated today, if not more, by race and ethnicity and income, than before *Brown* (1954). We have presented evidence regarding how our nation has attempted to maintain the privileged status of White Americans, from its inception to as recently as the last decade of the twentieth century. This preference for privilege may be still with us or re-emerging (Toobin, 2010). We have also described the intense and sustained struggles of civil rights activists and their supporters to transform our nation from one particularistic in law and custom to one universal in law and custom. The fact that we ever needed to struggle, one group against the other, to gain equality and equity is abhorrent enough—especially after we engaged in a Civil War. But we are fortunate in the sense that our *milieu*—the dramatic stage of our national context upon which our embedded contradictory beliefs of Americanness have played themselves out—affords us the opportunity to do so. And so the struggle continues. As does our fragmentation and its effects, which translates inevitably to the development of distinct microcultures that constrain our metacultural cohesion. The words of Jennings (2000) resonate with the above points:

> Something in Anglo-American history has preserved most of us from the ultimately worst governmental cruelty to persons. The rhetoric of liberty has behind it centuries of struggle by common people and elite sympathizers who detest the denial of life and dignity to other persons....[Ours has been a history] of raising the people to become *part* of the state instead of merely being *under* it.... The people's perceived definition of themselves as a White race became immensely important as a means of organizing power and equally as a source of delusion. It inspired and energized conquest, but sooner or later the offspring of Europe must encounter the multitudinous offspring of Asia, and those vastly numerous Asians will not tolerate presumptions of White superiority.... It would be best all around to discard

the delusions of race and to accept the need to share power and cooperate. (pp. 317–318)

There are currently many disturbing systemic conditions that threaten our well-being as individuals and as a nation and that demand our keen awareness if we are to effectively contend with and resolve them. Some of these conditions are the evidence of injustice due to racial, ethnic, religious, gender or other factors—each category, a trumped-up transgression applicable to a whole group; the three-decade-long economic deterioration of the general American public, particularly the poor and middleclass; the steady degradation of our nation's educational performance; the accelerating wealth gap between the very wealthy Americans and all other Americans (5 percent now own 62 percent of all wealth [Friedman, 2010]); and the rapid development of countries such as China, that are simultaneously resource-hungry and resource-rich, that compete vigorously and effectively for scarce resources and markets, and from whom we borrow and purchase in extraordinary amounts.

The list goes on, but the point is that we will not rise to the challenge of successfully confronting and resolving these issues if we are not united as a metaculture. This has been our purpose: to provide evidence of sustained privilege, albeit weakened by law in the latter half of last century, that conflicts with our founding rhetoric and spirit and influences the pace and commitment we have toward unity. The naïve logical fallacy of equating democracy with individualism and capitalism, and social programs that address our collective well-being with socialism, diminishes our reform alternatives and reinforces not only the status quo scenario of securing wealth for the few and depleting the asset base of the many, but also the unfortunate anti-intellectual modality to which we are prone. We cannot afford to continue down either of these nationally threatening trajectories.

At the same time, groups who were forcibly segregated, survived and developed their alternate cultures as best they could within the greater boundaries of the national culture. Inequalities prevailed as the segregated groups did not have rights to access the nation's institutions nor did they have the resources or rights to build their own. Thus, differences developed in the past that included language (standard vs. non-standard, elite vs. popular), education (formal vs.

informal; completion vs. non-completion; high quality vs. low quality); employment (sustained, upwardly mobile, dependable wage-salary, blue collar-to-professional vs. temporary, relative static mobility, unpredictable wage structure, laborer); sustained status differentials between privileged group and other groups ("We" vs. "the Other"); and culture (dominant vs. subordinate). Again, there are other outcomes, but our point is to emphasize that the dominant group will develop a cultural image and expression that is distinct from, and considered superior to, the subordinate cultures—and the dominant culture will be the standard that all others will be judged by, regardless of the degree to which they had access to it.

Our schools similarly have developed in distinct ways. So much so that our inner city schools are unrecognizable as an institution representative of the dominant culture—such schools are considered representative of the cultures of the students who inhabit them. With these types of misguided and antagonistic perceptions, there is little chance that reform agendas can be effective, as Anyon (1995, 2005, in Berliner, 2011) states:

> It has become increasingly clear that several decades of educational reform have failed to bring substantial improvements to schools in America's inner cities. Most recent analyses of unsuccessful school reform (and prescriptions for change) have isolated educational, regulatory, or financial aspects of reform from the social context of poverty and race in which inner city schools are located. [1995]

> Currently, relatively few urban poor students go past ninth grade: The graduation rates in large comprehensive inner-city high schools are abysmally low. In fourteen such New York City schools, for example, only 10 percent to 20 percent of ninth graders in 1996 graduated four years later. Despite the fact that low-income individuals desperately need a college degree to find decent employment, only 7 percent obtain a bachelor's degree by age twenty-six. So, in relation to the needs of low-income students, urban districts fail their students with more egregious consequences now than in the early twentieth century. (Anyon, 2005 in Berliner, 2011, pp. 514–515)

And, as the cultures of the schools have developed distinctly, so have the neighborhoods in which the students live and interact. This context forms their reality and the greater the cultural distance from the dominant culture, the less either one will reflect the other or that they will understand one another in terms of behavior or even values. We have socialized formally along difference and now we need to socialize for unity, which is only possible at the metacultural level for we have also socialized along lines of dominance and subordination, and we have to abandon that practice and destroy that legacy. The differences are striking, as evinced in the passionate statement by Connell (1993, quoted in Apple, 1996):

> I would like to shout this from the rooftops every time I hear another argument for "talented and gifted" programs, for tougher "standards" and stricter discipline, for streaming or tracking, for merit awards and opportunity schools and honors programs—in short, for any of the hundred and one affronts to equal provision of education. An education that privileges one child over another is giving the privileged child a corrupted education, even as it gives him or her a social or economic advantage. (p. 94)

For reform to work, we, the people, must transform. We must see the disadvantage in extending and sustaining privilege and the advantage in providing quality schooling contexts, leaders, teachers, curricula and instruction for traditionally underserved students. This heightened sense of internally-directed perception is in the interest of metacultural self-preservation, as Guo Shuqing, Chairman of China Construction Bank, understands (Shuqing, 2010):

> In increasingly tense international competition, differences in costs, wages and land prices are becoming less important than factors such as human capital, the law, market regulation and the environment. For this reason, international competition is to a large extent a country's competition with itself. (p. 151)

We must understand the contribution that the sustained practice of equity will make to our populous and nation, as all will have access to quality schooling experiences, be able to participate meaningfully and regularly in all facets of learning and subject matter, and derive benefit from that access and participation. Similarly, through core communication experiences, in face-to-face and technology-mediated interactions, all students can develop as individuals, social beings, professionals and service-oriented community members who negotiate and contribute productively at local, national and global levels. We will have arrived at the nexus of our rhetoric and practice, and experienced the unity that has eluded us for centuries. We will have transformed from a culture of conflict to a culture of purpose. Above all, whatever sacrifices we must make at present to achieve this vision, once achieved, future generations will judge us to have invested well and wisely in our nation's people and future.

Notes

Chapter 2

1. "An arboreal anthropoid ape (simia satyrus), which inhabits borneo and Sumatra. It is over four feet high, when full grown, and has very long arms, which reach nearly or quite to the ground when the body is erect. Its colour is reddish brown. In structure, it closely resembles man in many respects" (http://www.biology-online.org/dictionary/Orang-outang). "Hottentot (1677), a member of a native South African race, the first met by the Dutch; [the Dutch word] *Hottentot* is supposed to mean 'stutterer or stammerer', and was applied to them because of the frequency of clicks in their speech" (Llewellyn, 1936).

2. The use of the term "immigrant" is necessary as, from 1790 to 1943, Chinese were not eligible for naturalization as American citizens regardless of the time they had been in the country; in 1952, the passage of the McCarran-Walter Immigration and Nationality Act repealed the exclusion laws against the immigration and naturalization of Asians.

Chapter 4

1. Kelly Miller (1863–1939) and George Schuyler (1895–1977) were intellectual activists and writers, who were contemporaries of DuBois (1868–1963) and differed from him regarding the presence of segregation in the North ("little or no"), preferring to attribute, however inaccurately, its presence to the American South. Miller was a noted scholar who first studied mathematics and then taught sociology at Howard University. Schuyler (1895–1977) was a well-known, controversial, even contentious, journalist and writer, as well as an anti-racist and vocal Socialist—although anti-Communist—who later in his life became a self-proclaimed conservative, even writing for the John Birch Society publication, *American Opinion* (Reed, 1999).

2. Lew and Bea Wechsler, former activists in Communist-led organizations and activities from the 1930s to the mid-1950s, were now residents of Levittown and owners of the house next door to the one the Myers would purchase. The Wechslers befriended the Myers family and were instrumental in recruiting them, as well as morally supporting them prior to and after their move to Levittown (Kushner, 2009).

3. See, for example, the documentary produced in 1957 and narrated by New York New York University Professor of Education Dan W. Dodson regarding attitudes of Whites toward the presence of the Myers family in Levittown, Pennsylvania, available at http://www.youtube.com/watch?v=bp22YlJlfHo&feature=PlayList&p=D9D691839B350F13&index=51.

4. Access is a necessary but not sufficient element of equity. DeVillar (1986, 1994, 2000) and DeVillar and Faltis (1987, 1991, 1994) have characterized equity as comprising three essential elements— access, participation and benefit—in the absence of which the United States cannot achieve its goal of universal *quality* schooling and *competitive* academic outcomes that are independent of race, ethnicity, class, gender or other features that singly or in combination have traditionally marked a particular group and hindered its learning and earning potential, as well as substantive civic participation and political influence.

Chapter 7

1. A native of Chicago, Saul Alinsky, 1909–1972, was a leading figure in community organizing.

Chapter 8

1. Carey states that the "TQI is a composite of six school-level measures of teacher qualifications that research suggests are associated with classroom effectiveness: Percentage of teachers with bachelor's degrees from more competitive colleges, as determined by Barron's Guide to College; percentage of teachers with less than four years of teaching experience; percentage of

teachers with emergency or provisional credentials; percentage of teachers who failed the state-required "Basis Skills Test" at least once; score on the Teachers' composite ACT score and Teachers' English ACT score.

2. The Supreme Court case is interesting also from a race-based policy and practice perspective. Homer Plessy, the plaintiff, who refused to change train cars—that is, from his seat from the "White" section of the train to the "colored" section of the same train, traveling within the state of Louisiana—was seven-eighths White, having only an African-origin great-grandmother among his recent immediate parentage (Hall, 1992, p. 637). Nevertheless, the United States officially adhered to and acted upon the "one-drop" rule, which designated all individuals as non-White who had any "colored blood" in their ancestry. The current racial designation policy and practice of the United States remains ambiguous and contradictory, particularly with respect to individuals of more than one race. In U.S. cultural parlance, Plessy could "pass" for White, and, indeed, why is a person of mixed race accorded the designation of one race, and the "subordinate" (hypodescent) one at that—even today? As F. James Davis (1991) states: "The concept of 'passing' rests on the one-drop rule and on folk beliefs about race and miscegenation, not on biological or historical fact."

References

ABC News (2006, December 4). Debate over segregation in schools to hit Supreme Court today. ABC Good Morning America. Retrieved from http://abcnews.go.com/GMA/story?id= 2698225&page=1.

ACLU (2004, September 15). Federal court rules South Dakota violated voting rights of Native Americans. American Civil Liberties Union news release. Retrieved from http://www.aclu.org/voting-rights/federal-court-rules-south-dakota-violated-voting-rights-native-americans.

Adelman, L. (2003). A long history of racial preferences—for Whites. Background readings. Race—The power of an illusion. PBS Home Programs. Retrieved from http://www.pbs.org/race/000_About/002_04-background-03-02.htm.

Adler, R. (2008, November-December). Counting on the middle class. *Miller-McCune*, 1(6), 20–23.

Ailon, G. (2008). Mirror, mirror on the wall: *Culture's Consequences* in a value test of its own design. *Academy of Management Review, 33*(4), pp. 885–904.

Allen, G. E. (n.d.). Flaws in eugenics research. Image Archive of the American Eugenics Movement. Retrieved from http://www.eugenicsarchive.org/eugenics/list2.pl.

Allport, G. (1954/1958). *The nature of prejudice*. New York: Doubleday Anchor.

Alvarez, R. R., Jr. (1986, spring). The Lemon Grove incident: The nation's first successful desegregation court case. *Journal of San Diego History, 32* (2). Retrieved from https://www.sandiegohistory.org/journal/86spring/index.htm.

American Renaissance.com (2006, April 3). Racial IQ research. Article originally published in *Times* (London), April 2, 2006. Retrieved from http://www.amren.com/mtnews/archives/2006/04/racial_iq_resea.php.

Anderson, N. (2010, December 7). International test score data show U.S. firmly mid-pack. *The Washington Post*. Education. Washington.com. Retrieved from http://www.washingtonpost.

com/wp-dyn/content/article/2010/12/07/AR2010120701178. html?wpisrc=nl_education&sid=ST2010120701251.

Andrews, M. (2010, January). The cost of healthcare. *National Geographic, 217*, p. 27.

Andrews, Molly (2004). Counter-narratives and the power to oppose. In M. Bamberg and M. Andrews (Eds.), Considering counter narratives: Narrating, resisting, making sense. Amsterdam, the Netherlands: John Benjamins, pp. 1–6.

Apple, M. W. (1996). *Cultural politics and education*. New York: Teachers College Press.

Aristotle (350 B.C.). *Nicomachean ethics* [Book V]. (W. D. Ross, Trans., 1925). *The Internet Classics Archives*. Retrieved from http://classics.mit.edu/ Aristotle/ nicomachaen.mb.txt.

Aristotle (350 B.C.). *Politics*. (B. Jowett, Trans., 1885). *The Internet Classics Archives*. Retrieved from http://classics.mit.edu/ Aristotle/politics.4.four.html.

Arndt, M. (2009, December 29 & 2010, January 4). Ben Franklin, where are you? *Bloomberg Businessweek*, 29.

Aud, S., Hussar, W., Planty, M., Snyder, T., Bianco, K., Fox, M., Frohlich, L., Kemp, J., and Drake, L. (2010, May). *The condition of Education 2010* (NCES 2010–028). Report of the National Center for Education Statistics, Institute of Education Sciences. Washington, D.C.: U.S. Department of Education.

Autism National Committee (n.d.). The I.Q. fallacy, A three part series. Retrieved February 4, 2010, from http://www.autcom.org/ articles/IQFallacy1.html.

Baertlein, L. (2009, December 18). FACTBOX: Facts about U.S. food stamps. *Reuters*. Retrieved from http://www.reuters.com/article/ idUSTRE5BH2DO20091218.

Bai, M. (2010, September 15). G.O.P. uses Obama 'Otherness' as campaign tactic. Politics section. *The New York Times*. Retrieved from http://www.nytimes.com/2010/09/16/us/politics/16bai.html.

Baker, C. (2006), *Foundations of bilingual education and bilingualism* (4th edition). Clevedon, England: Multilingual Matters, p. 194.

Baker, C. and Prys Jones, S. (1998). *Encyclopedia of bilingualism and bilingual education*. Clevedon, England: Multilingual Matters.

Banks, W. C., McQuater, G. V., Anthony, J. R., and Ward, W. E. (1992). Delayed gratification in Blacks: A critical review. In A. K. H. Burlew, W. C. Banks, H. P. McAdoo, and D. A. Y. Azibo (Eds.), *African American psychology: Theory, research and practice*. Newbury Park, CA: SAGE, pp. 330–345.

Barboza, D. (2010, August 15). China passes Japan as second-largest economy. *The New York Times*. Retrieved from http://www.nytimes.com/2010/08/16/business/global/16yuan.html.

Barnett, A. D. and Chappell, K. (2010, September). Education nation. *Ebony*, pp. 68–73.

Barraclough, G. (Ed.) (1978). The making of the United States. Excerpt from *The Times Atlas of World History*. London: Times Books, pp. 220–221. Retrieved from http://www.globalpolicy.org/component/content/article/155/25946.html.

Beard, C. A. and Beard, M. R. (1941). *The rise of American civilization*. New York: Macmillan.

Bennett, D. (2010, October 25–31). The inequality delusion. *Bloomberg Businessweek*, 8–11.

Berliner, D. C. (2011). Our impoverished view of educational reform. In A. R. Sadovnik (Ed.), *Sociology of education, A critical reader* (2nd edition). New York: Routledge, pp. 513–542.

Birnbaum, M. (2010, March 18). Historians speak out against proposed Texas textbook changes. *The Washington Post*. Retrieved from http://www.washingtonpost.com/wp-dyn/content/article/2010/03/17/AR2010031700560.html.

Bloomberg News (2010, August 16). China GDP surpasses Japan, capping three-decade rise. *Bloomberg Businessweek*. Retrieved from http://www.businessweek.com/news/2010-08-16/china-gdp-surpasses-japan-capping-three-decade-rise.html.

Bond, C. and Williams, R. (2007, December). Residential segregation and the transformation of home mortgage lending. *Social Forces*, 86 (2), pp. 671–698.

Boswell, S. and McConaghy, L. (1996, November 10). A resource divided. *The Seattle Times*. Retrieved from http://seattletimes.nwsource.com/special/centennial/november/resource.html.

Bourdieu, P. (1986). The forms of capital. In J. Richardson (Ed.), *Handbook of theory and research for the sociology of education*. New York: Greenwood, pp. 241–258.

Boyer, P. S. (Ed.) (2001). *The Oxford companion to United States history*. New York: Oxford University Press.

Bramlett, M. D. and Mosher, W. D. (2002, July). Cohabitation, marriage, divorce, and remarriage in the United States. Vital and Health Statistics 23(22). National Center for Health Statistics. Retrieved from http://www.cdc.gov/nchs/data/series/sr_23/sr23_022.pdf.

Brown, E. S. (1920). *The Constitutional history of the Louisiana Purchase, 1803–1812*. Berkeley, CA: University of California Press.

Brown v. Board of Education, 347 U.S. 483 (1954) (USSC+). [*Brown I*]. The National Center for Public Policy Research. Retrieved from http://www.nationalcenter.org/brown.html.

Brown v. Board of Education, 349 U.S. 294 (1955). [*Brown II*]. The National Center for Public Policy Research. Retrieved from http://www.nationalcenter.org/index.html.

Buckley, C. (2010, November 1–7). The "Mad as Hell" marketing strategy. [Review of the book *Tears of a clown: Glenn Beck and the tea bagging of America*]. *Bloomberg Businessweek*, 86–87.

Bureau of Labor Statistics (2010, August 6). Economic News Release. Employment Situation Summary. U.S. Department of Labor. Retrieved from http://www.bls.gov/news.release/empsit.nr0.htm.

Burris, C. C. and Welner, K. G. (2005). Closing the achievement gap by detracking. *Phi Delta Kappan*, 86(8), pp. 594–598.

Caldas, S. J. and Bankston, C. L., III. (2005). *Forced to fail: The paradox of school desegregation*. Westport, CT: Praeger.

Calhoun, C. (Ed.) (2002). *Dictionary of the social sciences*. New York: Oxford University Press.

Campi, A. (2004, June). The McCarran-Walter Act: A contradictory legacy on race, quotas, and ideology. Immigration Policy Center (American Immigration Law Foundation). Retrieved from http://www.ilw.com/articles/2004,0708-Campi.shtm.

Carlsen, E. (n.d.) Scientific origins of eugenics. Image Archive of the American Eugenics Movement. Retrieved from http://www. eugenicsarchive.org/ html/eugenics/essay2text.html.

Carr, C. (2006). *Our town: A heartland lynching, a haunted town, and the hidden history of white America.* New York: Crown.

Carey, K. (2007, January 7). How low teacher quality sabotages advanced high school math. Washington, D.C.: Education Sector. Retrieved from http://www.educationsector.org/publications/ how-low-teacher-quality-sabotages-advanced-high-school-math.

Castañeda v. Pickard, 648 F.2d 989 (5th Cir. 1981). Retrieved from http://www.stanford.edu/~kenro/LAU/IAPolicy/IA1bCastanedaF ullText.htm.

Caiazza, A., Shaw, A., and Werschkul, M. (2004, July). The status of women in the States: Women's economic status in the States: Wide disparities by race, ethnicity, and region. Washington, D.C.: Institute for Women's Policy Research. Retrieved from http:// www.iwpr.org/pdf/R260.pdf.

Central Intelligence Agency (2009a). Country comparison: Life expectancy at birth. *The World Factbook.* Retrieved from https://www.cia.gov/library/publications/the-world-factbook/ rankorder/2102rank.html.

Central Intelligence Agency (2009b). Country comparison: Infant mortality rate. Retrieved January 3, 2010, from https://www. cia.gov/library/publications/the-world-factbook/rankorder/2091 rank.html.

Central Intelligence Agency (2009c, November 27). Economic overview, United States. *The World Factbook.* Retrieved from https://www.cia.gov/library/publications/the-world-factbook/geos/ us.html.

Chappell, D. L. (2001). States' rights. In P. S. Boyer (Ed.), *The Oxford companion to United States history.* New York: Oxford University Press, p. 744.

Charles I, 1640. "Act for Adventurers'." *Statutes of the Realm, volume 5, 1628-80* (1819), pp. 173–174. Retrieved from http://www. british-history.ac.uk/report.aspx?compid=47246.

Chi, E. H., Munson, S., Fischer, G., Vieweg, S., and Parr, C. (2010, July 21). Design of social participation systems. National Science

Foundation Workshop on TMSP. Retrieved from http://www.
tmsp.umd.edu/TMSPreports_files/2.IEEE-Computer-TMSP-
Design.pdf.

Child Trends Data Bank (n.d.). Percentage of births to unmarried
women. Retrieved from http://www.childtrendsdatabank.org/
?q=node/196.

Children of the Camps Project (1999). Internment history. Retrieved
from http://www.pbs.org/childofcamp/index.html.

China surpasses U.S. in energy consumption (2010, July 19). *Business
News*. UPI.com. Retrieved from http://www.upi.com/Business_
News/2010/07/19/China-surpasses-US-in-energy-consumption/
UPI-36681279571734/.

Christman, J. (2009, August 11). Autonomy in moral and political
philosophy. *The Stanford Encyclopedia of Philosophy*. Retrieved
from http://plato.stanford.edu/entries/autonomy-moral/#AutPat.

CNBC.com (2007, September 4). A history of recessions. Retrieved
from http://www.cnbc.com/id/20510977/A_History_of_Recessions.

CNN (2010, August 24). Sherrod declines USDA job offer. *CNN
Political Ticker*. Retrieved from http://politicalticker.blogs.
cnn.com/category/usda/.

Cochran-Smith, M. (2003). The multiple meanings of multicultural
teacher education. *Teacher Education Quarterly, 30*(2), pp. 7–26.

Cochran-Smith, M., Davis, D., and Fries, K. (2004). Multicultural
teacher education: Research, practice and policy. In J. A. Banks
and C. A. Banks (Eds.), *Handbook of research on multicultural
education* (2nd edition). San Francisco, CA: Jossey Bass, pp. 931–
975.

Cohen, A. K. (1955). *Delinquent boys*. Glencoe, IL: Free Press.

Columbus Board of Education v. Penick, 443 U.S. 449 (1979).
FindLaw. Retrieved from http://caselaw.lp.findlaw.com/scripts/
getcase.pl?navby=case&court=us&vol=443&page=449.

Colvin, S. S. and Allen, R. D. (1923). Mental tests and linguistic ability.
The Journal of Educational Psychology, 14(1), pp. 1–20.

Comas, J. (1951/1969). Racial myths. *Race and science*. New York:
Columbia University Press, pp. 13–55. [Note: Second printing and
Columbia paperback edition, 1969.]

Congressional Oversight Panel (2009, December 9). Taking stock: what has the Troubled Asset Relief Program achieved? Congress of the United States. Washington, D.C. Retrieved from http://cop.senate.gov/reports/library/report-120909-cop.cfm.

Cookson, P.W. and Persell, C. H. (1985). *Preparing for power: America's elite boarding schools.* New York: Basic Books.

Costa, R. (2010, September 11). Gingrich: Obama's 'Kenyan, anti-colonial' worldview. *National Review Online.* Retrieved from http://www.nationalreview.com/corner/246302/gingrich-obama-s-kenyan-anti-colonial-worldview-robert-costa.

Courteau, S. L. (2009, Autumn). Ghosts of the heartland. [Review of the books *Hollowing out the middle: The rural brain drain and what it means for America* and *Methland: The death and life of an American small town*]. *Wilson Quarterly, 33,* pp. 101–102.

Crawford, J. and MacSwan, J. (2008, December 15). Letter to President-Elect Barack Obama. Institute for Language and Education Policy. Retrieved from http://www.elladvocates.org/documents/Statement_for_Obama_Transition.pdf.

Cronbach, L. J. (1975). Five decades of public controversy over mental testing. *American Psychologist, 30*(1), pp. 1–14.

Cummins, J. (1999). The ethics of doublethink: Language rights and the bilingual education debate. In R. A. DeVillar and T. Sugino (Eds.), One world, many tongues: Special issue on language policies and the rights of learners. *TESOL Journal, 8,* pp. 13–17.

Cummins, J. (1994). The socioacademic achievement model in the context of coercive and collaborative relations of power. In R. A. DeVillar, C. J. Faltis, and J. P. Cummins (Eds.), *Cultural diversity in schools: From rhetoric to practice.* Albany: State University of New York Press, pp. 363–390.

Cummins, J. (1991). Foreword. In R. A. DeVillar and C. J. Faltis, *Computers and cultural diversity.* Albany: State University of New York Press, pp. vii–ix.

Cummins, S. (2009, March 2). Maine towns opposed Indian Removal Act. *Old News from Southern Maine.* Retrieved from http://www.someoldnews.com/?p=36.

Cunningham, R. T. (1997). Market segmentation: The role of race in housing markets. In R. L. Bartlett (Ed.), *Introducing race and gender into economics*. New York: Routledge, pp. 42–51.

Curtis, M. K. (1992). Fourteenth Amendment. In K. L. Hall (Ed.), *The Oxford companion to the Supreme Court of the United States*. New York: Oxford University Press, pp. 309–311.

Daniels, R. (2008). Aspects of the Asian American experience: Rights denied and attained. *American Studies Journal, 51*. Retrieved from http://asjournal.zusas.uni-halle.de/archive/51/105.html.

Daniels, R. (1992). *Asian America: Chinese and Japanese in the United States since 1850*. Seattle, WA: University of Washington Press, 2nd printing.

Daniels, R. (1991). *Coming to America: A history of immigration and ethnicity in American life*. New York: HarperPerennial.

Daniels, R. and Kitano, H. H. L. (1970). *American racism: Exploration of the nature of prejudice*. Englewood Cliffs, NJ: Prentice-Hall.

Darcy, N. T. (1963). Bilingualism and the measurement of intelligence: Review of a decade of research. *The Journal of Genetic Psychology, 103*, pp. 259–282.

Darling-Hammond, L. (2010). *The flat world and education: How America's commitment to equity will determine our future*. New York: Teachers College Press.

Darling-Hammond, L. (2006). Securing the right to learn: Policy and practice for powerful teaching and learning. *Educational Researcher, 35*(7), pp. 13–24.

Davis, F. J. (1991). *Who is black?: One nation's definition*. University Park: The Pennsylvania State University Press. Excerpt retrieved from http://www.pbs.org/wgbh/pages/frontline/shows/jefferson/mixed/onedrop.html.

Davis, J. C. (Ed.) (2008). *On religious liberty: Selections from the works of Roger Williams*. Cambridge, MA: The Belknap Press of Harvard University Press.

Davis, K. C. (2010, October). God and country. *Smithsonian, 41*(6), pp. 86–96.

Davis, R. L. F. (n.d.). Creating Jim Crow: An in-depth essay. The history of Jim Crow Web site: http://www.jimcrowhistory. org/history/creating2.htm.

Day, J. C. (1996, February). Population projections of the United States by age, sex, race, and Hispanic origin: 1995 to 2050. U.S. Bureau of the Census. Current Population Reports, P25–1130. Washington, DC: U.S. Government Printing Office.

Debo, A. (2003). *A history of the Indians of the United States.* London: The Folio Society. Originally published 1970; Addenda, 1983; ninth printing, 2009.

Decker, P. T., Mayer, D. P., and Glazerman, S. (2004, June 9). *The effects of Teach for America on students: Findings from a national evaluation.* Mathematica Policy Research, Inc. Contract No.: CAPE 2001-004-01/Carnegie B7302; DB7302-R01, MPR Reference No.: 8792-750. Princeton, NJ.

Dedman, B. (1988a, May 1). Atlanta Blacks losing in home loans scramble. Banks favor white areas by 5-1 margin. *The Atlanta Journal-Constitution*, p. A1.

Dedman, B. (1988b, May 3). A test that few banks fail—in federal eyes. Regulators say 98% obey lending law, but skeptics say communities shorted. *The Atlanta Journal-Constitution*, p. A1.

Dedman, B. (1988c, September 11). Feds: Banks reject more black loans. *The Atlanta Journal-Constitution*, p. A1.

Dedman, B. (1988d, July 17). Federal study finds bias in lending across nation. *The Atlanta Journal-Constitution*, p. A1.

Dedman, B. (1988e, May 15). Black boycott forestalled by loan plan. Negotiations with ministers, publicity spur bankers to act. *The Atlanta Journal-Constitution*, p. A1.

Dedman, B. (1988f, May 25). Banking chief reverses stand calling for fair-lending laws. *The Atlanta Journal-Constitution*, p. A1.

Dedman, B. (1998g, May 2). Southside treated like banks' stepchild? Blacks may shun some home-loan lenders because they're shunned first, critics say. *The Atlanta Journal-Constitution*, p. A1.

Dell, M. (2009, February 3). Keynote. Northern Virginia Technology Council. Washington, D.C. Retrieved from http://content. dell.com/us/en/corp/d/speeches/MichaelDell-NVTCSpeech.aspx.

Democratic Policy Committee (2004, October 7). The American Indian vote: Celebrating 80 years of U.S. citizenship. Retrieved from http://democrats.senate.gov/dpc/dpc-new.cfm?doc_name= sr-108-2-283#foot11.

Dempsey, J. (2010, February 9). China passes Germany as world's top exporter. *The New York Times*, p. B9.

DeNavas-Walt, C., Proctor, B. D. and Smith, J. C. (2010, September). *Income, poverty, and health insurance coverage in the United States: 2009.* U.S. Census Bureau, Current Population Reports, P60–238. Washington, DC: U.S. Government Printing Office.

Desmond, H. (1907). The American Protective Association. *The Catholic Encyclopedia.* New York: Robert Appleton. Retrieved from New Advent Web site: http://www.newadvent.org/cathen/01426a.htm.

DeVillar, R. A. (2010, October). *Chinese scientific socialism in global perspective: Geopolitical implications for Latin American and the United States.* Paper presentation, China Goes Global Conference, John F Kennedy School of Government, Harvard University, Cambridge, MA.

DeVillar, R. A. (2000). Literacy and the role of technology: Toward a framework of equitable schooling. In J. V. Tinajero and R. A. DeVillar (Eds.), *The power of two languages, 2000: Effective dual-language use across the curriculum.* New York: McGraw-Hill School Division, pp. 320–336.

DeVillar, R. A. (1994). The rhetoric and practice of cultural diversity in U.S. schools: Socialization, resocialization, and quality schooling. In R. A. DeVillar, C. J. Faltis, and J. P. Cummins (Eds.), *Cultural diversity in schools: From rhetoric to practice.* Albany: State University of New York Press, pp. 25–56.

DeVillar, R. A. (1987, July–August). Los ordenadores y la equidad educativa en los Estados Unidos [Computers and Educational Equity in the United States]. TELOS, Cuadernos de Comunicación, Tecnología y Sociedad, número 10, ISSN: 1575-9393.Valencia, Spain, pp. 16–32. Available at Quaderns Digitals.net: http://www.quadernsdigitals.net/index.php?accionMenu=hemero teca.VisualizaArticuloIU.visualiza&articulo_id=4368.

DeVillar, R. A. (1986). Computers and educational equity within the United States: An overview and examination of computer uses in education. Stanford University-UNESCO International Symposium on Computers and Education, March 12–16, 1986, Stanford, California.

DeVillar, R. A. (1977, December). *The effect of bilingualism on measured intelligence with the school: A review and reappraisal of the literature, 1915–1960.* Unpublished manuscript, Stanford University, California, pp. 1–48.

DeVillar, R. A. and Faltis, C. J. (1994). Reconciling cultural diversity and quality schooling: Paradigmatic elements of a socioacademic framework. In R. A. DeVillar, C. J. Faltis, and J. P. Cummins (Eds.), *Cultural diversity in schools: From rhetoric to practice.* Albany: State University of New York Press, pp. 1–22.

DeVillar, R. A. and Faltis, C. J. (1991). *Computers and cultural diversity: Restructuring for school success.* Albany: State University of New York Press.

DeVillar, R. A. and Faltis, C. J. (1987). Computers and educational equity in American public schools. *Capstone Journal of Education, VII* (4), pp. 3–10.

DeVillar, R. A. and Jiang, B. (2007). Education and Hispanics in hypergrowth areas: The Georgia question in American schooling. In R. A. DeVillar (Ed.), Hispanic immigration, education and empowerment in the U.S. South. [Special Issue]. *Journal of Global Initiatives, 2*(1), pp. 84–103.

DeVillar, R. A. and Sugino, T. (1999). Democratic discourse on the language rights of learners: Lessons learned from visiting scholars. In R. A. DeVillar and T. Sugino (Eds.), One world, many tongues: Special issue on language policies and the rights of learners. *TESOL Journal, 8,* pp. 4–5.

Downes v. Bidwell, 182 U.S. 244 (1901). Justia.com. U.S. Supreme Court Center. Retrieved from http://supreme.justia.com/us/182/244/case.html.

D'Souza, D. (2010, September 26). How Obama thinks. *Fortune Magazine.* Retrieved from Forbes.com at http://www.forbes.com/forbes/2010/0927/politics-socialism-capitalism-private-enterprises-obama-business-problem.html.

D'Souza, D. (1995). *The end of racism.* New York: Free Press Paperbacks. New preface, 1996.

D'Souza, D. (1991). *Illiberal education: The politics of race and sex on campus.* New York: The Free Press.

DuBois, W.E.B. (1902, September). Of the training of Black men. *The Atlantic Monthly, 90*(539), pp. 289–297.

DuBois, W.E.B. (1903/1989). Of our spiritual strivings, in *The souls of black folk.* New York: Penguin Books, pp. 3–12.

DuBois, W.E.B. (1903/1989). Of the dawn of freedom, in *The souls of black folk.* New York: Penguin Books, pp. 13–35.

DuBois, W.E.B. (1934, April). Segregation in the North. *The Crisis,* vol. XLI, 115–117. Reprinted in J. H. Bracey, Jr., A. Meier, and E. Rudwick (Eds.) (1970), *Black nationalism in America.* New York: Bobbs-Merrill, pp. 288–298.

Dugas, C. (2009, June 3). Bankruptcy filings rise to 6,000 a day as job losses take toll. *USA Today.* Retrieved from http://www.usatoday.com/money/economy/2009-06-03-bankruptcy-filings-unemployment_N.htm?obref=obinsite.

Dugas, C. (2009, November 19). More members of middle class file for bankruptcy. *USA Today.* Retrieved from http://www.usatoday.com/money/perfi/general/2009-11-19-bankruptcy19_CV_N.htm.

Duncan, A. (2010, November/December). Back to school: Enhancing U.S. education and competitiveness. *Foreign Affairs, 89*(6), pp. 65–74.

Dyson, M. E. (2004). Foreword. In M. Forman and M. A. Neal (Eds.), *That's the joint! The Hip-Hop studies reader.* New York: Routledge, pp. xi–xiv.

Eckholm, E. (2009, July 4). In prisoners' wake, a tide of troubled kids. *The New York Times.* Retrieved from http://www.nytimes.com/2009/07/05/us/05prison.html.

Einhorn, R. (2010, October 18). Founder fatigue. [Review of the book *Revolutionaries, A new history of the invention of America*]. *The Nation, 291*(16), pp. 32–34.

Ellis, J. J. (2007a). *American creation: Triumphs and tragedies at the founding of the Republic.* New York: Knopf.

Ellis, J. J. (2007b). Joseph Ellis: An American creation. Forum Network. Presentation given November 1, 2007. Retrieved from http://forum-network.org/lecture/joseph-ellis-american-creation.

Engels, F. (1881/1971). [Letter from] Engels to Jenny Longuet, February 24, 1881. Original source: *Marx and Engels on the Irish question*. Progress Publishers, Moscow 1971, pp. 326–329; transcribed by E. O'Callaghan. Retrieved from http://www.marxists.org/archive/marx/works/1881/letters/81_02_24.htm.

Facing up to China. (2010, February 6). *The Economist*, p. 11.

Fallows, J. (2010, January/February). How America can rise again. *The Atlantic*, pp. 38–55.

Fengler, R. (2006). Thomas Jefferson's Indian Policy, 18 January 1803. Documenting American History project. University of Wisconsin–Green Bay. Retrieved from http://www.historytools.org/sources/Jefferson-Indians.pdf.

Ferguson, N. (2010, March/April). Complexity and collapse: Empires on the edge of chaos. *Foreign Affairs*, 89(2), pp. 18–32.

Fiction Mags Index (n.d.). Stories, listed by author. Retrieved from http://www.philsp.com/homeville/FMI/s938.htm#A32201.

FindLaw (2010). U.S. Constitution: Fourteenth Amendment. Retrieved from http://caselaw.lp.findlaw.com/data/constitution/amendment14/.

Finkelman, P. (1992). Segregation, de facto. In K. L. Hall (Ed.), *The Oxford companion to the Supreme Court of the United States*. New York: Oxford University Press, p. 766.

Fisher, G. M. (1994). From Hunter to Orshansky: An overview of (unofficial) poverty lines in the United States from 1904 to 1965—summary. Fifteenth Annual Research Conference of the Association for Public Policy Analysis and Management in Washington, D.C. Retrieved from http://aspe.hhs.gov/poverty/papers/htrssmiv.htm.

Fisher, G. M. (1997). The development and history of the U.S. poverty thresholds—A brief overview. Newsletter of the Government Statistics Section and the Social Statistics Section of the American Statistical Association, Winter 1997, pp. 6–7. Retrieved from http://aspe.hhs.gov/poverty/papers/ HPTGSSIV.htm.

Flanagan, C. (2010, January/February). Cultivating failure: How school gardens are cheating our most vulnerable students. *The Atlantic, 305*(1), pp. 101–111.

Flurry, G. (2010, September). The hope that politicians can't give you. *The Philadelphia Trumpet*, p. 1.

Folkenflik, D. (2010, October 21). NPR ends Juan Williams' contract after Muslim remarks. *NPR.com*. Retrieved from http://www.npr.org/templates/story/story.php?storyId=130712737.

Foner, P. S. (Ed.) (1970). *W.E.B. DuBois speaks: Speeches and addresses 1890–1919*. New York: Pathfinder.

Fox, J. (2009, December 21). The real jobless rate. *Time*, p. 39.

Franklin, J. H. (1965). The two roles of race: A historical view. *Daedalus, Journal of the American Academy of Arts and Sciences, 94*, pp. 899–920.

Fraser, R. (2010, September). Reconstructing NATO. *The Philadelphia Trumpet*, pp. 22–24.

Frazier, E. F. (1957). *Race and culture contacts in the modern world*. Boston: Beacon Press.

Freedman, K. and Liu, M. (1996). The importance of computer experience, learning processes, and communication patterns in multicultural networking. *Educational Technology Research and Development, 44* (1), pp. 43–59.

Freese, P. (2008). American national identity in a globalized world as a topic in the advanced EFL-classroom. *Journal of American Studies, 51*. Retrieved from http://asjournal.zusas.uni-halle.de/archive/51/103.html.

Frere-Jones, S. (2008, June 2). Usher 2.0. *The New Yorker*. Retrieved from http://www.newyorker.com/arts/critics/musical/2008/06/02/080602 crmu_music_frerejones.

Friedkin, N. E. (2004). Social cohesion. *Annual Review of Sociology, 30*(1), pp. 409–25.

Friedman, L. (2010, December 13). Time for a wealth tax. *The Nation*, pp. 4, 6.

Fry, R. (2010, May 13). *Hispanics, high school dropouts and the GED*. Washington, DC: Pew Hispanic Center. Retrieved from http://pewhispanic.org/files/reports/ 122.pdf.

Gándara, P. (2010, February). The Latino. education crisis. *Educational Leadership, 76*(5), *pp.* 24–30.

Gándara, P. and Orfield, G. (2010, October 14). Déjà vu: The access/success pendulum. *Diverse*, pp. 20–21.

Gans, H. J. (1967). *The Levittowners: Ways of life and politics in a new suburban community.* New York: Pantheon Books.

Gillette, W. (2001). Fifteenth Amendment (1870). In Boyer, P. S. (Ed.), *The Oxford companion to United States history.* New York: Oxford University Press, p. 264.

Glass, G. V. (2008). *Fertilizers, pill, and magnetic strips: The fate of public education in America.* Charlotte, NC: Information Age.

Glass, G. V. (2002). School reform proposals: The research evidence. Retrieved from http://epsl.asu.edu/epru/documents/EPRU%202002-101/Chapter%2005-Glass-Final.htm.

Goffman, E. (1981/1983). *Forms of talk.* Philadelphia: University of Pennsylvania Press (2nd printing).

Gold, M. (2010, October 21). In wake of NPR controversy, Fox News gives Juan Williams an expanded role. *Los Angeles Times.* Retrieved from http://articles.latimes.com/2010/oct/21/news/la-pn-juan-williams-20101022.

Goldman, D. (2009, December 29). Bailout's big mistake: Loans to small banks. *CNNMoney.com.* Retrieved from http://money.cnn.com/2009/12/24/news/economy/bailout_payback/index.htm.

Gong Lum v. Rice, 275 U.S. 78 (1927). Justisia.com. US Supreme Court Center. Retrieved from http://supreme.justia.com/us/275/78/case.html.

Gonzales, P., Williams, T., Jocelyn, L., Roey, S., Kastberg, D., and Brenwald, S. (2008). Highlights from TIMSS 2007: Mathematics and science achievement of U.S. fourth- and eighth-grade students in an international context (NCES 2009–001). National Center for Education Statistics, Institute of Education Sciences, U.S. Department of Education. Washington, DC.

Google Scholar (2010). Westminster School Dist. of Orange County v. Mendez, 161 F. 2d 774. April 14, 1947. As Corrected August 1, 1947. (9th Cir. 1947). Retrieved from http://scholar.google.com/scholar_case?case=8464528661773237273&hl=en&as_sdt=2&as_vis=1&oi=scholarr.

Gordon, M. (1964). *Assimilation in American life: The role of race, religion, and national origins.* New York: Oxford University Press.

GPO Access (2008, April 15). Core documents of U.S. democracy. U.S. Government Printing Office. Retrieved from http://www.gpoaccess.gov/coredocs.html.

Graham, A. (2009). Race in early American film. America in the 1930s. American Studies at the University of Virginia Web site: http://xroads.virginia.edu/~ug99/ graham/race.html.

Greider, W. (2004, April 22). Debtor nation. *The Nation.* Retrieved from http://www.thenation.com/doc/20040510/greider.

Gutiérrez, R. A. (n.d.). Mexican-origin people in the United States. Retrieved from http://www.jrank.org/cultures/pages/4188/Mexican-Origin-People-in-United-States.html.

Hall, K. L. (Ed.) (1992). *The Oxford companion to the Supreme Court of the United States.* New York: Oxford University Press.

Harris-Lacewell, M. (2010, May 3). Black by choice. *The Nation,* *290*(17), p. 10.

Hennessy, J. (2010, November/December). Higher education's new challenges. *Stanford,* p. 6.

Herc, DJ Kool (2005). Introduction. In J. Chang, *Can't stop, Won't stop: A history of the hip-hop generation.* New York: Picador, pp. xi–xiii.

Herrnstein, R. J. and Murray, C. (1994). *The bell curve: Intelligence and class structure in American life.* New York: Free Press.

Hilliker, J. (2010a, September). How to raise a man: Bible-based wisdom on bringing up boys. *The Philadelphia Trumpet,* pp. 3–5, 31.

Hilliker, J. (2010b, September). There is no such thing as two fathers: America's government is working feverishly to redefine family. *The Philadelphia Trumpet,* p. 35.

Hirschorn, M. (2010, November). Truth lies here. *The Atlantic,* *306*(4), pp. 58, 62–64.

History matters: The U.S. survey course on the web (2005). Center for History and New Media (Fairfax, Virginia: George Mason University) and American Social History Project/Center for Media and Learning (New York: City University of New York). Retrieved from http://historymatters.gmu.edu/ credits.html.

Hodgkinson, H. (2000/2001). Educational demographics: What teachers should know. *Educational Leadership, 58*, pp. 6–11.

Hodgson, D. (1991, March). The ideological origins of the Population Association of America. *Population and Development Review, 17*(1), pp. 1–34.

Hofstede, G. (2001). *Culture's consequences: Comparing values, behaviors, institutions, and organizations across nations* (2nd edition). Thousand Oaks, CA: Sage Publications.

hooks, bell (2009). *Belonging: A culture of place.* New York: Routledge.

Horsman, R. (1981). *Race and manifest destiny: The origins of American racial Anglo-Saxonism.* Cambridge, MA: Harvard University Press.

How they see us: Is the Tea Party a real threat (2010, February 26). *The Week*, p. 14.

Hoyt, H. (1933). *One hundred years of land values in Chicago: The relationship of the growth of Chicago to the rise in its land values, 1830–1933.* Chicago, IL: University of Chicago Press.

Hudgins, E. L. (1985, September 24). The U.S. as a debtor nation: What it really means. The Heritage Foundation. Retrieved from http://www.heritage.org/research/ economy/em92.cfm.

Hughes, L. (1922/1995). The south. In A. Rampersad (Ed.) and D. Roessel (Assoc. Ed.), *The collected poems of Langston Hughes.* New York: Vintage Books, A Division of Random House, p. 26.

Huntington, S. P. (2004, March/April). The Hispanic challenge. *Foreign Policy.* Retrieved from http://cyber.law.harvard.edu/ blogs/gems/culturalagency1/SamuelHuntingtonTheHispanicC.pdf.

Hurun Report (2009, October 13). Hainan Clearwater Bay 2009 Hurun Rich List. Retrieved from http://www.hurun.net/ listen162.aspx.

Hutchinson, D. J. (1992). Brown v. Board of Education, 347 U.S. 483 (1954). In K. L. Hall (Ed.), *The Oxford companion to the Supreme Court of the United States.* New York: Oxford University Press, pp. 93–96.

Hymowitz, K. S. (2010, November 11). The fragile family effect: It's instability, not poverty, that does the greater damage to children. Op-Ed. *Los Angeles Times*. Retrieved from http://articles.latimes.com/2010/nov/11/opinion/la-oe-hymowitz-families-20101111.

Income, poverty and health insurance coverage in the United States: 2009 (2010, September 16). Summary of Findings. Newsroom. Washington, D.C.: U.S. Census Bureau. Retrieved from http://www.census.gov/newsroom/releases/archives/income_wealth/cb 10-144.html.

Ingram, B. (n.d.). Amos 'n' Andy, Standard and stain. Retrieved from http://www.tvparty.com/50amos1.html.

Institute on Assets and Social Policy (2010, May). The racial wealth gap increases fourfold. *Research and Policy Brief*. The Heller School for Social Policy and Management, Brandeis University. Retrieved from http://iasp.brandeis.edu/pdfs/Racial-Wealth-Gap-Brief.pdf.

International Baccalaureate Organization (2010). Find an IB world school. Retrieved from http://www.k12academics.com/national-directories/international-school/United+States.

Irwin, N. (2010, January 2). A lost decade for U.S. economy, workers. *The Washington Post* (Washingtonpost.com.). Retrieved at http://www.msnbc.msn.com/id/34664092/ns/business-washington_post.

Jackman, M. R. (1994). *The velvet glove: Paternalism and conflict in gender, class and race relations*. Berkeley: University of California Press.

Jacobson, J., Olsen, C., Rice, J. K., Sweetland, S., and Ralph, J. (2001, July). *Educational Achievement and Black-White Inequality*. U.S. Department of Education, National Center for Education Statistics., NCES 2001-061. Washington, DC: U.S. Government Printing Office.

Jacques, M. (2009). *When China rules the world: The end of the Western world and the birth of a new global order*. New York: Penguin Press.

Jennings, F. (2000). *The creation of America: Through revolution to empire*. New York: Cambridge University Press.

Jensen A. R. (1969, Winter/Summer). How much can we boost IQ and scholastic achievement? *Harvard Educational Review*, *39*, pp. 1–123.

Johnson, D. W. and Johnson, R. T. (2009a, June/July). An educational psychology success story: Social interdependence theory and cooperative learning. *Educational Researcher*, *38*(1), pp. 365–379.

Johnson, D. W. and Johnson, R. T. (2009b, January/February). Energizing learning: The instructional power of conflict. *Educational Researcher*, *38*(1), pp. 37–51.

Johnson, D. W. and Johnson, R. T. (1994). Cooperative learning in the culturally diverse classroom. In R. A. DeVillar, C. J. Faltis, and J. P. Cummins (Eds.), *Cultural diversity in schools: From rhetoric to practice*. Albany: State University of New York Press, pp. 57–73.

Johnson, D. W. and Johnson, R. T. (1975). *Learning together and alone: Cooperation, competition, and individualization*. Englewood Cliffs, NJ: Prentice-Hall.

Johnson, D. W., Johnson, R. T., and Stanne, M. B. (2000, May). Cooperative learning methods: A meta-analysis. Retrieved from http://www.tablelearning.com/uploads/ File/EXHIBIT-B.pdf.

Johnson, D. W., Johnson, R. T., and Holubec, E. Johnson (1986). *Revised circles of learning: Cooperation in the classroom*. Edina, MN: Interaction Book Company.

Johnson, L. B. (1965, March 15). Address to Congress: We shall overcome. Retrieved from http://wiretap.area.com/Gopher/Gov/US-Speech/johnson.spJohnson, R. E. (1979). *Juvenile delinquency and its origins: An integrated theoretical approach*. New York: Cambridge University Press.

Jones, J. M. (2010, February 3). Asian-Americans lean left politically. Gallup.com Retrieved from http://www.gallup.com/poll/125579/asian-americans-lean-left-politically.aspx.

Judson, B. (2009). *It could happen here: America on the brink*. New York: Harper.

Just the Stats (2010, November 11). *Diverse: Issue in Higher Education*, p. 18.

K12 Academics. *Directory of international schools: United States.* Retrieved from http://www.k12academics.com/national-directories/ international school/ United+States.

Kahlenberg, R. D. (2010, March 3). Disadvantages [Review of the book *No longer separate, not yet equal: Race and class in elite college admission and campus life*]. The Book, Online Review at *The New Republic.* Retrieved from *http://www.tnr.com/book/ review/disadvantages.*

Kalwarski, T. (2009, December 28 & 2010, January, 4). Surveying a dismal decade for the U.S. economy. *Bloomberg Businessweek*, p. 19.

Katzman, D. M. (1975). *Before the ghetto, Black Detroit in the nineteenth century.* Urbana: University of Illinois Press.

Kenrick, K. (2003). Al Jolson: A biography. Music 101. Retrieved from http://www.musicals101.com/jolsonbio.htm.

Keppel, F. P. (1942, December 15/1944). Foreword. In G. Myrdal, *An American dilemma: The Negro problem and modern democracy.* New York: Harper & Brothers Publishers, pp. v–viii.

Kevles, D. J. (1979, January). Eugenics in the United States and Britain, 1890 to 1930: A comparative analysis. Humanities Working Paper 19. California Institute of Technology. Retrieved from http://authors.library.caltech.edu/ 14563/1/HumsWP-0019. pdf.

Khanna, P. (2008). *The second world: Empires and influence in the new global order.* New York: Random House.

Kilkenny, S. (2010, July 14). Growth in the number of Black-owned businesses outpaces national and overall minority rates. *The Network Journal, Black Professionals and Small Business Magazine.* Retrieved from http://www.tnj.com/news/black-american/growth-number-black-owned-businesses-outpaces-national-and-overall-minority-rate.

Kimes, M. (2009, August 25). Bankruptcy's repeat offenders. *Fortune.* Retrieved from http://money.cnn.com/galleries/2009/fortune/ 0908/gallery.bankruptcies.fortune/index.html.

Kirsch, I., Braun, H., Yamamoto, K., and Sum, A. (2007, January). *America's perfect storm: Three forces changing our nation's future*. Policy Information Report. Policy Evaluation and Research Center. Princeton, New Jersey: Educational Testing Service.

Kleiman, M. A. R. (2010, March–April). The outpatient prison. *The American Interest Online*. Retrieved from http://www.the-american-interest.com/article.cfm?piece=786.

Kroeber, A. L. (1948/1963). *Anthropology: Biology and race*. New York: Harbinger Books. Originally published 1923; revised 1948; 1963 printing.

Kroll, A. (2010, May 13). Introduction to *Tomgram*: Does the Tea Party Run on Race?, by G. Grandin. *TomDispatch.com*. Retrieved from http://www.tomdispatch.com/post/175247/tomgram%3A_greg_grandin%2C_does_the_tea_party_run_on_race/.

Kornblith, G. J. and Murrin, J. M. (2005). The dilemmas of ruling elites in revolutionary America. In S. Fraser and G. Gerstle (Eds.), *Ruling America: A history of wealth and power in a democracy*. Cambridge, MA: Harvard University Press, pp. 27–63.

Kurland, P. (1963). The legal background of the school segregation cases. Appendix 1 in K. B. Clark, *Prejudice and your child*, 2nd edition. Boston, MA: Beacon Press, pp. 143–155.

Kurtz, H. (2010, October 21). Was Juan Williams fired unfairly? *The Daily Beast*. Retrieved from http://www.thedailybeast.com/blogs-and-stories/2010-10-21/juan-williams-behind-his-firing-by-npr/.

Kwok, Pui-Lan (2005). *Postcolonial imagination & feminist theology*. Louisville, KY: Westminster John Knox Press.

Kwok, Pui-Lan (1988). *Chinese women and Christianity 1860–1927*. Atlanta, GA: Scholars Press.

Labov, W. (1969). The logic of non-standard English. In J. Alatis (Ed.), *Georgetown Monograph on Languages and Linguistics 22*, pp. 1–44.

Ladson-Billings, G. (2006). From the achievement gap to the education debt: Understanding achievement in U.S. schools. *Educational Researcher, 35*(7), pp. 3–12.

Lahr, J. (2010, November 29). Manifest comedy: John Guare on New Orleans and the Louisiana Purchase. The Theatre. *The New Yorker*, pp. 88–89.

LaMarche, G. and Bhargava, D. (2010, November 8). Looking back, moving forward. *The Nation*, 9–17.

Lane, J. (2008, April). Meat vs. fuel: Grain use in the U.S. and China, 1995–2008. *Biofuels Digest.* Retrieved from http://www.biofuelsdigest.com/ MeatvsFuel.pdf.

Lau v. Nichols, 414 U.S. 563 (1974). Find Law for Legal Professionals. Retrieved from http://caselaw.lp.findlaw.com/scripts/getcase.pl?court=US&navby=case&vol=414&invol=563.

Lay, S. M. (2010). *A 2020 vision student success: A report of the Commission on the Future.* Sacramento, CA: Community College League of California.

Le, C. N. (2010, November 9). Religion, spirituality, and faith. *Asian-Nation: The Landscape of Asian America.* Retrieved from http://www.asian-nation.org/religion.shtml.

Lee, J. M., Jr. and Rawls, A. (2010). *The college completion agenda progress report, 2010. Executive summary.* New York: College Board Advocacy and Policy Center. Retrieved from http://completionagenda.collegeboard.org/sites/default/files/reports_pdf/Progress_Executive_Summary.pdf.

Lehman, D. (2009). *A fine romance: Jewish songwriters, American songs.* New York: Nextbook.

Leiter, A. (2010/2004). *Thomas Dixon, Jr.: Conflicts in history and literature.* University Library, The University of North Carolina at Chapel Hill. Documenting the American South Web site: http://docsouth.unc.edu/southlit/dixon_intro.html#note5.

Lepore, J. (2010, September 6). The uprooted: Chronicling the Great Migration. [Review of the book *The warmth of other suns: The epic story of America's Great Migration*]. *The New Yorker,* pp. 76–80.

Leuchtenburg, W. E. (1991, November). The conversion of Harry Truman. *American Heritage Magazine, 42.* Retrieved from http://www.americanheritage.com/articles/magazine/ah/1991/7/1991_7_55.shtml.

Library of Congress (2003, October 31). From slavery to freedom: The African-American pamphlet collection, 182201909. American Memory, Rare Books and Special Collections Division. Retrieved from http://memory.loc.gov/ammem/aapchtml/aapcpres09.html.

Library of Congress (n.d.). [President Andrew Jackson's] Second Annual Message to Congress on December 6, 1830. A Century of

Lawmaking for a New Nation: U.S. Congressional Documents and Debates, 1774–1875. American Memory Web site: http://memory.loc.gov/cgi-bin/ampage?collId=llrd&fileName=010/llrd010.db&recNum=438.

Library of Economics and Liberty (2008). *David Hume: Essays, moral, political, and literary*. Liberty Fund, Inc. Retrieved from http://www.econlib.org/cgi-bin/searchbooks.pl?searchtype=Book SearchPara&id=hmMPL&query=Jamaica.

Lincoln, A. (1858). *The writings of Abraham Lincoln*, volume IV: Lincoln and Douglas fourth joint debate. Retrieved from http://www.classic-literature.co.uk/american-authors/19th-century/Abraham-lincoln/the-writings-of-abraham-lincoln-04/.

Linder, D. (2009). *Exploring Constitutional law*. University of Missouri-Kansas City Law School Web site: http://www.law.umkc.edu/faculty/projects/ftrials/conlaw/home.html.

Lipski, J. M. (2005). *A history of Afro-Hispanic language: Five centuriesfive continents*. Cambridge, England: Cambridge University Press.

Little, K. L. (1952). *Race and society*. Paris: UNESCO.

Llewellyn, E.C. (1936/2007). *The influence of Low Dutch on the English vocabulary*. London: Oxford University Press. Leiden, Holland: digitale bibliotheek voor de Nederlandse letteren. Retrieved from http://www.dbnl.org/tekst/llew001inflo1_01/llew001inflo1_01_0016.php.

Locke, A. (1925a). Harlem. *Survey Graphic, vi(6), pp.* 629–630. Reprint: Black Classic Press, 1980, Baltimore, MD, pp. 629–630.

Locke, A. (1925b). Enter the New Negro. Reprinted in J. H. Bracey, Jr., A. Meier, and E. Rudwick, Eds. (1970), *Black nationalism in America*. New York: Bobbs-Merrill, pp. 334–347. Originally published in *Survey Graphic, vi(6), pp.* 631–634 and reprinted by Black Classic Press, 1980, Baltimore, MD.

Logan, J. (2007). Settlement patterns in metropolitan America. In M. C. Waters and R. Ueda (with H. B. Marrow) (Eds.), *The new Americans, A guide to immigration since 1965*. Cambridge, MA: Harvard University Press, pp. 83–97.

Loislaw Federal District Court Opinions (2010). Lopez v. Seccombe, 71 F. Supp. 769 - Dist. Court, SD California 1944. Available at http://www.loislaw.com/livepublish8923/doclink.htp?alias=FDC R&cite=71+F.+Supp.+769.

Long Island University (n.d.[a]). African American Freedom Fighters: Soldiers of Liberty. C. W. Post Campus. B. W. Schwartz Memorial Library Web site: http://www.liu.edu/cwis/cwp/library/aaffsfl. htm#CIVIL.

Long Island University (n.d.[b]). The African American: A journey from slavery to freedom. C. W. Post Campus. B. W. Schwartz Memorial Library Web site: http://www.liu.edu/cwis/cwp/ library/aaslavry.htm#dred.

Loong, Tse Min (2009, July 4). China seen overtaking Japan by 2010. *The Star Online*. Retrieved from http://biz.thestar.com.my/news/ story.asp?file=/2009/7/4/business/4254034&sec=business.

Lopez v. Seccombe, 71 F. Supp. 769 - Dist. Court, SD California 1944. Available at http://www.loislaw.com/livepublish8923/doclink. htp?alias=FDCR&cite=71+F.+Supp.+769.

Louisiana State Museum (n.d.). *Territory to statehood*. New Orleans, LA: Author. Retrieved from http://lsm.crt.state.la.us/cabildo/ cab5.htm.

Louisiana State University Libraries (n.d.). *The Louisiana Purchase: A heritage explored*. Baton Rouge, LA: Author. Retrieved from http://www.lib.lsu.edu/special/purchase/history.html#native2.

Madrick, J. (2010, July 19/26). Symposium: Inequality in America and what to do about it. *The Nation*, pp. 21–22.

Manganiello, S. C. (2004). *The concise encyclopedia of the revolutions and wars of England, Scotland, and Ireland, 1639–1660*. Lanham, MD: Scarecrow.

Marshall, T. (2010, February 11–12). Unity and diversity in technology mediated social participation literature. Position paper, National Science Foundation Workshop on TMSP. Retrieved from http://www.tmsp.umd.edu/position%20papers/Marshall-TMSP. pdf.

Marx, K. (1867/1960). On the Irish question. Speech presented to the German Workers' Educational Society in London, December 16, 1867. First published in K. Marx and F. Engels, *Collected Works*, 2nd Russian edition, 1960. Retrieved from http://www.marxists. org/archive/marx/iwma/documents/1867/irish-speech.htm.

Massey, D. S. and Denton, N. A. (1993). *American apartheid: Segregation and the making of the underclass.* Cambridge, MA: Harvard University Press.

Mauer, M. (2009, October 29). Racial disparities in the criminal justice system. Prepared for the House Judiciary Subcommittee on Crime, Terrorism, and Homeland Security. Testimony of Mark Mauer. The Sentencing Project: Research and Advocacy for Reform. Retrieved from http://www.sentencingproject.org/doc/publications/rd_mmhousetestimonyonRD.pdf.

Mayer, J. (2010, August 30). Covert operations. A report at large. *The New Yorker*, pp. 44–55.

McAllister, G. and Irvine, J. J. (2000). Cross cultural competency and multicultural teacher education. *Review of Educational Research, 70*, pp. 3–24.

McCarty, M. (2010, April 15). Commentary: A Tea Party member appalled by remarks. *Dayton Daily News.* Retrieved from http://www.daytondailynews.com/news/dayton-news/commentary-a-tea-party-member-appalled-by-remarks-654061.html.

McConnell, E. D. and Miraftab, F. (2009, December). Sundown town to "Little Mexico": Old-timers and newcomers in an American small town. *Rural Sociology, 74* (4), pp. 605–629.

McKinsey & Company (2009, April). The economic impact of the achievement gap in America's schools. Social Sector Office. Retrieved from http://www.mckinsey.com/clientservice/Social_Sector/Meet_Our_People.aspx.

Media Matters for America (2006, November 15). CNN's Beck to first-ever Muslim congressman: "[W]hat I feel like saying is, 'Sir, prove to me that you are not working with our enemies.' Retrieved from http://mediamatters.org/mmtv/200611150004.

Medina, J. F., Saegert, J., and Gresham, A. (1996). Comparison of Mexican-American and Anglo-American attitudes toward money. *Journal of Consumer Affairs*, Summer. Retrieved from http://findarticles.com/p/articles/mi_hb3250/is_n1_v30/ai_n28669945/?tag=content;col1.

Mekay, E. (2005, February 18). China overtakes US as world's leading consumer. *Asian Times Online.* Retrieved from http://www.atimes.com/atimes/China/GB18Ad01.html.

Miles, J. (2009, October 24). A wary respect. A special report on China and America. *The Economist*, 3–4.

Miller, A. (2006, August 23). McCarthyism. *American Masters*. PBS. Retrieved from http://www.pbs.org/wnet/americanmasters/episodes/arthur-miller/mccarthyism/484/.

Miller Center of Public Affairs (2009). A life in brief. Andrew Johnson (1808–1875). American President: An Online Reference Resource Web site: http://millercenter.org/academic/americanpresident/johnson.

Miller, Kara (2010, February 8). Do colleges redline Asian-Americans? *The Boston Globe*. Retrieved from http://www.boston.com/bostonglobe/editorial_opinion/oped/articles/2010/02/08/do_colleges_redline_asian_americans/.

Miller, Kelly (1925, March). The harvest of race prejudice. *Survey Graphic*, *VI*(6), pp. 682–683 and 711–712. [Black Classics Press Reprint 1980].

Mintz, S. (2007). Landmarks in immigration history. *Digital History*. Retrieved from http://www.digitalhistory.uh.edu.

Molnar, S. (1998). *Human variation: Races, types, and ethnic groups* (4th edition). Upper Saddle River, NJ: Prentice Hall.

Morley, R. (2010, September). The president, Black Panthers, and the coming racial explosion: Truth is trampled in the street and judgment is turned around backward. *The Philadelphia Trumpet*, pp. 8–9.

Morrison, W. M. (2009, March 5). China's economic conditions. CRS Report for Congress. Congressional Research Service, Washington, D.C. Retrieved from http://www.fas.org/sgp/crs/row/RL33534.pdf.

Mourshed, M. and Whelan, F. (2010, August 16). How to close the achievement gap. The world's best schools offer important lessons about what works. *Newsweek Mobile Reader*. Retrieved from http://www.newsweek.com/2010/08/16/secrets-of-the-world-s-best-school-systems.html.

MPI Data Hub (2010). The United States social and demographic characteristics (immigrant and native-born populations in the United States in 2008). Washington, DC: Migration Policy

Institute. Retrieved from http://www.migrationinformation.org/datahub/state.cfm?ID=US.

Munns, D. and Metzger, T. (2009, October 12). Bankruptcy filings, state by state, 2005–2009: 3rd quarter of '09 puts filings on record-setting track. *Credit Cards.com*. Retrieved from http://www.creditcards.com/credit-card-news/state-bankruptcy-filings-statistics-1276.php.

Myrdal, G. (1944). *An American dilemma: The Negro problem and modern democracy*. New York: Harper.

National Archives (1996, February). The Louisiana Purchase, Treaty between the United States of America and the French Republic. Retrieved from http://www.archives.gov/exhibits/american_originals/louistxt.html.

National Archives (n.d.). Chinese immigration and the Chinese in the United States. Retrieved from http://www.archives.gov/locations/finding-aids/chinese-immigration.html.

National Bureau of Economic Research (2010, September 20). Business Cycle Dating Committee, National Bureau of Economic Research. Cambridge, MA. Retrieved from http://www.nber.org/cycles/sept2010.html.

National Public Radio (2010, January 10). Diversity efforts uneven in U.S. companies. *NPR News*. Retrieved from http://www.google.com/ig?hl= en#max10.

National Science Foundation (2003, July). *Women, minorities, and persons with disabilities in science and engineering: 2002*, Division of Science Resources Statistics, NSF 03-312. Arlington, VA: Author. Retrieved from http://www.nsf.gov/statistics/nsf03312/pdf/front.pdf.

Naturalization Act (1790). Major Acts of Congress. *Encyclopedia.com*. Retrieved from http://www.encyclopedia.com/doc/1G2-340740 0229.html.

Neighborhood Scout (2010a). Web-based organization specializing in nationwide relocation software, retail site selection, and real estate investment advising. Retrieved from http://www.neighborhood scout.com/nj/willingboro/town-center/.

Neighborhood Scout (2010b). Web-based organization specializing in nationwide relocation software, retail site selection, and real estate investment advising. Retrieved from http://www.neighborhood scout.com/ny/levittown/.

Neighborhood Scout (2010c). Web-based organization specializing in nationwide relocation software, retail site selection, and real estate investment advising. Retrieved from http://www.neighborhood scout.com/pa/levittown/.

Neil, D. (2009, November). Why America Should Pay More Attention to Korean Cars. Esquire 152(5). Retrieved from http://www. esquire.com/features/cars/korean-cars-1109?click=main_sr.

New Look Foundation (2008). Retrieved from http://www. ushersnewlook.org/news_media.

Newman, K. and Pedulla, D. (2010, July 19/26). Symposium: Inequality in America and what to do about it. *The Nation*, pp. 17–18.

Ngai, M. M. (2003, Spring). The strange career of the illegal alien: Immigration restriction and deportation policy In the United States, 1921–1965. *Law and History Review*, 21, 100 pars. 42, 46, 97–99. Retrieved from http://www.historycooperative.org/journals/lhr/21.1/ngai.html#REF53.

Nihart, T., K., Lersch, M., Sellers, C., and Mieczkowaski, T. (2005). Kids, cops, parents and teachers: Exploring juvenile attitudes toward authority figures. *Western Criminology Review, 6(1)*. Retrieved from http://wcr.sonoma.edu/v6n1/nihart.htm.

NNDB (2009). Thomas D. Rice. Soylent Communications. Retrieved from http://www.nndb.com/people/275/000203663/.

Norgren, J. (1992). Lone Wolf v. Hitchcock, 187, U.S. 553 (1903). In K. L. Hall (Ed.), *The Oxford companion to the Supreme Court of the United States*. New York: Oxford University Press, p. 511.

Nussbaum, M. C. (2010, October 25). Representative women. [Review of the book *The feminist promise, 1792 to the present*]. *The Nation*, pp. 27–31.

Oakes, J. (2005). *Keeping track: How schools structure inequality* (2nd edition). New Haven, CT: Yale University Press.

Oakes, J. (1985). *Keeping track: How schools structure inequality*. New Haven, CT: Yale University Press.

Obama, B. (2009, February 24). Remarks of President Barack Obama – As prepared for delivery Address to Joint Session of Congress,

Tuesday, February 24th, 2009. Washington, D.C.: The White House. Retrieved from http://www.whitehouse.gov/the_press_office/Remarks-of-President-Barack-Obama-Address-to-Joint-Session-of-Congress/.

O'Donovan, C. (n.d.). The Cromwellian Settlement. Clare County Library, Ireland. Retrieved from http://www.clarelibrary.ie/eolas/coclare/history/ cromwell_settlement.htm.

O'Keefe, E. (2010, July 20). NAACP, White House respond to ouster of USDA worker Shirley Sherrod. Federal Eye Column. *The Washington Post.* Retrieved from http://voices.washingtonpost.com/federal-eye/2010/07/usda_worker_quits_over_racism. html.

O'Neil, D. (2008, March 14). Kinship: An introduction to descent systems and family organization. Palomar College. San Marcos, CA. Retrieved from http://anthro.palomar.edu/kinship/default.htm.

Orfield, G. (2001, July). *Schools more separate: Consequences of a decade of resegregation.* Cambridge, MA: The Civil Rights Project at Harvard University.

Orfield, G. and Lee, C. (2007, August). *Historic reversals, accelerating resegregation, and the need for new integration strategies.* Los Angeles, CA: The Civil Rights Project/*Proyecto Derechos Civiles,* UCLA.

Orfield, G. and Lee, C. (2006). *Racial transformation and the changing nature of segregation.* Cambridge, MA: The Civil Rights Project at Harvard University.

O'Sullivan, J. L. (1839, November). The great nation of futurity. *The United States Democratic Review, 0006,* pp. 426–430. Retrieved from http://digital.library.cornell.edu/cgi/t/text/pageviewer-idx?c=usde;cc=usde;rgn=full%20text;idno=usde0006-4;didno=usde0006-4;view=image;seq=354;node=usde0006-4%3A6;page=root;size=s;frm=frameset.

Panikkar, K. M. (1959). *Asia and Western dominance: A survey of the Vasco Da Gama epoch of Asian history 1498–1945.* London: George Allen & Unwin.

Patterson, O. (2010, July 19/26). Symposium: Inequality in America and what to do about it. *The Nation,* pp. 18–20.

Peal, E. and Lambert, W. E. (1962, 1972 reprint). The relationship of bilingualism to intelligence. In W. E. Lambert, *Language, psychology and culture: Essays by Wallace E. Lambert*. Selected and introduced by A. S. Dil. Stanford, CA: Stanford University Press, pp. 111–159. (Originally published in 1962, in *Psychological Monographs, 76*(27), pp. 1–23).

Perie, M., Moran, R., and Lutkus, A.D. (2005, July). *NAEP 2004 trends in academic progress: Three decades of student performance in reading and mathematics* (NCES 2005-464). U.S. Department of Education, Institute of Education Sciences, National Center for Education Statistics. Washington, DC: Government Printing Office.

Peterson, K. (2005). *Diversity fuels student enrollment boom.* Retrieved from http://www.stateline.org/live/ViewPage.action?siteNodeId=136&languageId= 1&contentId=35088.

Pew Hispanic Center (2010, January 21). *Statistical portrait of Hispanics in the United States, 2008.* Washington, DC: Author. Retrieved from http://pewhispanic.org/files/factsheets/hispanics2008/Table%2022.pdf.

Plessy vs. Ferguson, Judgement, Decided May 18, 1896; Records of the Supreme Court of the United States; Record Group 267; *Plessy v. Ferguson*, 163, #15248, National Archives. Retrieved from http://www.ourdocuments.gov/ doc.php?flash =true&doc =52.

Pooley, K. B. (2003, June). The other Levittown: Race and place in Willingboro, NJ. *Next American City* magazine. Retrieved from http://americancity.org/magazine/article/the-other-levittown-pooley/.

Poverty rising in the U.S. (2010, October/November). *Poder Hispanic* magazine, p. 22.

Pressley, J. (2010, January 25). The meltdown according to Stiglitz. [Review of the book *Free fall: America, free markets, and the sinking of the world economy*] *Bloomberg Businessweek*, pp. 66–67.

Prison Policy Initiative (n.d.). *U.S. incarceration rates by race.* Northampton, MA: Author. Retrieved from http://www.prisonpolicy.org/graphs/raceinc.html.

Public Broadcasting System [PBS] (2003). Go deeper: Race timeline. *Race: The power of an illusion.* California Newsreel. Retrieved from http://www.pbs.org/race/000_General/000_00-Home.htm.

Quindlen, A. (2009, November 2). Why liberals need to stop worrying and learn to embrace incrementalism. *Newsweek,* pp. 32–35.

Racial IQ Research (2006, April 2). *Sunday Times* (London). Posted in *Times Online* (London). Retrieved from http://www.timesonline.co.uk/tol/comment/article701059.ece.

Ramirez, J. D., Yuen, S. D., Ramey, D. R., and Pasta, D. J. (1991). *Final report: Longitudinal study of structured English immersion strategy, early-exit and late-exit transitional bilingual education programs for language-minority children,* Volume I (Contract No. 300-87-0156, U.S. Department of Education, Washington, DC). San Mateo, CA: Aguirre International. Retrieved from http://www.timesonline.co.uk/tol/comment/article 701059.ece.

Ramirez, J. D., Pasta, D. J., Yuen, S. D., Billings, D. K., and Ramey, D. R. (1991). *Final report: Longitudinal study of structured English immersion strategy, early-exit and late-exit transitional bilingual education programs for language-minority children,* Volume II (Contract No. 300-87-0156, U.S. Department of Education, Washington, DC). San Mateo, CA: Aguirre International.

Reed, I. (1999). Introduction. In G. Schuyler, *Black no more.* New York: Modern Library, pp. ix–xiii. Reprint of 1931 novel with new (1999) Introduction.

Reich, R. (2010b, July 19/26). Symposium: Inequality in America and what to do about it. *The Nation,* pp. 13–15.

Reler, S. (2000, June 10). Half a century later, economist's "creative destruction" theory is apt for the Internet age: Schumpeter: The prophet of bust and boom. *The New York Times.* Retrieved from http://www.nytimes.com/2000/06/10/your-money/10iht-mschump.t.html?pagewanted=1.

Remnick, D. (2010, February 15 & 22). The Promise: Veterans of the civil-rights movement. Portfolio by Platon. *The New Yorker,* pp. 94–115.

Ripley, A. (2010, December). Your child left behind. *The Atlantic*, *306*(5), pp. 95–98.

Ripley, K. (2010, May 22). Texas textbook controversy. *Gather News*. Retrieved from http://news.gather.com/viewArticle.action?article Id=281474978252238.

Roberts, D. and Engardio, P. (2009, November 23). China's end run around the U.S. *Businessweek*, 22–24.

Roberts, J. M. (1990). *The Penguin history of the world*. London: Penguin.

Robertson, E. (1988, January). Race as a factor in Mussolini's policy in Africa and Europe. *Journal of Contemporary History*, *23*(1), pp. 37–58.

Rogers, J. A. (1925, March). Jazz at home. In *Survey Graphic*, *vi*(6), pp. 665–667, 712. Reprint: Black Classic Press, 1980, Baltimore, MD.

Romano, C. (2009, February 7). A fine first biography of thinker Alain Locke. [Review of the book *Alain Locke: The biography of a philosopher*] Alain Locke Society. Retrieved from http://alainlocke.com/?p=18.

Romo, R. (1975/1994). Responses to Mexican immigration, 1910–1930. In A. S. Lopez (Ed.), *Latino employment, labor organizations and immigration—Latinos in the United States: History, law and perspective*. New York: Routledge, pp. 24–46. (Originally published in *Atzlan: International Journal of Chicano Studies Research 6* [1975]: 173–194).

Rose, C. (2010a, November 1–7). Charlie Rose talks to Jacob Hacker, Arianna Huffington, Pearlstein, and Kenneth Rogoff. *Bloomberg Businessweek*, p. 18.

Rose, C. (2010b, October 25–31). Charlie Rose talks to Robert Reich. *Bloomberg Businessweek*, p. 40.

Rose, C. (2010c, January 16). Sir Howard Stringer: Why Sony is about to snap back *Bloomberg Businessweek*, pp. 15–16.

Rose, C. (2010d, January 11). Paul Volcker, the lion gets loose. *Bloomberg Businessweek*, pp. 11–13.

Rose, F. (2002, March). The father of creative destruction. *Wired*, *10*(03). Retrieved from http://www.wired.com/wired/archive/10.03/schumpeter.html.

Rothman, A. (2005). The "slave power" in the United States, 1783–1865. In S. Fraser and G. Gerstle (Eds.), *Ruling America: A history of wealth and power in a democracy*. Cambridge, MA: Harvard University Press, pp. 64–91.

Sager, R. (2010, January 7). *Native Americans in Texas during the U.S.-Mexican War, 1846–1848*. Retrieved from http://cnx.org/content/m33062/1.2/.

Salomone, R. C. (1986). *Equal education under law: Legal rights and federal policy in the post-Brown era*. New York: St. Martin's.

Sánchez, J. P. (1989, Winter). The Spanish Black legend: Origins of anti-Hispanic stereotypes. *Encounters*. Retrieved from https://people.cohums.ohio-state.edu/ahern1/Spanish555/pdffiles/Black%20Legend,%20330-555,%205%20pages.pdf.

Sawhill, I. V. (2008). Trends in intergenerational mobility. In J. B. Isaacs, I. V. Sawhill, and R. Haskins, *Getting ahead or losing ground: Economic mobility in America*. Washington, D.C.: The Brookings Institution, pp. 27–36. Retrieved from http://www.brookings.edu/reports/2008/02_economic_mobility_sawhill.aspx.

Schaffer, M. P. (n.d.). Laws in Ireland for the suppression of popery, commonly known as the penal laws. Retrieved from http://local.law.umn.edu/irishlaw/ intro.html#BACKGND.

Schneider, L. and Lysgaard, S. (1953). The deferred gratification pattern. *American Sociological Review, 18*(2), pp. 142–49.

Schoultz, L. (1998). *Beneath the United States: A history of U.S. policy toward Latin America*. Cambridge, MA: Harvard University Press.

Schultz, S. K. (2006). American history 102: Civil War to the present. Board of Regents of the University of Wisconsin System. Syllabus retrieved from http://us.history.wisc.edu/hist102/lectures/lecture08.html.

Scruton, R. (1982). *A dictionary of political thought*. New York: Hill and Wang.

Seth Kaller, Inc. (2009). The Thirteenth Amendment, ending slavery: A "Congressional" copy. Retrieved from http://www.sethkaller.net/component/content/article/570-the-thirteenth-amendment-ending-slavery-a-congressional-copy.

Seybert, T. (n.d.). Slavery and Native Americans in British North America and the United States: 1600 to 1865. History. Slavery in America Web site: http://www.slaveryinamerica.org/history/hs_es_indians_slavery.htm.

Shafer, B. E. (1999). American exceptionalism. *Annual Review of Political Science, 2,* pp. 445–463.

Shapiro, T. M., Meschede, T., and Sullivan, L. (2010, May). The racial wealth gap increases fourfold. *Research and Policy Brief.* Institute on Assets and Social Policy. The Heller School for Social Policy and Management, Brandeis University. Retrieved from http://iasp.brandeis.edu/pdfs/Racial-Wealth-Gap-Brief.pdf.

Shaw, J. (2007, July–August). Debtor nation: The rising risks of the American Dream, on a borrowed dime. *Harvard Magazine, 109* (6), pp. 40–49. Retrieved from http://harvardmag.com/pdf/2007/07-pdfs/0707-40.pdf.

Shiller, R. J. (2009) Unlearned lessons from the housing bubble. *The Economists' Voice, 6*(7). Retrieved from http://ideas.repec.org/s/bpj/evoice.html.

Short, K. (2009, July 24). Poverty measures that take account of changing living arrangements and childcare expenses. Retrieved from http://www.census.gov/hhes/www/povmeas/papers/child careandcohab.jul24.pdf.

Short, K., Iceland, J., and Dalaker, J. (2002). Defining and redefining poverty. Paper presented at the annual meetings of the American Sociological Association of America, Chicago, Illinois, August 16–19, 2002. Retrieved from http://www.census.gov/hhes/www/povmeas/papers/define.pdf.

Shuqing, S. (2010). China's balancing hand. *The World in 2011.* London: *The Economist*, p. 151.

Shurkin, J. (2006). *Broken genius: The rise and fall of William Shockley, creator of the electronic age.* New York: Macmillan.

Si, Tingting and Fu, Jing (2009, March 10). Nation may top Japan GDP in '09. *China Daily* (Chinadaily.com.cn). Retrieved from http://www.chinadaily.com.cn/bizchina/2009-03/10/content_75 58359.htm.

Silverstein, K. (2010, July). Tea Party in the Sonora: For the future of G.O.P. governance, look to Arizona. *Harper's Magazine, 321* (1922), pp. 35–39 & 42.

Simkin, J. (n.d.). Ku Klux Klan. USA history: Civil rights, 1860–1980. Spartacus Educational Web site: http://www.spartacus.schoolnet. co.uk/USAkkk.htm.

SINA (2009, November 20). China's millionaires club expands despite financial crisis. Retrieved from http://english.sina.com/ business/ 2009/1119/ 286845.html.

Slavin, R. E. (1983). Non-cognitive outcomes of cooperative learning. In J. M. Levine and M. C. Wang (Eds.), *Teacher and student perceptions: Implications for learning*. Hillsdale, NJ: Lawrence Erlbaum, pp. 341–365.

Smith, R. N. (2010, February 22). Era of no consensus. *Time*, p. 22.

Southern Education Foundation (n.d.). 1916–1931: Jim Crow segregation. Retrieved from http://www.sefatl.org/1916.asp.

Southern Poverty Law Center (2007). We must turn every stone to seek justice for martyrs: A message from SPLC president Richard Cohen. Retrieved from http://www.splcenter.org/news/item. jsp?aid=330.

Spickard, P. (2007). *Almost all aliens: Immigration, race, and colonialism in American history and identity*. New York: Routledge.

Spivak, G. C. (1988). Subaltern studies: Deconstructing historiography. In R. Guha and G. C. Spivak (Eds.), *Selected subaltern studies*. New York: Oxford University Press, pp. 3–34.

Steele, A. (2006, December 14). Zai Beijing: A cultural study of Hip Hop. Stanford Project for U.S.-China Dialogue. Retrieved from http://dialogue.stanford.edu/ zaibeijing.html.

Steele, C. M. (2004). A threat in the air: How stereotypes shape intellectual identity and performance. In J. A. Banks and C. A. McGee Banks (Eds.), *Handbook on research in multicultural education* (2nd edition). San Francisco: Jossey-Bass, pp. 682–698.

Steele, C. M. (1992, April). Race and the schooling of Black Americans. *The Atlantic, 269*(4), pp. 67–78. Retrieved from http://www.theatlantic.com/past/docs/unbound/flashbks/blacked /steele.htm.

Stein, R. and St. George, D. (2009, May 14). Number of unwed mothers has risen sharply in U.S. *The Washington Post*. Retrieved from http://www.washingtonpost.com/wp-dyn/content/article/2009/05/13/ AR2009051301628.html.

Stein, S. (2010, August 23). Sam Stein on Mitch McConnell's comments about Obama's religion: "The whole idea is to seed doubt." Huff Post TV. Retrieved from http://www.huffington post.com/huff-tv/sam-stein-discusses-mitch_b_691821.html.

Strickland, R. J. (1992). Native Americans. In K. L. Hall (Ed.), *The Oxford companion to the Supreme Court of the United States*. New York: Oxford University Press, pp. 577–581.

Takaki, R. (1993). *A different mirror: A history of multicultural America*. Boston: Little, Brown.

Takaki, R. (1989). *Strangers from a different shore: A history of Asian Americans*. Boston: Little, Brown.

Talvi, S. J. A. (2004, December). Homo sapiens 1900, a 1999 documentary directed by Peter Cohen. *Z Magazine, 17* (12). Woods Hole, MA. http://zmagsite.zmag.org/Dec2004/talvi1204. html.

Tannenbaum, F. (1946). *Slave & citizen: The Negro in America*. New York: Vintage Books.

Terrazas, A. and Batalova, J. (2009, October). Frequently requested statistics on immigrants and immigration in the United States. Migration Policy Institute. Washington, D.C. Retrieved from http://www.migrationinformation.org/Feature/display.cfm?ID=7 47.

Theodorson, G. A. and Theodorson, A. G. (1969). *Modern dictionary of sociology*. New York: Thomas E. Crowell Company (Apollo Edition, 1970).

Thernstrom, A. M. (1992). Right to vote. In K. L. Hall, (Ed.), *The Oxford companion to the Supreme Court of the United States*. New York: Oxford University Press, pp. 899–902.

Thevenot, B. (2010, March 26). Texas textbooks' national influence is a myth. *Texas Tribune*. Retrieved from http://www.texastribune. org/texas-education/state-board-of-education/texas-textbooks-national-influence-is-a-myth/.

Thomas, E. (2010, February 15). Obama's other deficit. *Newsweek*, pp. 26–29.

Thomas, H. (2001). Culture and economic development: Modernisation to globalisation. *Theory and Science*. Retrieved from http://theoryandscience.icaap.org/content/vol002.002/thompson.html.

Tiekin, M. C. (2010, Summer). Editor's review: *Belonging: A culture of place*. [Review of the book *Belonging: A culture of place*.] *Harvard Educational Review*, *80* (2), pp. 275–282.

Time (2009, December 21). The world: Tribal justice. Retrieved from http://www.time.com/time/magazine/article/0,9171,1946944-2,00.html.

Toobin, J. (2010, December 6). Comment: Precedent and prologue. *The New Yorker*, pp. 27–28.

Totenberg, N. and Kaufman, W. (2007, June 29). Supreme Court quashes school desegregation. NPR [National Public Radio]. Retrieved from http://www.npr.org/templates/story/story.php?storyId=11598422.

Truman, H. S. (1948, February 2). Special message to the Congress on civil rights, February 2, 1948. *Public Papers of the Presidents of the United States*. January 1 to December 31, 1948. Washington, DC: United States Government Printing Office, 1964, no. 20. The Gilder Lehrman Center for the Study of Slavery, Resistance & Abolition, Yale University. Retrieved from http://www.yale.edu/glc/archive/972.htm.

Tubb, B. R. (2009). Minstrel songs, old and new. A collection of minstrel and plantation songs, including the most popular of the celebrated Foster melodies, arranged with piano-forte accompaniment. Originally published by Oliver Ditson & Co., Boston (1883). Retrieved from http://www.pdmusic.org/minstrel.html.

U.S. Census Bureau (2010a, July 15). Facts for features: Hispanic heritage month 2010: September 15–October 15. Retrieved from http://www.census.gov/newsroom/releases/archives/facts_for_features_special_editions/cb10-ff17.html.

U.S. Census Bureau (2010b, March 2). Facts for features: Asian/Pacific American heritage month: May 2010. Retrieved from http://www.census.gov/newsroom/releases/archives/facts_ for_features_special_editions/cb10-ff07.html.

U.S. Census Bureau (2010c, July). Current population survey. Annual social and economic supplement, 2008.

U.S. Constitution Online (2010). U.S. Constitution—Amendment 15. Retrieved from http://www.usconstitution.net/xconst_Am15. html.

U.S. Department of Justice (2009, February 18). Attorney General Eric Holder at the Department of Justice African American History Month Program, Remarks as prepared for delivery. Retrieved from http://www.justice.gov/ag/speeches/2009/ag-speech-090218.html.

U.S. Department of Labor, Bureau of Labor Statistics (2009, July 28). International comparisons of GDP per capita and per employed person, 17 countries, 1960–2008. Retrieved from http://www. bls.gov/fls/flsgdp.pdf.

U.S. Department of State (n.d.). Repeal of the Chinese Exclusion Act, 1943. Diplomacy in action. Retrieved from http://www. state.gov/r/pa/ho/time/wwii/86552.htm.

U.S. Equal Employment Opportunity Commission (n.d.). Title VII of the Civil Rights Act of 1964. Retrieved from http://www. eeoc.gov/laws/statutes/titlevii.cfm.

U.S. Hispanic population continues to grow. (2010, June 10). Hispanosphere. *Orlando Sentinel.* Retrieved from http://blogs. orlandosentinel.com/news_hispanicaffairs/2010/06/u-s-hispanic -population-continues-to-grow-census-shows.html.

U.S. History (2000, November 1). Meet the historians: Professor Joseph Ellis [speaking on] Thomas Jefferson. Retrieved from http://www.ushistory.org/us/historians/ellis.asp.

U.S. National Archives & Records Administration (n.d.). The Emancipation Proclamation. *Featured Documents.* Retrieved from http://www.archives.gov/exhibits/featured_documents/ emancipation_proclamation/.

UNESCO (1969). *Race and science: The race question in modern science.* New York: Columbia University Press.

Unintended Consequences (2006, November 30). *The Economist.* Retrieved from http://www.economist.com/node/8366426.

United States Holocaust Memorial Museum (2009, May 4). The Holocaust. *Holocaust Encyclopedia*. Retrieved from http://www. ushmm.org/wlc/en/?ModuleId=10005143.

University of Texas, Arlington (2006, September). Improving achievement and closing gaps: Pre–K through college.

Vandenbroucke, G. (2006, November). The U.S. westward expansion. IEPR Working Papers 06.59, Institute of Economic Policy Research (IEPR).

Ventura, S. J. (2009, May). Changing patterns of nonmarital childbearing in the United States. NCHS (National Center for Health Statistics) Data Brief, No. 18. Retrieved from http:// www.cdc.gov/nchs/data/databriefs/db18.pdf.

Vygotsky, L. S. (1978). *Mind in society: The development of higher psychological processes*. Cambridge, MA: Harvard University Press.

Vygotsky, L. S. (1962/1934). *Thought and language*. Cambridge, MA: MIT Press.

Walker, C. L. (1987). Hispanic achievement: Old views and new perspectives. In H. T. Trueba (Ed.), *Success for failure? Learning & the language minority student*. Cambridge, MA: Newbury House Publishers, pp. 15–32. (Cited in DeVillar, 1994.)

wary respect, A (2009, October 24). A special report on China and America. *The Economist*, p. 3.

Washington, B. T. (1896, September). The awakening of the Negro. *The Atlantic Monthly*, 78(466), pp. 322–328.

Washington, J. (2010, November 6). Blacks struggle with 72 percent unwed mothers rate. *Comcast.net News*. Retrieved from http:// www.comcast.net/articles/news-national/20101106/US.Unwed. Births.72.Percent/.

Washington v. Fishing Vessel Assn., 443 U.S. 658 (1979). Retrieved from http://supreme.justia.com/us/443/658/.

Washington Times (2005, March). Disparity found in degreed women's earnings. Retrieved from http://www.washtimes.com/ business/20050328-125309-1639r.htm.

Weiss, S. F. (1987). *Race hygiene and national efficiency: The eugenics of Wilhelm Schallmayer*. Berkeley: University of

California Press. Retrieved from http://ark.cdlib.org/ark:/13030/ft596nb3v2/.

Wheelock, A. (1992). *Crossing the tracks: How "untracking" can save American schools.* New York: The Free Press. Introduction to book is available by permission at http://www.middleweb.com/Whlcktrack.html.

Widner, J. F. (1998). *Amos 'n' Andy.* Old Time Radio Days. Retrieved from http://www.otr.com/amosandy.html.

Wildeman, C. (2009, November/2010, May [revised]). *Imprisonment and infant mortality.* Research Report 09-692. Population Studies Center. Ann Arbor: University of Michigan. Retrieved from http://www.psc.isr.umich.edu/pubs/pdf/rr09-692.pdf.

Wildeman, C. (2009, May). Parental imprisonment, the prison boom, and the concentration of childhood disadvantage. *Demography*, *46*(2), pp. 265–280.

Wilkerson, I. (2010). *The warmth of other suns: The epic story of America's Great Migration.* New York: Random House.

Wilkinson, A. (2010, August 9). New York is killing me: The unlikely survival of Gil Scott-Heron. *The New Yorker*, pp. 26–32.

Williams, J. (1987/2002). *Eyes on the prize: America's civil rights years, 1954–1965.* New York: Penguin Books. (15th anniversary edition, 2002.)

Willig, A. C. (1988). A case of blaming the victim: The Dunn monograph on bilingual Hispanic children on the U.S. mainland. In R. R. Fernández (Ed.), Achievement testing: Science vs. ideology. Special Issue. *Hispanic Journal of Behavioral Sciences*, *10*(3), pp. 219–236.

Willing, A. C. (1985). A meta-analysis of selected studies on the effectiveness of bilingual education. *Review of Educational Research*, *55*(3), pp. 269–317.

Wilson, C. A. (1996). *Racism: From slavery to advanced capitalism.* Thousand Oaks, CA: Sage.

Wolf, R. (2010, May 13). Afghan war costs now outpace Iraq's. *USA Today*. Retrieved from http://www.usatoday.com/news/military/2010-05-12-afghan_N.htm.

Wollenberg, C. M. (1978). *All deliberate speed: Segregation and exclusion in California schools, 1855–1975*. Berkeley: University of California Press.

Woolley, J. T. and Peters, G. (2006, January 30). Harry S. Truman, XXXIII President of the United States: 1945–1983. Special message to the Congress on civil rights, February 2, 1948. Santa Barbara, CA. The American Presidency Project Web site: http://www.presidency.ucsb.edu/ws/?pid=13006.

Wright, E. O. and Rogers, J. (2010). *American society: How it actually works*. New York: W. W. Norton. Retrieved from http://www.ssc.wisc.edu/~wright/ContemporaryAmericanSociety.htm.

Wuthnow, R. (2005). *America and the challenges of religious diversity*. Princeton, NJ: Princeton University Press.

Yao, Shujie and Zhang, Jing (2009, November 10–11). On economic theory and recovery of financial crisis. Paper presented at 2nd China Conference of GEP at UNNC, Ningbo, China, November 10–11, 2009. Retrieved from http://www.gep.org.uk/shared/shared_levevents/conferences/Shujie_Yao_Financial_Crisis_On_E conomic_Theory_and_Recovery_of_Financial_Crisis_GEP.pdf.

Younge, G. (2010, November 8). Forgetting Afghanistan. *The Nation*, p. 8.

Yu, Pei (2008), "The October Revolution and the historical destiny of scientific socialism: In commemoration of the 90th anniversary of the October Revolution." *Social Sciences in China*, http://www.informaworld.com/smpp/title~content=t792221890~db=all~tab=issueslist~branches=29 - v2929(1), 29–49.

Zakaria, F. (2008). *The post-American world*. New York: W. W. Norton.

Zinn, H. (1980/2003). *A people's history of the United States, 1492 to the present*. New York: HarperCollins.

Zuckerberg, M. (2010, July 21). 500 million stories. The Facebook Blog. Retrieved from http://blog.facebook.com/blog.php?post=409753352130.

Index